KV-370-523

Made Simple   POTTERY

This new instructive series
has been created
primarily for self-education
but can equally well
be used as
an aid to group study.
However complex the subject,
the reader is taken
step by step,
clearly and methodically,
through the course. Each volume
has been prepared by experts,
using throughout the
Made Simple technique of teaching.
Consequently the gaining
of knowledge now becomes
an experience to be enjoyed.

Accounting
Acting and Stagecraft
Additional Mathematics
Advertising
Anthropology
Applied Economics
Applied Mathematics
Applied Mechanics
Art Appreciation
Art of Speaking
Art of Writing
Biology
Book-keeping
British Constitution
Chemistry
Childcare
Commerce
Commercial Law
Computer Programming
Cookery
Cost and Management
    Accounting
Economics
Electricity
Electronic Computers
Electronics

English
French
Geology
German
Human Anatomy
Italian
Journalism
Latin
Law
Management
Marketing
Mathematics
New Mathematics
Office Practice
Organic Chemistry
Philosophy
Physics
Pottery
Psychology
Rapid Reading
Russian
Salesmanship
Spanish
Statistics
Typing

POTTERY   Made Simple

Laurie Primmer, A.T.D.

Made Simple Books
W. H. ALLEN   London
A division of Howard & Wyndham Ltd

Copyright © 1974 by Laurie Primmer
All rights reserved, including the right
of reproduction in whole or in part in
any form whatsoever

Printed and bound in Great Britain by
Butler and Tanner Ltd, Frome and London
for the publishers
W. H. Allen & Co. Ltd, 44 Hill Street
London W1X 8LB

This book is sold subject to the condition
that it shall not, by way of trade or
otherwise, be lent, re-sold, hired out,
or otherwise circulated without the publisher's
prior consent in any form of binding or cover
other than that in which it is published and
without a similar condition including this
condition being imposed on the subsequent
purchaser

ISBN 0 491 01630 1 casebound
ISBN 0 491 01640 9 paperbound

Acknowledgments

The Publishers and Author gratefully acknowledge the assistance of: the Victoria and Albert Museum for granting permission to reproduce thirty-one photographs (*Crown Copyright reserved*); Lyn Curtis for the photographs showing examples of her work, plates thirty-one to thirty-five (some of which were produced by a combination of evening-class and home work, while the more recent come from her own studio); K. A. Smith, Ph.D., for photographing Lyn's work; and, especially, the Author's wife, Margaret Primmer, A.R.C.A., A.T.D., for producing all the line drawings in this book.

Preface

It is not surprising that many people feel a desire to make things from clay at some time in their lives. People have been creating useful objects and expressing feelings and ideas in clay since the earliest days of civilisation. This is because clay has always been widely available and also because its plastic nature lends itself to a great variety of forms, which become permanently rigid by heating to a readily attainable temperature.

Although extremely sophisticated work has been produced, displaying incredible virtuosity in shape and decoration, pottery is basically a primitive craft of true spontaneity and therein lies its universal appeal. Part of the primitive nature of pottery-making is the simplicity and directness of the methods used. There are no mysteries in the early stages beyond the mystery of clay itself. A warning here: do not rush out into the garden and dig up your own clay expecting to use it to make pottery, until you have had some experience. It may be good enough for bricks, but is unlikely on its own to be of the right quality for pots. Really workable clays are mixtures and have to be prepared for potting, but once you have obtained suitable materials you can make pottery in your own kitchen. The sixteen-page black-and-white photographic section does, in fact, include a sample of the sort of work that can be achieved by working at home.

This book is based on twenty years' experience of teaching pottery to adults in evening classes as well as students in school. Due to the limitations of two-hour evening-class sessions with a week's break between, students were often encouraged to commence or complete the making of their pots at home. With this in mind, the earlier chapters are designed to take readers through the basic processes of the craft: they contain simple and well-illustrated stage-by-stage instructions; explain the relevant techniques, materials and tools; and start readers to work at once on exercises (*Practical Work Tasks*), which can be accomplished at home or can amplify and consolidate evening-class work. Pupils at school, taking pottery as their craft in Ordinary or Advanced Level G.C.E. Art or Craft examinations, should find the book helpful as an additional source of instruction and as a means of recapitulation. For the mature student the Imperial system of measurement has been retained, but in each case these measurements are followed by their *approximate* metric equivalent for those who are using the metric system.

The simplest methods and equipment, much of which can be improvised, are suggested for the earlier work in order to minimise expense and save disappointment IF the craft fails to appeal. The various mechanical aids available for pottery-making are described in some detail and illustrated either in the text or in Appendix One— Pottery Machinery and Equipment. (Other Appendices include a comprehensive pottery vocabulary; a list of museums worth visiting; a recommended reading list and visual aids; and a list of firms who supply all the equipment and materials necessary to the modern potter.)

For those people who are interested in the subject, I would recommend attendance at recreational evening and day classes in pottery, for practical encouragement, using the facilities existing in schools, art schools and evening institutes, which are provided by most education authorities in this country. If you are interested enquire at your local library, which should have a list of classes available locally. Enrolment for the annual session usually takes place in mid-September and the fee is likely to be about £3. Classes are always over-subscribed, so to be sure of a place you are advised to join the queue for enrolment as early as possible. Evening-class experience has shown that the majority of ordinary people (not born artists!) find pottery so satisfying that they continue its practice for many years.

LAURIE PRIMMER

Table of Contents

CHAPTER ONE

THE CLAY YOU USE

Introduction to Clay

Although a real understanding of clay can come only with experience in handling it, a few hints about the nature and behaviour of the material should help you in your approach to making pottery. Clay, formed by erosion and glacial action over the ages, is composed of extremely fine particles and its chief characteristic is **plasticity**. This plasticity is the result of magnetic attraction between tiny molecules and the ease with which they are lubricated by the introduction of water. Whereas in the dry state of clay the molecules cling together to form a stable solid, when combined with water they slide about freely without losing their basic mutual attraction. Increasing or decreasing the amount of water in clay affects the condition of the material temporarily, but the persistent tendency is for it to dry out by evaporation. Anybody who lives on clay soil will know how a heavy rainstorm can turn his garden into a morass or, on the other hand, two weeks of sunshine will cause fissures in his lawn.

This means that plasticity in clay can be maintained only if steps are taken to prevent evaporation and that the physical state of clay can be altered to suit various practical purposes, provided no chemical change has taken place as a result of heating to a high temperature. What then are the physical states of clay? Let us try to identify them as they occur in making pottery. A broad classification, based on the amount of water present, is shown below. It is useful to remember the terminology of the states of clay, since they are referred to frequently. (The extensive pottery vocabulary, Appendix Two on page 270, should also be helpful to the beginner in explaining the specialised words and terms.)

The Physical States of Clay

1. Clay Wash. In this form water predominates. In clay wash there is just sufficient clay present to colour the water, but not enough to thicken it noticeably. It is used to separate plaster from other plaster during casting processes.

2. Slurry. Slurry is a wet, formless clay which is produced by steeping dry clay in water or from throwing with clay on the wheel.

3. Slip. Slip is a creamy liquid formed by adding further water to

1

slurry which is then stirred well, and passed through a sieve until it has an even consistency. It can be as thin as single cream or as thick as double cream, depending on the process for which it is to be used. It has several applications, including casting, decorating and joining pieces of clay together.

 4. **Viscous Clay.** More simply—very sticky clay—it is the intermediate state between liquid clay and plastic clay. In this condition clay is almost unmanageable. It is mixed with sand to make a soft clay used for sealing the gaps around kiln doors, which is known to potters as **clamming**.

 5. **Plastic Clay.** This is the state of clay in which there is a happy balance between fluid and solid, making it tactile, pliable and sympathetic to the pressure of fingers and tools.

 6. **Pliable Clay.** As plastic clay dries it loses moisture and its volume is reduced, so it becomes firmer and less tactile. However, in sheet form it can still be bent into gentle curves, and the surface will yield to firm tool pressure.

 7. **Leather-hard Clay.** This is a term frequently used by potters. After losing further moisture the clay becomes rigid. It can be cut with sharp tools and the surface can be incised, but it yields very little to pressure. It is liable to crack if handled unsympathetically. Attachments, such as handles, are made when pots are leather-hard.

 8. **Dry Clay.** Dry clay is rigid and brittle, practically all moisture having evaporated. The test for dampness is to hold the clay to your cheek. If it is still damp it will feel cold.

The Chemical Nature of Clay

 The chemical formula for theoretically pure clay is: $Al_2O_3 \cdot 2SiO_2 \cdot 2H_2O$. This means that clay is a combination of four elements: **aluminium, silicon, hydrogen** and **oxygen**. In the formula the first three elements combine with the fourth to form **oxides** so, in effect, it is a compound of three oxides: aluminium oxide, silicon oxide and hydrogen oxide (water). If you are at all familiar with chemistry this will mean something to you. If you are not, the practical significance is that water is part of the body or if you like, the flesh of the clay— just as water is a part of your body. This water is not lost by evaporation, unlike the water which is physically combined with clay.

 However, when clay is heated above 500°C the chemically combined water is driven off. It can be seen as a thin trickle of steam issuing from the spyhole in the kiln door. This happens during the first firing and afterwards the clay is rigid and, being porous, will absorb water—but water can never change its state again. If it was removed from the kiln at this temperature, it would be very porous and rather fragile, but the initial firing continues until a temperature of about 1100°C is attained, when the particles begin to melt into each other. The clay is then well baked or **mature**. If the temperature is increased further the melting action continues and eventually complete melting of many earthenware clays results, which is called 'fusion'.

Fusion means that the unmelted components will not support the melted components and the clay collapses. Consequently, when the clay reaches the maturing temperature the first firing of earthenware is terminated. It is then classed as **biscuit** pottery. If you recall that biscuit is the French word for 'twice-cooked' this seems a bit of a misnomer! However, once-fired clay does have a colour similar to that of biscuits.

Types of Clay

Prepared earthenware clays are based on plastic clays, which have been deposited after their removal from their original sites by glacial action and other natural forces. They exist in great variety and in their journeying have acquired additional material, especially iron oxide, familiar to us all in the form of rust!

Ball clay is a clay of very fine grain and hence of great plasticity, which contains a minimum of iron oxide. An important source of ball clay is the Purbeck area of Dorset—the clay used to be moved to the coast for shipping in large 'balls' carried on horseback. After digging, ball clay is grey-to-black in colour, due to the amount of decayed vegetation incorporated in it, and this adds to its natural plasticity. The vegetable impurity burns out when it is fired and it then becomes a pale-to-dark cream biscuit, depending on the amount of iron oxide present. For hand-made pottery, ball clay on its own is much too plastic: it shrinks too much, and therefore, cracks and warps when fired. The potter would say it is **too fat**—clays which lack plasticity are termed **lean**.

You are likely to meet three main types of prepared earthenware clays. A description of their characteristics will help you to choose between them and to decide which will suit you best in your work.

White, Ivory or Cream Clay

This is ball clay from which the traces of iron have been removed by magnets while it was in the slip state and non-plastic china clay has been added to counteract its fatness and improve the colour. It is prepared for commercial mass-production methods and is difficult to use in a hand-built pottery. However, if you are offered such a clay and your taste is very much for a smooth white or cream surface you may be tempted to use it, but it will require perseverance to master.

Frankly it will be more satisfactory to experiment later on with a white slip coating to give you the qualities you require.

Red Clay

Red clay is common in peasant pottery. The typical red-brown colour is due to the presence of an average of five per cent of red iron oxide, which lowers the melting-point of the clay. Its warm colour is natural to it and is retained after firing, though it darkens somewhat as the temperature is increased. Its pleasant feel makes it attractive to work with, especially to children, for whom the pleasure is enhanced by the extraordinary mess they can make when using it! It distorts and collapses easily if it is over-fired.

Grey Clay

Clays which are grey in the raw state are usually described as **buff** in the catalogues, because they fire to a darker-than-cream colour: this is the biscuit colour already referred to, which indicates the presence of a small percentage of iron oxide. The natural colour is caused by rotted vegetation. Fusion would take place at about 1400°C, which means that these clays can often be used for high-fired pottery (**stoneware**) as well as earthenware. Grey clays are as kind to beginners as they are to experienced hands. They have pleasant working properties and do not wilt or crack easily, either in making or in firing.

A grey clay which can be recommended from long personal experience is Podmore's P1034, a 'Buff School Clay', with ten per cent of **grog** added. **Grog** is the term for fired clay which has been ground to anything between a coarse grit and a floury powder. Grogs are graded by the mesh size of the sieve through which they have been passed. A mesh having sixty holes to the linear inch will give a medium grade. P1034 contains a fireclay grog which is **refractory**. The term 'refractory' means that it contains only very small quantities of easily-melted materials; therefore the grog assists the clay to stand up to high temperatures. Fireclay is a natural refractory material and can be added to other clays to strengthen them and coarsen their texture, which is necessary when making large pieces. The recommended firing range of P1034 is 1120°C–1280°C, and so it provides a good earthenware biscuit at the lower temperature and stoneware at the higher temperature.

If possible try both red and buff clay—they are easy to use and are great fun. If you are limited to one clay, buff clay is better as it is more tolerant. It is good for children's spontaneous work as it presents fewer technical difficulties. A straight buff clay, which has not had grog or sand added, may be improved by adding up to ten per cent grog which can be purchased at the same place as the clay. (Sand has not been mentioned before. It is an alternative additive material—some catalogues will list 'sanded and/or grogged clays'.) You can do this yourself: the method is described under Wedging on page 8.

Metrication

Since we are in the process of changing over to the metric system of measurements, wherever measurements occur throughout the book they are given in the old (imperial) form together with their **approximate** metric equivalent. As clay is a plastic material, measurements are intended as a general guide and it is unnecessary to be as accurate as, for example, when working with wood or metal.

Purchasing Clay

Clay can be purchased from a commercial pottery, a manufacturer who specialises in supplying schools, or studio potters, and a list of suppliers is provided in Appendix Five on page 286. On the other hand, if you are lucky, you may find a friendly individual potter in the neighbourhood who will supply you. Clay, before metrication, was put up in 1 cwt and $\frac{1}{2}$ cwt bags, but you are now more likely to obtain it in quantities of 100, 50, 25/20 kg. The larger the quantity of clay you buy the cheaper per kilogramme it will be. As a general rule you may expect a price of approximately 6p per kilogramme, varying with the types of clay and the quantity you buy. The price is, of course, 'ex-works' and will apply only if you can fetch it in your own car. If it has to be transported the cost may double. This is a point to consider if you are thinking of attending adult education classes as, although there is a tuition fee to pay, materials should be cheaper because they are bought in bulk.

Some potters dig their own clay, which has to be purified by breaking it up and making **slip**, from which the impurities can be removed by sieving. There follows a long period of drying, conditioning and adjusting the clay to make it suitable for handwork and successful firing. Should you fancy potting in the traditional manner, try finding some clay rather than buying it. Recently something about a pile of drying grey sludge on a nearby canal bank, apparently dredged up, evoked a faint inkling that it might be a workable clay. My instinct was justified, for the grey sludge, when reduced to a slip, sieved and dried to a plastic condition, was very malleable and as smooth as butter; its qualities as a throwing clay were good and it remained well behaved throughout. Its smooth finish and rich red-brown colour, when fired, are reminiscent of the Roman pottery found at Verulamium (St. Albans) nearby and I wonder if there is a connection?

The fun of finding clay for oneself can compensate for the time and work involved, and of course it is cheaper, transport being the only expense. If your 'found' clay warps or cracks add fine sand or fine grog. Traditional potters making simple ware lived next to their clay pit, dug the clay and used it without special preparation, which is why flower pots often had stones embedded in them.

Preparing Clay for Use

Thorough preparation of the clay is a discipline which is essential to pottery making. The clay you buy will be in good condition, having passed through a pug-mill, which is like a meat mincer but much larger and electrically driven. One firm even advertises that its clays have been artificially aged by introducing organisms from aged clays! Nevertheless a thoroughly uniform body must be ensured by vigorous hand-mixing, the water and clay completely integrated and evenly distributed; all air expelled by banging and compressing the clay. Uniform clay means uniform shrinkage. Uneven shrinkage causes the tensions which produce warping and cracking.

Kneading

Take as large a block of clay as you can comfortably handle and pull it towards you with the left hand. Almost simultaneously, with the weight of your shoulders behind the right arm, push into the clay

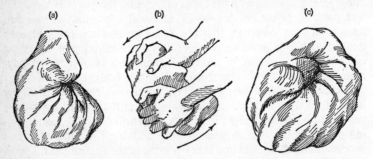

(a)   (b)   (c)

Fig. 1. (a) and (c) Two views of spirally kneaded clay; (b) the kneading action.

with the heel of the palm, giving the clay a twist with your left hand as you do so.

Continue this as a rhythmic process—it is splendid exercise— imparting a succession of waves which spiral from the outside inwards, constantly moving the clay to the centre. It is a knack, of course and difficult to describe. Try to see it done if you can.

Do it for at least five minutes: you will be breathless but you should feel better for it. In any case the clay will be well mixed! If you would like to check the thoroughness of your kneeding, cut slices of red and grey clay and sandwich them together before kneading them. When you have a mass of uniformly pinky-grey clay then you have wedged it thoroughly. Incidentally this is a very pleasant mixture which fires to an attractive pink biscuit.

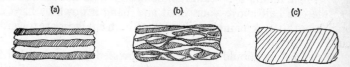

Fig. 2. (a) Stack of red and grey clay slices; (b) initial mixing giving streaky colour; (c) thoroughly mixed clay of uniform colour.

Wedging

If you find kneading a good exercise you will find that wedging is better. It is a splendid outlet for aggressive instincts.

A really strong table or bench is necessary because the clay has to be banged forcibly on it. On top of this table, if possible, have a

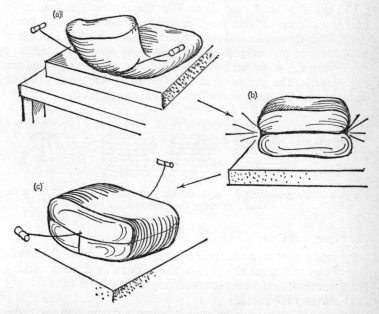

Fig. 3. Wedging clay: (a) lift and halve the lump; (b) slam the cut halves together; (c) turn the lump through ninety degrees and cut again.

paving-slab or a thick slate, as a wedging-block. For cutting the clay you will need a nylon or wire claycutter, similar to a cheese cutter. Wire is sharper but breaks more readily than nylon. These cutters, or the wire to make your own, can be bought from the usual suppliers.

Cut a piece of clay straight from the end of your bag of clay, about a quarter of a 25 kg bag will do to start. Bang it down on the edge of the block with the front tilted so that you can cut upwards and halve it; half should drop towards the block. With both hands free raise the one half above your head and bang it down as hard as possible onto the remaining half, so that both cut faces are towards you.

The two halves should have been compressed into each other if you have done it properly, somewhat flattened out, of course. Twist the clay block towards you at right angles to its original direction and repeat the action. Keep going, pausing to examine the cut faces occasionally for light or dark streaks (dark streaks indicate dampness, light streaks dryness: clay becomes lighter in colour as it dries) and for air-bubbles. When there is no evidence of these and the clay obviously has a good even grain, it will be ready for use.

Grogging

Cut the clay block into slices. Wet the top surfaces and cover thickly using ten per cent grog, by weight. Make a sandwich stack, cut through the middle and restack rather as for wedging, but do not bang hard at first or you will be splattered with water and soft clay. When the water has been absorbed then wedge and knead the clay properly. The grog in the clay will probably tear the clay surface when you cut it; this is normal and can be disregarded.

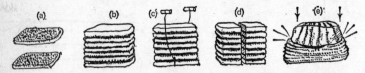

Fig. 4. (a) Grogged slices; (b) sandwich stack of slices; (c) and (d) halve the stack; (e) wedge the halved stacks.

The Storage of Clay

Provision must be made for the storage of your clay as the condition of clay is of great importance. The various methods of making pottery necessitate different states of clay, but in general a good supply of plastic clay is essential.

Your clay is likely to be supplied tightly wrapped in polythene sheeting or in a polythene bag, protected by a stout paper bag or sack. It can be stored like this for a long time, in a cool cellar or a stout plastic bin indoors, without losing moisture. However, when you open the sack and start to use the clay you will find the round-shaped bin inconvenient. For small quantities a biscuit tin will do, provided you keep a damp cloth inside to maintain a moist atmosphere and place a sheet of polythene over the opening, before closing down the lid tight. For larger quantities an old sink or cistern, rectangular in shape, is more convenient. A duckboard in the base raised on low supports with 1 in (2·5 cm) of water underneath moistens the air inside; a wooden lid with polythene sheeting tacked

Fig. 5. Clay stored in old sink or cistern.

on the underside will make it airtight. Clay can be stored in this in convenient lumps. Put all clay back after working and if it is a little dry wrap it in damp cloth.

Remember that restoring clay to a plastic state is a difficult and time-consuming task. It is worth going to the trouble of storing your clay efficiently.

Re-conditioning Clay

Clay is not so cheap nowadays that it can afford to be wasted. In spite of careful discipline in storage you will accumulate clay scraps and unfired ware which has been damaged, or discarded as unsatisfactory. Collect all this waste and dry it thoroughly. DO NOT include old biscuit: it has been fired and will not break down in water. Remember this especially if you are a member of to class. (There is nothing more annoying for an instructor than having to root around in the waste clay bin removing old biscuit!) A small experiment will demonstrate why the clay should be dry. Fill two jam jars with water, place a lump of damp clay in one and a lump of bone-dry clay in the other. You will see that the dry clay very rapidly disintegrates whereas the damp clay will hardly change.

When all the clay discards are dry, enclose them in a cloth and break them up with a hammer into small fragments. The fragments placed in a bucket or bin, are covered with water and left to stand for a day or two. Then they should be chopped and stirred with a boy's spade or a lawn edge-trimmer until a slurry is formed. Leave the slurry until surplus water has ceased to collect on top, then drain it off. Stir the slurry again as often as you like (children love this job!) and when it seems reasonably well mixed, decant it onto a board in the garden in fine weather, or onto a plaster block if it has to be done

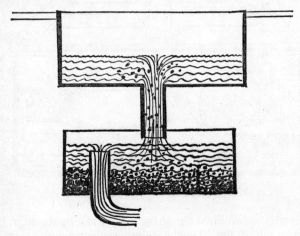

Fig. 6. Sink trap.

indoors. If the slurry is too thick to pour, wear rubber gloves and scoop it out by hand, or use a bowl.

If you get sticky clay on your clothes do not sponge or rub it (you will rub it into the texture of the cloth) but let it dry thoroughly so it can be brushed off easily. Do not wash too much clay down the sink; if this is done frequently you may block the drains. In a studio there is an auxiliary sink underneath the main one known as a 'sink-trap', where the clay settles, so that only the water goes into the drain.

If you use a plaster block it will absorb the moisture from the slurry quickly and as soon as drier clay forms turn it over, so that the wetter stuff on the top gets a chance to dry. Later, when it is dry enough to handle give it some kneading on the plaster block. On a board clay will not dry so quickly, but when it is at all manageable form it into round sausages and bend them into U-shapes, placing them on the

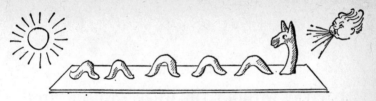

Fig. 7. Drying clay.

board so that they stand on their legs. This will expose a maximum of surface to the air and give even drying.

After wedging the clay it should be left to 'sour' for some weeks as it has lost much of its nature and would prove soft and pulpy if you tried to use it straightaway. **Souring** really implies a long period of storage during which decomposition of the organic life in the clay continues, adding greatly to its plasticity and making it smell far more than the most mature cheeses! The potters of ancient China lived for their work and handed the craft from father to son. It is said that they prepared clay and set it aside to sour for use by the third generation.

CHAPTER TWO

POTTERY WITHOUT THE WHEEL: THUMB POTS

The essential character of pottery forms is their simplicity and strength. This is the result of very direct techniques, which in their turn arise from the nature of clay. Plastic clay is wonderfully responsive to lively fingers and lively minds and, as it dries quickly, it encourages spontaneity. Because of the comparative speed with which you will have to work it is necessary to work methodically and tidily.

Work on a board such as a pastry-board or a thick plywood board, with a fairly absorbent surface. Clay sticks like glue to smooth, impervious surfaces such as Formica. Never leave your pots to dry on a smooth surface: if the base of a pot sticks to the surface it stands on, then when it dries and shrinks, the clay is bound to give and it will crack. Always remember that soft clay cannot be attached to harder clay or *vice versa*. Clays of different texture cannot be joined together; in both cases differences in shrinkage would cause them to part before, or after, firing. Remember that unless clay is grogged any piece of clay more than 1 in (2·5 cm) thick must be hollowed out and also that hollow pottery with air enclosed must have a hole, however minute, from which the air may escape.

Tools and Equipment

Listed below are the tools mentioned in this chapter.

Tools

(a) Old kitchen knives. Thin, narrow blades are essential because clay closes in and binds the blade.

(b) Craft tools with replaceable blades. Stanley and Swann-Morton types are both very useful.

(c) A potter's knife if you are ordering from a catalogue.

(d) Pieces of hacksaw blade and any old blades from small saws like pad-saws, fret saws, etc. Used for scraping and texturing.

(e) A boxwood modelling tool from a catalogue or the local art and craft shop. A serrated edge at one end is desirable.

(f) A small brush, preferably with square-ended bristles, such as a paste brush. For applying water or slip.

(g) A clay cutter, either from a catalogue, or purchase brass-wire or a nylon fishing line and make your own. Three-strand nylon is good, whereas wire cuts better but breaks more easily.

(h) 6 in (1·50 dm) or so of $\frac{3}{8}$ in (10 mm) wooden dowel, for forming grooves and poking holes—also useful as handles for clay cutters.

(i) An old fork for patterns and texture.

(j) Two sponges. A small natural sponge from Boots or from a catalogue. A decorator's sponge for cleaning up generally: must be a good mopper-upper.

Equipment

(a) A really stout table with strong, firm legs for working (and banging!) on.

(b) A large pastry-board, or thick plywood board about 3 ft × 2 ft (9 dm × 6 dm).

(c) A paving-slab, 2 ft × 2 ft approximately (6 dm × 6 dm), or piece of thick slate.

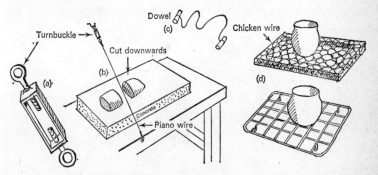

Fig. 8. (a) Turnbuckle for adjusting tension; (b) fixed cutting wire; (c) hand clay cutter; (d) supports for drying pottery.

(d) A special clay cutter for wedging, as shown in Fig. 8 (c).

(e) Ceramic sink or water tank.

(f) 2 in/3 in (5 cm/7·5 cm) thick plaster slab.

(g) Wire cooling tray or wooden frame covered with chicken wire.

(h) Plastic bags, plastic sheet, pipe cleaners or twists.

(i) Plastic bin, plastic buckets.

Tools which are not illustrated in the text may be found in Appendix One, on page 255.

Firing Your Work

Until you join an organised class or obtain your own kiln (please see Chapter Nine on kilns for details of home kilns) you will have to explore your district for individual or commercial potters who may be willing to fire your work.

Practical Work Tasks

Forming Five Basic Shapes

Task One: Forming Cubes. In order to understand how to shape the clay you can best begin by forming solid basic shapes. Cut a neat block from the clay with the wire cutter and divide it into cubes, about 2 in (5 cm) wide. Use the fingers and the palm to pinch and pat one piece of clay into as perfect a cube as possible. It will have soft edges and somewhat concave sides but it should be smooth: stroke away creases in the clay. Form a second cube by gently tapping it on the working surface and constantly turning the faces. The clay should make your fingers slightly damp. If the clay adheres to them it is too wet, so leave it a while to dry. If the clay persists in opening up into cracks, especially on the edges, it is too dry. Break it up, wet it and knead it together again before you recommence shaping.

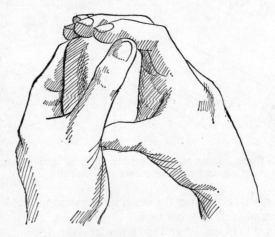

Fig. 9. Forming a cube of clay.

Task Two: Forming Spheres. Loosely cupping both hands, roll the clay around between the palms. Form as perfect a ball as possible, with an unbroken surface. Then try forming the perfect sphere by rolling the clay around on the working surface. If you do not succeed, use the previous method to finish off. Keep what you have made in an airtight plastic bag for use later, securing the neck of the bag with a twist or pipe cleaner.

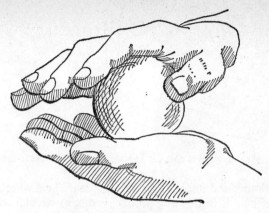

Fig. 10. Rolling a ball of clay.

Task Three: Forming Cones. Pinch and stroke a ball of clay so that it becomes somewhat pointed at one end. Roll it carefully on the board until a smooth cone is formed. Form a second cone and tap the point before rolling it again to form a truncated cone (bucket shape). Keep these shapes.

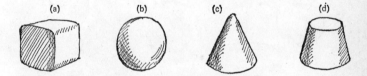

Fig. 11. Basic shapes: (a) cube; (b) sphere; (c) cone and truncated cone.

Task Four: Forming Tiles. Make a somewhat larger cube of clay, about 3 in (7·5 cm) square. Cut it into four slices—carefully cutting downwards with the wire cutter. Press each of the four slices with the heel of the hand and pat them; stand them on end; and tap them, until four regular shaped tiles about $\frac{1}{2}$ in (13 mm) thick have been shaped. Now use your index finger, your thumb, and your nails to make regular impressions on three tiles. It is suggested that the impressions are arranged in rows as a pattern: if each indentation is gently pushed up against the preceding one some interesting effects will be achieved. On the fourth tile, using the end of a dowel rod, experiment with impressions (see Fig. 12 on page 16).

Task Five: Forming Discs. Make a ball of clay and gently press on it as it lies on the working surface, with the heel of the hand. Smooth together any cracks which appear in the rim, then holding it

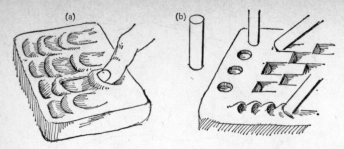

Fig. 12. Making impressions: (a) with the finger; (b) with the dowel rod.

between thumb and finger at the centre, use it like a wheel, and roll it on your board. In this way produce a disc as circular as possible with a firm edge of about $\frac{1}{2}$ in (13 mm) thick. Decorate it with finger or dowel rod marks arranged like the spokes of a wheel— try to broaden them as they get closer to the rim. Discs are useful as bases in forming hand-built pots.

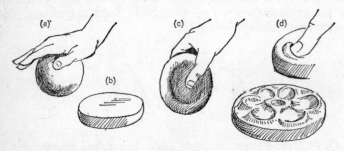

Fig. 13. (a) Rolling a ball of clay; (b) flattened to a disc; (c) wheeled between finger and thumb; (d) finger impressions.

Making Pinch and Thumb Pots

Make a ball of clay and place it in the hollow of the left palm. Press your thumb in very deliberately four times around the centre, letting the hollows formed overlap, so that you have one hole with an outline of four equal arcs (Fig. 14).

DO NOT press too deep: you are forming a bowl which should have a shell of uniform thickness, so the base must be kept equal to the walls. Now squeeze the wall of your bowl firmly between thumb and index finger (this is the **pinching** action) while rotating the ball, cupped in the left-hand palm. Pinch evenly all round the shell and avoid producing a thin rim. Squeeze towards the centre, not outwards, or the bowl will spread and lose shape. If your bowl does spread, and

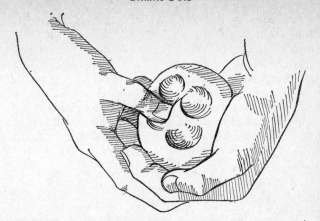

Fig. 14. Thumb pot: making the first four impressions.

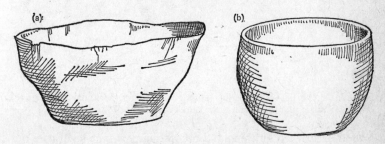

Fig. 15. (a) The result of uneven pressure; (b) a good shape for a thumb pot.

the perimeter is thin, ragged and wavy, scrap it and start again with fresh clay.

Keep trying until you produce a strong shape of about ¼ in (6·5 mm) uniform thickness: it will look like a half a Jaffa orange. Smooth the inside with your thumb. Now, holding the wire taut in both

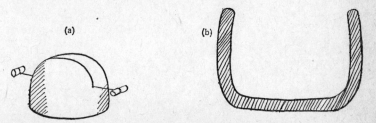

Fig. 16. (a) Halve the reversed bowl; (b) a section of the bowl showing even thickness.

B

hands, reverse the bowl on the board and cut through it diametrically, examining the sections critically for even thickness (Fig. 16).

Now make another ball. Hold it in the left hand and press the right thumb well in. Move the ball round with the left hand while pressing the right thumb outwards to thin the wall at the bottom, maintaining an even thickness of clay at every point. Complete the bowl by squeezing the thicker clay at the top and pulling it outwards. In this way you will have made a different type of bowl shape, which you will find useful for developing more complex forms.

Fig. 17. Thumb pot—alternative method: (a) making the initial opening; (b) enlarging the opening; (c) the development of the shape.

REMEMBER when finishing and decorating pots take great care not to hold them by the rim or edge, either reverse the bowl onto the board or hold it in the cupped hand. When pots have been finished off in the leather-hard state, they are ready for drying, and are referred to as **green**. They must be handled with care and picked up only by supporting the base. Never hold them by handles, rims or other thin parts. Never exert pressure. Breakage is very difficult to repair and to disguise.

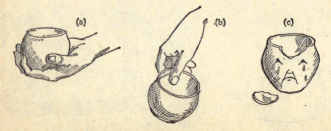

Fig. 18. (a) Method of holding the pot; (b) and (c) the result of holding a pot by the rim.

Pattern Arrangement

All types of patterns may be arranged either symmetrically, or arbitrarily and non-symmetrically. The usual forms are: (a) **bands**, (b) **panels** and (c) **'all-over'** repeats. When cutting bands on your pot, mark their position first with a felt pen. Stand the bowl upside down on an old gramophone turntable (if you have one) and hold the pen against it and rotate the turntable slowly.

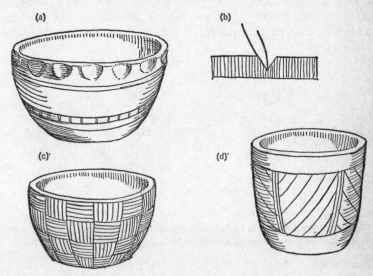

Fig. 19. (a) Impressed and incised bands; (b) section showing the tip of the knife incising; (c) all-over decoration; (d) decorative panels.

Finishing and Decorating Thumb Pots

Make six or eight thumbed bowls, varying the thickness and shape a little. Set them aside to dry to the leather-hard state, when their shape will not alter under moderate pressure and they will be ready for finishing and decorating.

Surface Finishes

For this you need four bowls.

Bowl 1. Hold a bowl securely by the base and smooth the surface with a damp (not wet) natural sponge. Do not forget the inside surface.

Bowl 2. Smooth the second bowl by pressing and stroking with fingers and thumbs. Avoid using moisture unless the clay is obviously too dry to respond, in which case a preliminary wipe with the sponge is in order.

Bowl 3. Smooth the third bowl by using a piece of hacksaw blade (or the serrated edge of a modelling tool) to roughen the surface and plough out all bumps and irregularities. Finally heal the surface and make it smooth by stroking it deliberately and with pressure, using the shaped end of the modelling tool. This will cause all the texture to disappear and give an almost polished appearance to the surface provided it is not too damp.

Bowl 4. Using a hacksaw, or serrated wooden tool again, score the surface of the fourth pot in a variety of directions aiming at an interesting random arrangement of textures. Keep this one for firing and glazing.

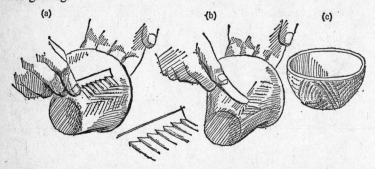

Fig. 20. (a) Scoring the pot surface with a piece of hacksaw blade; (b) smoothing the surface with a wooden modelling tool; (c) scored textures on a pot.

Decoration

Incising. Using the point of a thin kitchen knife (potato knife) or a craft knife, turn it sideways, and incise a pattern of lines in the outside surface of the bowl, which should not be deeper than half the thickness of the clay wall. The texture of the pot should resemble cheese for this process: there should be little or no burr.

Carving. (a) Try carving deep, wide lines in the clay with a wire gouge. Use a piece of thin but strong wire bent into a hairpin shape

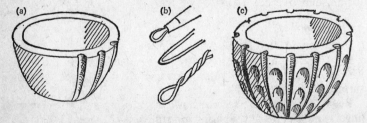

Fig. 21. (a) Lines gouged with a wire tool; (b) wire tools; (c) pot patterned with gouged marks and lines.

(a hairpin will do if you press the end to narrow the U-bend), or a special wire-ended modelling tool made for hollowing clay models (the smallest size obtainable).

(b) Try carving deep lines in the thickest bowl you have. Cut at an angle from both left, and right, to meet and produce a clean, deep line, as in the Roman letters carved on gravestones.

(c) Use a simple design, such as a circle in a square; carve and rout out the background with the wire tool, leaving the circle in relief.

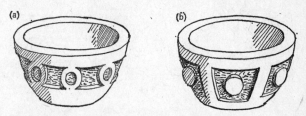

Fig. 22. (a) and (b) Examples of patterns based on the circle and square with the background gouged away.

If you make a mistake and cut through the clay wall, try a simple fretted pattern, cutting the background shapes away completely. This technique will have decorative possibilities later on if you make flower-pot holders, lamp-bases, etc.

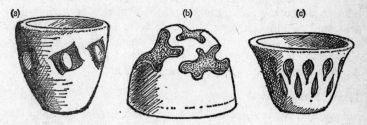

Fig. 23. (a) and (c) Flower-pot holders; (b) bowl reversed with a base added to make a pot for growing flowers. Three examples of cutting decorative shapes right through the clay.

All bases should be flattened and very smooth. Scratch your initials on the base and then rub or sponge off the burr.

Storing and Drying for Biscuit Firing

If the work in progress has to be left for a time, store it in an air-tight plastic bag. Finished leather-hard pots should be stored carefully in a draught-proof place to complete their drying. Ideally air should be able to get at every part of the pot, inside and out.

Small pots can be set to dry on the type of woven wire tray used for cooling cakes and larger pots on slatted wooden shelves. Do not dry pots before a fire: the drying would be fatally uneven.

When green ware is completely dry it feels warm to the cheek and is a light tone all over. It is then ready for the biscuit kiln.

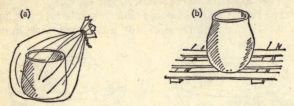

Fig. 24. (a) Pot stored in a polythene bag; (b) leather-hard pot stored for drying.

Shrinkage

It is obvious that the plastic clay with which we work contains about twenty-five per cent moisture, most of which is lost by evaporation, and the remainder during firing. The volume of the clay is thus reduced from start to finish by one-seventh to almost one-quarter according to the nature of the clay, the term for which is 'shrinkage'.

The most convenient measurements are usually linear. It will be of interest to you to make a number of strips of clay of varying thickness, and to measure their shrinkage from the plastic to the dry state, and also their ultimate shrinkage when biscuited. This will be a useful guide when Grandma asks you to make a replacement for the lid of her favourite teapot which the cat broke.

Three More Practical Tasks

Task Six. Make three bowls of somewhat similar size. Dry them leather-hard. Join them together: use a small ball or half cube of

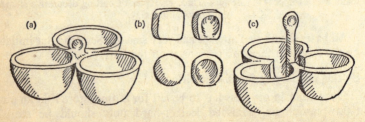

Fig. 25. (a) Three bowls with a pinched handle; (b) pinched handles formed from a cube or ball of clay; (c) an alternative design.

clay, pinched between thumb and finger, as a handle, placed at the junction of the pots.

Remember that the joining process is simple and effective if done carefully. All surfaces to be joined together are scratched deeply with the end of a knife, coated with thick slip and pressed together. Welding around the seam with the modelling tool completes a good joint. The slip is common to the surfaces where they join, and as it penetrates the scratches it bonds them together.

Fig. 26. Joining two pieces of clay: (a) making deep scratches; (b) coating the surface to be joined and filling the scratches with slip, applied with a brush; (c) the two surfaces joined.

To make a small quantity of slip take a wad of clay in the palm and form a rough shallow dish, which you fill with water. Brushing this water with the small stiff brush will mix it with the clay, and form a reservoir of slip. Apply handles and knobs by scratching and slipping (see Fig. 26).

Task Seven. Make a fairly large cone of clay and hollow it with the thumb: complete it by attaching a small disc of clay as a foot, or make a bowl from a truncated cone (no foot required). Make three conical bowls and join them together as in Task Six.

Task Eight. Make a solid cube and a solid truncated cone. Hollow the centre of both with the thumb. Take an egg and wiggle it around in the holes making a very loose fit to allow for shrinkage. These will make good egg-cups.

Improvisations

Task Nine. Enough of utility. This exercise is good practice in handling simple forms and it is good fun. Make something useless but amusing by the following methods:

Stage One. Make two thumbed bowls about the size of half an orange—the mouths must make as perfect a match as possible. Crumple up newspaper nice and soft and pack the bowls fairly tight.

Stage Two. Score the rims and apply slip heavily.

Stage Three. Place them rim to rim and press till they join. Forget the newspaper, it will burn to ash in the kiln.

Stage Four. Make deep criss-cross cuts through the entire join. It

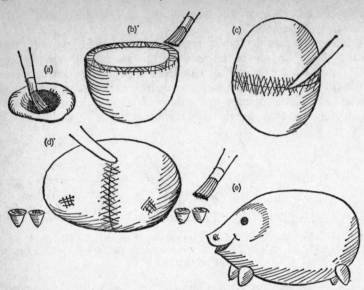

Fig. 27. (a) A pool of slip in a wad of clay; (b) scratching and slipping the rim; (c) the join being darned with deep cross-hatching; (d) smoothing over the join; (e) pig shape made from two thumb pots and four small cones.

will look as if the join is being darned. The object of the process is to mash up the clay on either side of the join and unify it.

Stage Five. Now clean up the join and restore the surface by using pressure from the blunt end of the modelling tool. When the join can no longer be seen, roll the clay on the table to smooth it and shape it further.

You now have a basic hollow enclosed shape from which many things can be improvised with a little imagination.

Reminder! A small hole is necessary to allow the air to escape when expansion due to heating takes place. It is fatal to your pottery to forget it.

Task Ten. Make ash trays from thick tiles of clay. Your ingenuity will doubtless suggest a dozen different forms. Make a groove for the cigarette with a short length of dowel rod (Fig. 28).

Task Eleven. Try making small, stylised animals from one piece of clay which is pinched, prodded and tooled into shape. Be as direct as possible in your modelling. Adapt forms to suit the directness of the methods (Fig. 29).

Task Twelve. Use the ovoid shape as in Task Nine and invent various stylised animal and bird forms. The hedgehogs have a variety of surface treatments: scratched, thick slip, roughed-up, deep incisions and tiny cones of clay stuck to the body (Fig. 30). (Do not forget to pierce a small hole for the air to escape!) Whiskers for animals could be formed of ordinary galvanised wire, which will stand the heat of an earthenware kiln, if it is not too thin.

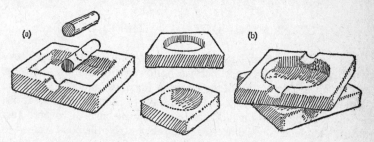

Fig. 28. Ash trays: (a) forming a depression with dowel rod; (b) designs for ash trays—example on the right is made from two tiles joined.

Fig. 29. Shapes pinched from one piece of clay.

Fig. 30. Stylised animal forms from thumb pots with different surface treatments.

CHAPTER THREE

POTTERY WITHOUT THE WHEEL: COILING

So far the exercises have been based on simple bowl shapes produced from a ball of clay, which was hollowed with thumb and fingers. Although tools were used, the essential form was modelled with the hands and a quite useful bowl could have been made without tools. While making bowls it is likely that you will have discovered two distinct tendencies which were difficult to control: the bowl seemed to insist on spreading and the clay persisted in becoming very thin around the rim of the bowl. Unless and until these tendencies were corrected and mastered, the bowls were irregular in shape and quite unstable.

The next method of forming pots may prove less arduous, depending more on patience and reason, though you will find that rolling clay ropes is a skill which some can never seem to acquire. However, there are alternatives, such as clay strips. Any method is only a means to an end, which in this case is to build taller shapes than are possible with pinched and thumbed pots. Some form of building is necessary to achieve the extra height —provided it is done methodically even blobs or balls of clay can be employed.

Tools

The equipment is the same as for chapter two with the following additions: (1) a potter's needle which can be purchased, or improvised from a crewel needle (used in embroidery) set in cork or dowel wood, for a handle; (2) a bamboo 'comb', or a wooden modelling tool with one serrated edge; and (3) a small bowl for water and a piece of natural, or fine plastic sponge.

Practical Work Tasks

Task One: Forming Coils

Take a small lump of well-prepared plastic clay (grogged clay is best) and, as a preliminary, roll it in your hands so that you have a somewhat cylindrical shape like a sausage roll. Squeeze it between thumbs and fingers so that it becomes more of a Cornish pasty shape, thinner at the two ends. You may find slapping the clay on the table or beating it with a stick, or wooden spoon, more effective. The taper-

26

ing of the ends is deliberate, since when you roll out coils there is a tendency to form heavy ends which flap about interrupting the rhythm of the rolling action.

Most beginners find themselves rocking the clay backwards and forwards, forming ropes of clay which are oval in section and, provided they are consistent, they can be used for coil building. But there is another fault inherent in the rocking action, for it tends to fold the clay over on itself, forming pockets of air, like puff pastry. The last thing you want is 'puff-clay', because the air expands when the clay is fired and it shatters the pottery. Therefore, roll the clay with a light, brisk action of the flattened hand, if possible avoiding any suspicion of rocking, and constantly moving your hands from the

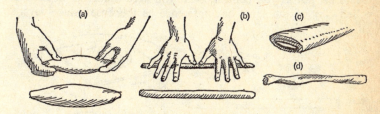

Fig. 31. (a) The first stage in forming a clay rope; (b) the position of the hands when rolling the clay; (c) air trapped in the clay rope; (d) clay rope rolled unevenly.

centre to the ends. If the pressure is too heavy or uneven the clay will form a very stringy rope of battered appearance. The true action for rolling is rhythmic and never jerky: once you've got it you will find you can roll long ropes, several feet long, circular in section and a smooth, even shape.

However, to start with, short lengths will do. Should the clay refuse to roll at all it is too wet and if it cracks and breaks, it is too dry. If you find yourself making oval-sectioned ropes, nevertheless, cut them with a fine wire and examine for air pockets. Try using slightly softer clay if air is present. Otherwise, you can either accept the oval section, or correct it by standing the coil on its thinner edge and pressing it to a square section, before carefully rolling it into a rounder shape. However, if you are not feeling too desperate, it is better to take fresh clay and persevere until you have mastered the knack. Some people are put off coiling by the difficulty they experience in forming these ropes of clay and, as shown on page 35, there are other ways of building up pottery forms. But it is useful to be able to make good ropes, because they also lend themselves to many decorative uses. The last word of warning is that you should avoid using clay *strings*; they should be ropes! Anything looking like macaroni

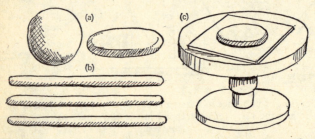

will lack strength, and will produce pots which are and look weak and ineffectual.

Task Two: Ring Coiling

First make a base on which to build, formed from a ball of clay in the palms of your hands and then pressed flat on a board, until it is a little more than $\frac{1}{4}$ in (6 mm) thick. Turn it over once or twice and wipe over the cracks which form with your thumb. If your clay is in the right condition no water need be added. Place this base on a square board of wood or asbestos of a convenient size, say 8 in (2 dm) square, and keep your pot on it all the time you are making it. If you have a turntable of any sort, it will help a great deal to man-œuvre the pot as you build it. Next you need a number of rings of coiled clay of the same circumference as the base. Make several

Fig. 32. Coiling a pot: (a) the base; (b) the ropes; (c) the base on a board on a bench whirler.

lengths of coiled clay and use one to find what length is needed. Then cut all your ropes to the same length, slicing them off at forty-five degrees at the ends.

Use a damp sponge to moisten the first rope, and then bend it with your fingers, with a compressing action to counteract the tendency of the rope to crack as it is eased round. Of course any cracks which do form can be wiped over with the thumb. Wet the cut ends with a brush and join them together. Smooth over the join, doing your best to integrate the ends of the clay to form a perfectly welded ring. If the clay is at all stiff you may have to scratch the surfaces to be joined with a potter's needle and coat them with slip before welding them together. Now the perimeter of the base re-quires slipping to a depth equivalent to the thickness of a rope, before a ring is pressed firmly onto it.

This is the first storey of the pot and it has to be flattened to re-ceive another ring. Do this by pressing it with a piece of flat board or the unglazed surface of a tile. After this it is only a matter of repeat-ing the process carefully and methodically. Quite a tall cylinder can be made, but it will be necessary to wait a while after the first half-dozen rings, to allow the clay wall to grow firm enough to support the weight of further rings.

This is a rule which has to be observed in all building, as the plastic nature of clay (due to the water in it) causes it to sink and spread. A sculptor, for instance, before he models a head, needs a wooden or metal armature to hold up the clay and maintain the shape. Your final pot should be firm, clearly exhibiting its manner of construction —a strong, even, symmetrical cylinder looking like a pile of tyres! Not very thrilling as a shape, but cleanly and neatly made. Of course it is only a first exercise, but it is a good springboard from which to jump. If you like working with this precision, you can modify the exercise by varying the size of the rings in gradual stages to produce pots with more interesting silhouettes.

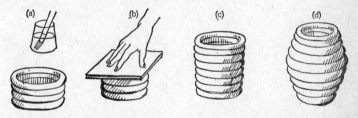

Fig. 33. (a) Separate clay coils stacked and joined with water; (b) flattening the surface with a board or tile; (c) simple coiled cylinder; (d) simple coiled convex pot.

Task Three: Spiral Coiling

A method of building up pots of intentionally irregular, as well as regular shapes, is coiling in a spiral. The equivalent of a continuous rope of clay is used, but the stages of growth are much less obvious than in the first technique. It is the method popularly adopted in schools and is usually combined with scratching and slipping to join the coils.

It is difficult to lay down any exact law regarding the use of water, slip, or slip combined with a scratched surface, to provide a key (a hold). Whenever two pieces of clay are joined together the primary consideration is that they should both be in the same state (i.e. they should contain the same percentage of water). Given this premise, the manner of joining depends on how wet, or damp, the clay is. Obviously if the two pieces are sloppy wet they will combine by slapping together and there will be no question of a join. If the clay is plastic, but sufficiently wet to soften easily when water is brushed on the surface, then the two pieces can be pressed together and the surfaces will integrate easily by rubbing the finger over the join until it disappears. But if the clay is plastic with rather a firm surface it may be wiser to use slip, and if this does not make a good join, then scratch the surfaces first to provide a key, which will help the slip to form a real bond.

One always comes back to this in pottery. 'It is all a matter of experience'—experience, incidentally, of the particular clay you are using because clays act differently and some join more easily than others. A grogged clay is easier to handle in this respect than its counterpart which is not grogged. When you have sufficient understanding of your clay, and you are able to assess its state with confidence, you will know by instinct the best way to make joins. Meanwhile the best thing is to try the various methods in these exercises, and to make a careful assessment of the results. Deep scratching

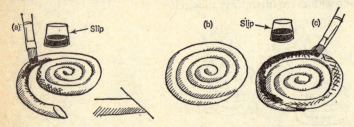

Fig. 34. (a) Forming a base with a coiled rope—note the chamfered end of the rope and the scratching and slipping; (b) the completed base; (c) scratching and slipping the top surface of the outer ring.

of the surfaces to be joined, which are then impregnated with slip, is the traditional method of joining leather-hard pieces of clay. The slip in the pieces to be joined intermingles and becomes common to both. Never try to join clay which has become dry, it is rarely possible and needs much experience.

For the base of a spirally coiled pot roll out a long rope and wind it round like a Catherine-wheel joining it with slip as you go. Scratch and slip if you are unsure. Chamfer off the end of the coil at a low angle and smooth it into itself, as shown in Figs. 34 and 35. Scratch and slip inside the perimeter.

Next make a long rope which can be picked up without breaking. Chamfer the end and stick it to the base, welding it on carefully. Start coiling it around the perimeter, and when you have completed one circle slip the top surface of this ring. Continue to build up the wall, slipping the top each time another coil is completed. If you are right handed you will probably work clockwise, but it does not matter. Press the clay rope down firmly with the fingers as you coil, making sure it adheres, but avoid pushing the wall out of shape as the pot grows taller.

When the first length of clay rope runs out, chamfer the end and blend it into the supporting coil. Your pot will probably need a rest now—when the wall has reached a height of five or six coils it is best to allow it time to harden a little before adding the weight of more clay. When it is ready, continue by forming a second rope and chamfer the end so that an invisible join can be made to the chamfered end of the first coil. Do not leave ropes of clay around to dry while the pot is drying as they will become too brittle. They can be stored in polythene bags.

Fig. 35. (a) Laying the first rope; (b) three coils completed; (c) joining ropes by scratching then slipping and smoothing with a modelling tool.

The idea of making another perfectly symmetrical jar shape is unlikely to appeal so this time vary the pattern by introducing a change in the way the ropes are assembled. After two or three ropes have been used try adding to the wall a stage formed from a clay rope bent into a continuous wave pattern and then gently pressed together, so that the waves become loops (they may need a little sponging to prevent cracking) and the loops meet each other as in Fig. 36.

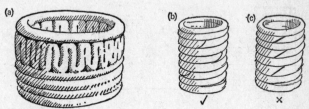

Fig. 36. (a) A horizontal and vertical arrangement; (b) correct—staggered joins; (c) incorrect—joins in line.

Take care in making a spirally coiled pot that the joins do not coincide in position, forming an obvious vertical line which could prove a weakness. The spiral nature of the coiling causes a slight rise where the rope passes over the initial join at the base, so that the pot is never exactly symmetrical. When the lip is reached you can accept the slight slope to the top as typical of the method, or it can be flattened by finishing off the end of the last rope in an extended taper instead of the usual chamfer. When the pot is firm enough it can be reversed and the top rubbed around on a piece of wet glass, which will soon give it a smooth, flat appearance.

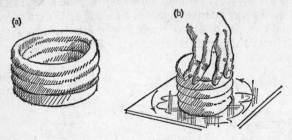

Fig. 37. (a) Irregular top; (b) smoothing and flattening the top on moist glass.

Alternatively you can aim from the start at forming a pot with curved sides. If you gradually increase the diameter of the coil as you build up, and then start to decrease again around half-way, you will have a satisfactory shape. It is a good idea to draw the curve you want on a piece of card, and cut it out as a template to guide you as you build. Aim at a shape with only a moderate outward bulge. A too quickly expanding shape, whether intentional or accidental, is almost certain to collapse. Do not forget to allow time for the lower half to become firm: this is especially necessary in a pot with an out-curving shape.

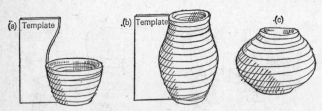

Fig. 38. (a) Using a template as a guide; (b) finished pot with the template; (c) an irregular bulge.

Task Four: Welded Coiling

Spiral coiling is a fairly free way of building and not so static as the ring method. **Welded coiling**, the complete integration of the coils as you build, is a very spontaneous way of handling the clay and consequently needs confidence and experience. However, if you dislike the more rigid use of coiling you may prefer the freedom of this method. It can be used to form almost any shape, symmetrical or otherwise, once you know what you are doing. The rope should be rather thicker than before, formed from well-grogged clay and soft enough to weld to itself without the use of water or slip. (The term 'weld' is generally used with reference to the joining of metal but, as the *Oxford Dictionary* defines it as *uniting into a homogeneous mass*, it is appropriate to the way the clay is used in this instance.) Make a pot by forming a base from a flattened ball of clay. The perimeter is pulled up by modelling it with fingers and thumb so that there is a slight wall and it turns into a shallow saucer-like shape.

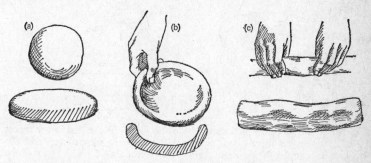

Fig. 39. Welded coiling: (a) the normal base; (b) producing a depression in the base, with a sectional view of the base; (c) forming a thick rope.

Once again aim at making a pot which bulges outwards slightly—keep it simple. Make a template as a guide. Lay the first rope inside the lip of the base, then with finger and thumb carefully squeeze the lip and the rope together, integrating them, and raising the clay wall by an upward and inward pulling action (Fig. 40).

Building can proceed in rings or spirally. The ropes are welded, each one lapped inside the preceding one and squeezed into it, either in stages or continuously. Whichever way you work there must be rests while the base clay stiffens sufficiently to support the top wall. (Boredom can be avoided by keeping two or three pots on the go at once!)

Every time five or six coils have been added, smooth the inside of the pot with your thumb or a rubber kidney (shown on page 268). If this smoothing is left until the pot is built, it may be too awkward to get at the inside, and you could ruin the shape in trying. Do not smooth the outside but examine it to make sure there are no holes or obvious dents. If there are any dents, make them good by welding in dabs of clay (support the area on the inside with the fingers of the other hand). Surface irregularities are easy to deal with, but a keen eye must be kept on the form of the pot, which can easily go wrong

Fig. 40. (a) Welding the first rope inside the base; (b) the first three ropes; (c) welding the first three ropes together; (d) adding the second stage with the template as a guide; (e) a whirler improvised from a round bread-board—note the washer between the board and its support.

when working in this spontaneous way. The charm of hand-made pottery is its comparative ruggedness—being nearer to nature than commercial pottery. There is a difference between intention and accident, however, so aim at giving the pot the shape you intend and **use a template conscientiously.**

Do not allow the first stage of your pot to dry too much or the next stage may part from it. In drying it will shrink more and this will cause cracking. The use of a turntable is almost a necessity when working in this way. A wooden one will suffice. This could be improvised from a circular bread-board mounted on a thick wooden base with a strong screw and a couple of washers to complete the assembly. Anything which turns freely while you are working will do. One of the earliest forms of potter's wheel resembled a millstone and was rotated by the feet—not so difficult as it sounds, because the weight of the wheel did most of the work.

Task Five: Strip Coiling

Use a thick rope of well-grogged clay, as for welded coils, only of a stiffer consistency and either beat it flat with a paddle, or press it flat with the heel of the hand. This is the strip which can be used for building in separate rings, stage by stage. Chamfer the ends of each piece of strip used to form a ring and weld these together using a scratched and slipped join.

You may have to 'darn' the join in order to conceal it effectively. The stages are also joined to each other by slipping and scratching and here too darning completes the job. The **process of darning** refers to the use of deep criss-cross scratches made with a potter's needle across the line of the join, followed by brushing thick slip into the scratches. The whole join is then firmly wiped over with a broad modelling tool, until the surface has been made good. If the join is

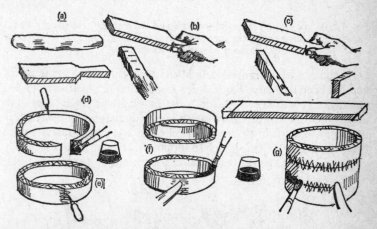

Fig. 41. Strip coiling: (a) rough clay rope and wooden paddle; (b) flattening the rope; (c) flattening the edge of the rope; (d) forming a ring from the rope; (e) darning the join; (f) adding one ring to another; (g) darning the external joins.

still obvious repeat the process. In fact you are softening up the clay surfaces on both sides of the join line and mashing them into each other until they become homogeneous.

This is a quicker way of building up a pot with high walls but, like the first ring method, it is rather static and the shapes produced are limited. Only a slight outward curve is possible until you are really skilled. However, if this technique appeals to you it can be used very effectively: all techniques are a means to an end and their use is a personal matter (see Plate 31).

Task Six: Building with Pieces

This is the freest technique for building. The clay required must be soft enough to weld easily (as with the Welded Coiling method described in Task Four), yet firm enough to retain its shape while being built outwards and upwards. It is best to use a well-grogged clay with little tendency to collapse; a sculptor's clay in fact. The forms themselves could be sculptural, three-dimensional in a very free way, rather than static or symmetrical.

Fig. 42. Building with pieces: (a) the base and the pieces; (b) shaping with the pieces; (c) welding the pieces together with a modelling tool; (d) an irregular shape produced by this method.

A saucer-like base is needed and balls of clay are rolled in the palms and flattened into large blobs which can be circular, oval, or rounded rectangles. These are welded into the base and into each other and, in this way, the pot can grow freely in any direction. As always, it is necessary to work in stages, never piling up too much weight before the early stages are firm enough to support it. How far you go depends on the nature of the clay and you can learn only by experience.

Fig. 43. Examples of irregular shapes built up with pieces of clay. Note the temporary prop in the example on the far left.

If you have little success in working this way, then give up for the time being, but return to it later when you are more experienced in the use of clay. Once you have tried the usual methods of making more conventional shapes, it is refreshing to invent new shapes which are rather difficult. Remember that temporary props or buttresses can be used to support shapes which would collapse in the plastic state, but which are perfectly stable when the clay is rigid.

Task Seven: Beating

A further technique which encourages spontaneity uses a basic, spirally-coiled cylinder made from fat ropes of grogged clay which is medium-stiff. The cylinder can be run up quickly and should be narrow, tall and thick walled. The beating is done with a wooden paddle (this can be a heavy wooden spoon, a butter pat, a miniature cricket bat, or just a hefty piece of wood shaped with a rudimentary handle). Support the cylinder inside with your hand or a piece of rounded wood. It is best to beat and see what happens, improvising the technique for yourself. Smooth the inside by smearing the coils together before and after beating. If you make a pot with a narrow neck, and you want a good finish on the inside, wait until it is leather-hard and then cut through the middle with a sharp knife. After smoothing with a rubber kidney join the two halves by scratching, slipping and darning. If support is needed stuff the inside with crumpled newspaper (see Plate 35).

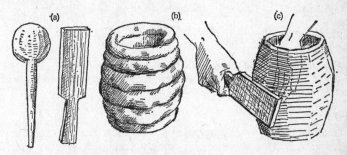

Fig. 44. Beating: (a) large wooden spoon and paddle; (b) pot coiled from extra-thick ropes; (c) thinning the walls and shaping.

Task Eight: Coiling Animal Forms

This is a good exercise for the imaginative use of clay. Animals, birds, fish, or insect forms, based directly on nature or invented, can be as fantastic as you choose. They may be of no practical use, although it is fun to make them holders for sweets, flowers, matches, cigarettes, or what you will. Avoid any impulse to attempt to reproduce natural forms faithfully, but try to transpose nature into pottery terms, exploiting the peculiar quality of the coiled clay rope in various thicknesses (quite thin coils are viable in decorative work). It is the equivalent of a thick line with which you can parody and caricature nature (see Plate 32).

1. Start by forming the body. This has been done previously by sticking two thumbed bowls together to form an ovoid shape. Now try forming the halves with coils. This could be done over two old cups without handles or two small glass bowls (cover them with damp tissue paper first). Remove the coils as soon as they are sufficiently firm.

2. At the same time coil cone shapes for the neck and legs. Keep

the latter chunky as thin legs are unstable and easily broken. A base may be necessary to support the legs.

3. Model the head by forming a ball, and squeezing it, flattening it, or drawing it out to an appropriate (simple) shape for a head.

4. Details such as tail and wings can be formed from one long rope bent into loops or folded. Ideas will occur to you as you work.

5. When all the parts are leather-hard assemble them by scratching and slipping.

Fig. 45. (a) Coiled bowl shape covered with moist tissue paper squares; (b) two bowls joined to form an egg shape; (c) base, legs, head and other coiled details; (d) assembled fired form.

Finishing

In all methods of building pots by hand there remains a characteristic surface. This surface may satisfy you as it stands. From a practical aspect, if the method has been executed properly, the pot will be leak-proof when fired and glazed—that is to say liquid will not penetrate the walls due to faulty workmanship or construction. Therefore whether one treats the pot surface any further is an aesthetic consideration. If you do not fancy the rugged but honest appearance of exposed coiling then there are ways of changing it. Again if your coiling has a distressingly haphazard look about it, you may wish to cover up by giving your pot a smooth or textured surface, to which further decoration could be added.

You will remember earlier (see page 19) finishing off thumb pots in the following ways. If a coiled pot is still soft enough when finished you can smear the coils into each other, or you can do this while making it. The final finish, however, is best given at the leather-hard stage. A bamboo comb or a piece of hacksaw blade will break through the coils if they are still evident; scraping with the hacksaw in a number of directions ploughs the surface and prepares it for smoothing by pressure with a large modelling tool. This gives a perfectly smooth surface but if the clay is a little too dry, sponge the surface lightly first. Reminder: a good way of ensuring a really smooth base, **which is a practical necessity,** is to rub it on a piece of damp glass, working it about so that it makes contact in all directions (see Fig. 37). Be careful to keep it moving in case it surprises you by sticking fast to the glass (due to the vacuum created when clay is pressed on to a very smooth surface).

As already suggested, both finishing and making coiled pots is easier done on a turntable, which can be improvised. However, a professionally made one is better and there are plenty to choose from in the catalogues. There are **banding** or **lining wheels** (designed for applying even bands of colour by brush) which are light and made of aluminium, and also heavy cast-iron **whirlers** (see page 255) which run more easily.

Decoration

Impressed Decoration

As the biscuit firing process has not been gone into so far, decoration is limited to those methods suitable for damp clay. The methods suggested for thumb pots apply to coiled pots also, although there are additional ones which can be used on coiled pots only. For instance, the coils can be embellished with impressions from the end of a tool. Naturally the tool shape prints itself on the plastic clay and so, with a set of modelling tools, there is a range of patterns you can produce. If you are handy at woodwork you can produce a number of shaped pieces of dowel specifically for printing on clay—dowel itself is useful for making a circular print, which forms a rich pattern when repeated at intervals. You may have seen the 'printing sticks' used in junior schools to print on paper: crosses, stars and other shapes are cut into the end surface of the dowel. They print very clearly on clay, in relief, and are also easily made at home.

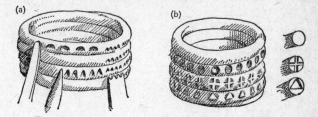

Fig. 46. (a) Tool marks on a coiled pot; (b) impressions from wooden printing sticks.

The marks from the modelling tools are not only decorative, they seal each rope of clay to the next, thus strengthening the surface of the pot. This form of decoration is, therefore, part of the construction of the pot and it is more effective if done stage by stage, along with the smoothing of the inside. Be careful not to spoil the shape of the pot when pressing on the outside; support the area you are decorating with your hand inside, or if your hand is too big, use a roller, or a wooden spoon, etc. Of course, there is no reason why such tool or stick marks should not be applied to welded or beaten pots also (although they will have no constructional significance in this case). Applied to a pot with a texture they provide a pleasant variety of surface.

Fig. 47. Joining marks made with: (a) a pointed tool; (b) a curved tool or knife; (c) a spatula-shaped tool.

Tool marks applied to a leather-hard pot are crisper, and require more pressure: they must be applied with restraint or the walls may cave in.

It has been mentioned already that horizontal coiling may be varied by occasional vertical coiling, which has a very positive pattern effect. A large part of the pot can be built in this way, in fact, and another variation is to introduce Catherine-wheels of clay. One student used to make all her pots in this way, including pots in which interstices were left. These were, of course, holders (not containers for liquid!) designed to accommodate glass jars. Such pots can also house growing plants which send out shoots through the holes.

Fig. 48. Coiled pots.

Applied Decoration

Another suggestion for decoration is that you apply coils, strips, or flattened balls of clay to some pots. (Keep the pots damp while the decorative detail is being prepared.) Before fixing them, scratching and slipping the pot surface, and the clay decorations, is necessary. Ensure that both clays are in the same state of dampness, or they will shrink away from each other. It is very exasperating to have part of your decoration fall off during the drying and it is very difficult to put right.

To summarise these methods of decoration, it is possible to have:

(a) A smooth surface which could be painted later.
(b) A surface with one or more textures.
(c) Exposed coils with or without tool marks (Figs. 46, 47, 49).
(d) Applied relief decoration in the form of strips, ropes or discs of clay (Fig. 48).

Any of these can be used in combination, but do not overload your work with ornamentation: aim to put it in the right place so that it looks as if it really belongs there.

Storage and Drying

Pots must dry slowly and evenly. Therefore, keep them cool with air circulating all round them, but not in a draught. Big pots are best dried on slatted shelves for good support. When dry store them safely, keeping them dry and clean until they can be fired. If they have to be transported to a kiln, pack them in straw or crumpled newspaper—do not squash them, but do not allow them to move. The packing should cushion the fragile dry clay, inside boxes stout enough to withstand the shock of transportation. **Remember** never to pick up a pot by the neck or rim until it has been fired and glazed and support it firmly with your hand under the base (see Fig. 18(a) on page 18).

Further Work

If the kind of work you have been trying out in this chapter is to your liking and you want to do more, without repeating exactly what you have done already, then make thumb pots and add to their height by coiling in one form or another.

Fig. 49. Thumb pots (base half) with added coils: (a) coils untreated; (b) coils joined with saw-blade texture; (c) coils joined with slip and with impressed pattern; (d) coils joined by tool impressions.

Alternatively make a large bowl, cylinder, or other simple shape and add smaller ones to it, or try a combination of different sizes with more than one shape.

Fig. 50. Composite pots.

What appears to be a difficult shape to make, such as a pot which expands quickly and just as quickly narrows to a small neck, is not so hard to achieve if it is made as two bowl shapes with exactly the same circumference particularly at the rim. When leather-hard, these are scratched and slipped along the joining edges and assembled as one pot. The seam is darned on the outside and can be smoothed on the inside with a profile or a sponge tied to a dowel rod or cane. Templates always help to achieve accuracy of shape.

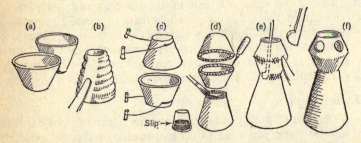

Fig. 51. (a) Coiled and smoothed 'flower-pot' shapes; (b) first stage coiled and smoothed; (c) removing the bases; (d) joining the three pieces; (e) welding the join externally with a modelling tool and internally with a profile; (f) finished pot with cut-out decoration.

CHAPTER FOUR

POTTERY WITHOUT THE WHEEL: PLIABLE ROLLED CLAY

An entirely different way of using clay is to roll it out in sheets with a rolling-pin and, while pliable, form it into shapes by bending. This technique is most suited to pieces of pottery with a large area and comparatively small height or depth, such as shallow dishes and bowls, plates and platters, etc. Also taller shapes, of a special character can be produced by folding and bending. It is a helpful method, when teaching numbers of children, as this technique gives quick results, which are presentable enough to satisfy even the most self-critical child. However, its speed and simplicity appeals to anybody who has limited time. Shapes with a broad, flat surface are tempting to decorate and give scope for real fun with the slip tracer and the slip brush. It is by far the simplest way of turning out ash trays, as generations of 'one evening a week' potters have proved every Christmas.

Tools

The new tools required in this chapter are: a domestic rolling-pin or beechwood roller; some hessian, linen, calico, sailcloth, or any fabric with a heavy weave and some weight; and kitchen paper, kitchen roll or newspaper. Hardwood guide strips will also be needed and these should be 18 in (4·5 dm) long and 1 in (2·5 cm) wide and between ¼ in (6·5 mm) and ⅜ in (10 mm) thick. They are easily made at home and as the thickness of the wood determines the thickness of

(a)   (b)

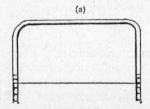
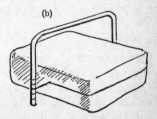

Fig. 52. (a) Clay cutter (bow or harp) with spaced notches; (b) cutting the clay lump.

43

the clay sheet, you will be able to suit yourself. Rectangular off-cuts of asbestos or hardwood of various sizes are used to support the pots to be made. You will also need a clay cutter or **harp**. These are metal frames of bow shape with slots cut at intervals, in the ends of which a cutting wire can be adjusted at various heights to cut different thicknesses of clay. Harps can be improvised if you have metal-work tools (Fig. 52).

The taut wire is parallel to the bench and the ends of the harp rest on the bench.

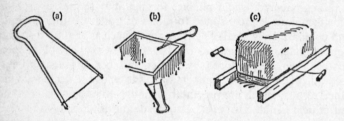

Fig. 53. (a) Bow trimmer; (b) using the bow trimmer; (c) cutting slices with a cutting wire and wooden guides.

The **bow trimmer** is a cutting wire set in a smaller, springy frame as shown in Fig. 53 and is used for slicing and trimming clay.

The materials mentioned, such as hessian and canvas, are useful for preventing the clay from sticking to the table-top. Whichever material you use its texture will make its imprint on the under-surface of the rolled clay. If the fabric is used loose it tends to ruck up and form creases, which mark the clay unpleasantly. You will find it best to secure it with staples, or to cover a board and glue it over the back (with waterproof glue!). For clay sheet, as for most hand-built work, a grogged clay is best. Wedge it thoroughly and get rid of all air-bubbles, unless you are cutting direct from a fresh block of clay. Clay sheet can be cut to thickness with the clay cutter (harp or bow), or it can be rolled to thickness using the guide strips.

Preparation

Clay comes to you from the merchant in block form in a bag and as clay sheet is more easily cut direct from the block, keep it in its polythene wrapping until you are ready to begin. Start by cutting sheets of clay $\frac{1}{4}$ in (6·5 mm) thick. The quick and easy way (especially when you want a number of sheets) is to use the bow. However, as you are unlikely to be using a bow or harp at this stage let us leave this for the moment. If you have a fresh block of clay, place rolling guides (thicker than the required thickness) on either side of your clay and draw an ordinary clay cutter through it, supporting the cutting wire on the guides. You should then be able to cut a reasonably even sheet. Lift the block away leaving the sheet ready for further preparation. It is far better to use guides but, if you do not have any, mark a line round the top of the clay and draw the cutting wire through with great care, making sure that the clay is thicker than you need it. If you are using the sheet of clay you have just sliced, beat it out with a mallet or paddle a little thicker than required, Work on it with the

Fig. 54. Rolling clay: (a) beating the clay to the approximate thickness; (b) rolling the clay using guide strips.

heel of your hand and spread it from the centre. Then trim it and (with $\frac{1}{4}$ in guides (6·5 mm) if possible) roll it out as even and as flat as you can.

Air may appear as blisters (squeezed to the surface by the pressure of rolling), so prick them, press out the air and restore the surface by wiping with the thumb. Fill in any dents with blobs of clay, wipe over and roll the surface again. Watch that the roller is kept clean since, if clay adheres to it, it will print fresh dents in the clay every time it is rolled. Keep a piece of cloth by you for wiping the roller. The clay should be turned over once at least during the rolling process, so that it is not compressed on one surface only.

If you do have the opportunity of cutting clay with a harp, set the cutting wire at the height required to give the desired thickness of clay sheet and holding it by the sides draw it through the clay block. Then raise the wire into higher notches to give twice the desired thickness and draw it through the clay once more. In this way you can cut two slices without disturbing the original block. Provided your harp has sufficient notches, this procedure can continue until several slices have been cut. If the clay is used in this way it gets little preparation of course, although the action of rolling helps to compress and condition the clay. The sensible compromise is to use the harp to cut approximately to the thickness required and then finish off by rolling, not forgetting to turn the clay and to get rid of all blisters. Clay sheets with a large area are difficult to handle, so do not attempt to roll out anything larger than you can lift without breaking.

Supports

In order to raise any form of wall and keep it in position until it becomes rigid, temporary supports are necessary. Props or buttresses of *clay* are used for this purpose because they shrink at the same rate as the object being formed and to prevent their adhering to each other thin paper guards are placed between them. When finished, the props are removed and returned to the bin for reconstitution.

Practical Work Tasks

Task One: Making a Round Dish

1. Make a cardboard disc as a template and place it on a sheet of rolled clay. Cut round it with a potter's needle. Alternatively, lightly press a tin lid of the right diameter on the clay and cut round it with the needle. Do not use the lid as a cutter; the clay will stick inside the lid, and it will be impossible to remove without spoiling its shape. A clay disc of 8 in (2 dm) diameter would be suitable for your first effort. Select the best area of the clay sheet, making sure it is of even thickness (if you have not been able to use guides).

2. Prepare the support required in this case by rolling a rope of clay about 1 in (2·5 cm) thick and of absolutely consistent shape. Use your wooden or asbestos pot board as a base and form the rope of clay into a ring a little less in diameter than the disc of clay. Weld the ends together to form a smooth, unbroken ring and cover the top surface with pieces of kitchen paper, damp enough to adhere.

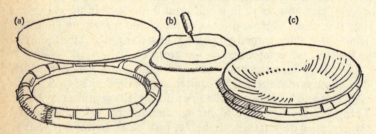

Fig. 55. (a) Clay ring covered with moist paper guards; (b) cutting a circle with a potter's needle; (c) the dish formed inside the supporting ring.

3. Place the clay disc centrally on the ring, gently press it down to meet the board, using a moist sponge. Do this very carefully to avoid marking or denting the clay surface. The disc has to be persuaded to cave in evenly and become a shallow bowl—the perimeter turning up, supported by the ring. Make sure you have pressed the centre flat, so that the bowl will stand firm.

4. Set it aside to dry leather-hard, when it can be removed from the supporting ring. Smooth off the edges with a damp sponge and impart roundness and smoothness by stroking between finger and thumb. Smooth the surfaces generally. If you do not like the fabric texture on the outside and underneath of the bowl, then sponge it lightly and work over it with a modelling tool until it is smooth.

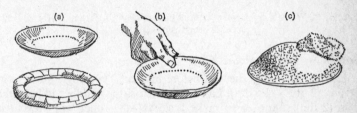

Fig. 56. (a) Dish removed when leather-hard; (b) smoothing the ring with moistened thumb and forefinger; (c) smoothing the under-surface with a moist sponge.

Variation on Task One. A popular variation is to produce a wavy-edged dish by using balls of clay placed in a circle as the support.

1. Cut the disc as before.

2. Form six balls of clay some $\frac{1}{2}$ in (13 mm) thick. Place these in order around the card template, and make paper guards for each one.

3. Place the flat clay disc centrally and press it down in the centre first.

Fig. 57. (a) Four balls of clay with paper guards ready to receive the clay disc; (b) shaping the disc over the clay balls; (c) the wavy-shaped dish.

4. The edge will be wavy already. Work on the undulations with the moist sponge, forming them over the supporting balls as evenly as possible. If you strain the clay it will crack. The depth of the wavy edge depends on the size, shape and number of supports—varying the number from four to eight will produce different patterns; larger balls make big waves; and a thick rope of clay cut into small cylindrical blocks can be used to form a flatter, wavy edge (Fig. 58).

Fig. 58. (a) Wavy dish formed over three balls of clay; (b) flatter dish formed over six short lengths of clay rope.

Task Two: Bending Rolled Clay

1. Roll out a clay sheet as before and cut a rectangle about 8 in × 6 in (2 dm × 1·5 dm). Lay a roller across the middle and bend the 8 in (2 dm) side over to make a sleeve—the roller will prevent it flattening. Wrapping damp paper round the roller will ensure its easy withdrawal later on.

2. Scratch and slip ½ in (13 mm) of clay inside both edges before pressing them together.

3. The end view will be a loop.

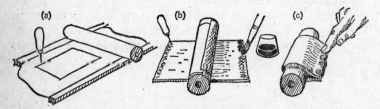

Fig. 59. (a) Cutting a rectangle from the middle of a rolled clay sheet; (b) bending the clay over a moist, paper-covered roller, with the edges scratched and slipped; (c) joining the edges with finger impressions.

4. Stand the 'sleeve' upright on the rest of the clay sheet and cut round it with the potter's needle. Take the shape you have cut out (this is the base), slip and scratch inside the perimeter and the bottom 'loop' of the clay sleeve. Place the sleeve on the base and weld it to the base so that no join shows.

5. Make good the lap join on the sleeve by squeezing it hard between thumb and forefinger, so that their impressions are left along the length.

Withdraw the supporting roller by easing it out with a wiggling motion, as soon as the pot is firm enough to stand up. If you cannot insert your hand to finish off the join at the base use the sponge on a rod, or a profile.

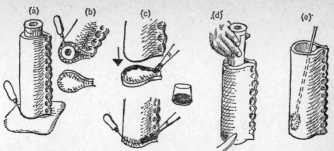

Fig. 60. (a) Marking out the base; (b) preparing the base for joining; (c) joining the base and sealing the external join; (d) smoothing the join and removing the roller; (e) smoothing the internal join with a sponge on a stick.

Task Three: *Using a Butt Join and Making a Handle*

Make another sleeve by wrapping the clay around a cylinder such as a jar (covered with damp paper). Make the two edges meet exactly and scratch and slip them before butting them together. As soon as possible withdraw the supporting cylinder. When it is leather-hard darn the butt join as thoroughly as possible (see Fig. 61(d)), internally and externally. Cut the base and join it to the cylinder. Insert a thin string of clay around the base and smooth it in. This will make it easier to clean inside. A popular exercise is to make a mug in this way. For the handle, roll a rope of clay and flatten it with finger pressure, incidentally forming a slight groove.

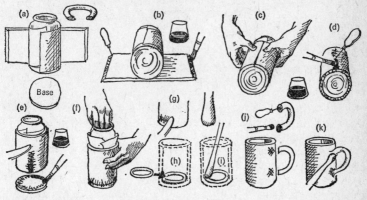

Fig. 61. (a) Clay sheet and base and handle with the jar wrapped in moist paper; (b) the jar in position on the clay sheet; (c) joining the clay round the jar; (d) darning the external join; (e) smoothing the external join and adding the base; (f) removing the jar and the paper; (g) smoothing the external join at the base; (h) adding a clay ring inside the base; (i) welding the ring into the base; (j) preparing the handle for joining; (k) joining the handle.

c

Make sure the edges are rounded for comfort in holding, then ease it round gradually into a C-curve. Try it for fit in your hand and then leave it to harden while you prepare the cylinder. When the cylinder is leather-hard and the joins have been attended to, chamfer the ends of the handle to fit snugly, scratch and slip them, and the places where they will be attached. Press the ends of the handle on firmly but gently as it could easily snap, and then weld the joins.

Task Four: Making a One-piece Box

1. For this you need well-grogged clay. If you have any red clay use it with as much grog as it will take without losing pliability. Roll it out and cut a true square—9 in (22·5 cm) would be a good size for this exercise, so that the box will be part of a (hollow) cube with 3 in (7·5 cm) sides.

2. Prepare a paper pattern. This is cruciform: two sets of parallel lines 3 in (7·5 cm) apart pass through each other at right angles to form five, 3 in (7·5 cm) squares.

3. Cut round the template with the potter's needle. Outline the central square of the clay cross with lightly impressed lines, using the top edge of a modelling tool held at a low angle (you are scoring the clay for folding).

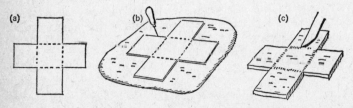

Fig. 62. (a) Paper pattern for a box; (b) cutting round the pattern; (c) marking the base by scoring.

4. Turn the clay cross over. Scratch all the cut edges and apply thick slip. Lift two adjacent walls carefully; when their edges meet press them together and squeeze the join a little.

5. Raise the other two walls in turn, joining them to the first two walls, and finally to each other. Inspect the junction of the base and walls and make good any cracks which have appeared by wiping them with thumb or tool.

6. Allow the clay to stiffen to *less* than leather-hard, then pick up the box and gently tap the sides on the working surface. Do this one at a time until they are all flat; darn the joins along the four edges and round them off smoothly. They will look more like pottery edges if you chamfer them before darning. Round off the top edges.

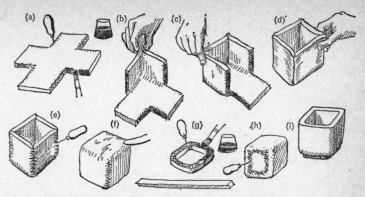

Fig. 63. (a) Scratching and slipping the edges; (b) pinching the edges together; (c) three sides joined; (d) four sides joined; (e) darning the joins; (f) smoothing and flattening the base; (g) foot formed from clay strip, scratched and slipped for joining; (h) preparing the base to receive the foot; (i) the finished box.

As your clay contains plenty of grog it may be too much in evidence on the surface. Pressure from the modelling tool will force the grog down and give a relatively smooth finish. A rectangular foot for the box could be made from thin strips of left-over clay sheet and applied with slip, etc.

Decoration

Any methods of decoration used already can be used on the pots in this chapter. They are all suitable for application on clay in the leather-hard state. Four further ways of decorating on damp clay which are especially suitable for the pots you have made from clay sheets are:

Slip coating the inside of dishes and the outside of pots;
Sgraffito (or scratched slip);
Brush and slip; and
Slip trailing: decoration through a nozzle using a **trailer** or **tracer** (alternative names).

Slip Coating

The use of a white slip (sometimes called 'engobe') to transform the familiar appearance of common red clay pots dates back a long way. White clay was not easy to obtain and so was expensive. A thin coat of white clay on a red pot solved the economic problem. Since then many coloured slips have been introduced for aesthetic rather than practical reasons; in your work it is best to retrace the steps of the early potters and confine yourselves to the basic clay colours.

If you have no red or white clay purchase a few kilos of dried clay for slip making from the potters' merchant who supplies your bulk clay: in this way you will be sure they match each other for shrinkage. Buy a clay powder recommended for slip tracing/trailing, NOT for slip casting—this is a different matter with which we shall deal on page 100. Powdered clay is sprinkled into water until it will absorb no more, allowed to stand for a while, stirred well, and allowed to stand again for several days, when surplus water is poured off. The consistency is controlled by the amount poured off. It must be sieved through a 60–80-mesh sieve before being used and needs an airtight container to prevent evaporation and undue thickening. It is possible also to buy slips prepared ready for use, but this is expensive. Plastic clay can be dried, pulverised, and then prepared in the same way. The possibilities you can explore are coating buff (or white) pots with red slip, and red or buff pots with white slip.

A practical use of the slip coating is to give a good finish to the inside of pots which have been difficult to smooth. A coat of slip inside an untouched coiled pot at the leather-hard stage will fill up small gaps and give a uniform finish. The slip should not be so thick that it fails to integrate with the clay it covers, or it will crack because it shrinks more. Too thin a slip is useless because it becomes patchily transparent under a clear glaze, and it will be neither a practical nor an aesthetic success. A very wet slip can penetrate the pot-body and soften it so that it falls apart.

(a) Pouring. To coat the inside of a pot or dish, pour in what you judge to be the necessary amount to provide all-over cover. This is rather like estimating the quantity of paint needed to cover a door! Sluice it around briskly but carefully and having covered all the surface, drain out the surplus, if any. If there is not enough pour a little more into the pot and swill it around until the inside is covered, the overlapping hardly shows. In the case of a dish it is best to remove the slip with a clean sponge, as you can salvage the slip and try again using more slip this time. Never fill the pot with slip or you will find it growing sticky in your hands and disintegrating before you can empty it.

Alternatively, the outside of a pot can be coated. **Never** attempt to coat both inside and outside—your pot will not withstand the double wetting. Choose a strong, simple shape such as a cylinder for your first attempt. As the slip will be poured over it, the pot must be supported above a bowl to catch the surplus. A small washing-up bowl with the guide strips placed across will do.

If this arrangement can be balanced safely on a turntable it will facilitate even pouring. A personal treasure is part of a 1920 vintage electric candelabra, consisting of three brass arms meeting centrally,

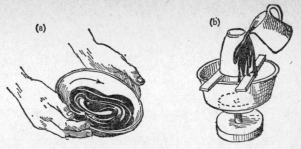

Fig. 64. (a) Slip coating the inside of a dish; (b) pouring slip.

which is invaluable as a support for slip-coating. Pottery provides many opportunities for improvising tools. Another useful support for pots being slipped or glazed is a piece of X.P.M—metal which has been punched with slits and then pulled out into a diamond mesh. It is used in the building trade and a finer type is used in radiators and wireless sets. It is an excellent support for drying pots, as it allows maximum air circulation. Reverse the pot and pour the slip from a jug in a steady stream, rotating the pot if possible.

Avoid covering the base with slip and any splashes can be removed easily with a sponge. Lift the support gently and tap it carefully, so that extra-thick slip is encouraged to run off the pot. Leave it to dry in a warm atmosphere until it can be handled safely. If you make marks on the slip there is little you can do to rectify it, so avoid touching it like the plague! If you insert your fingers through the neck opening and then spread your hand you can lift a pot safely while the slip is still somewhat tender. It is interesting to run streaks of another coloured slip down the pot immediately it has been coated. A pot which has been coated with red slip could be decorated

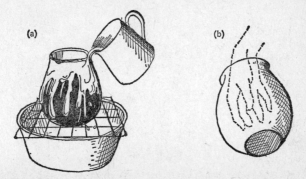

Fig. 65. (a) White slip dribbled over wet red slip; (b) picking up the pot.

with white slip poured (from a small jug) on a number of places around the neck. This decoration resembles veining in marble.

Please note that to do this the pot needs to be placed over another bowl and that it must have a good steady support (such as a cooling tray for cakes, or the X.P.M. already mentioned), otherwise the second slip will discolour the slip already in the bowl. If an assistant rotates the pot while you are pouring you may get interesting results. If your attempts are not very successful, or if you touch the slip with your fingers, try drawing a finger lightly across the surface so that the clay body shows through, and form a pattern of swirling lines with soft, thick edges. This is a traditional idea which is echoed in the finger painting popular in junior schools. Ideas for natural patterns in slip can be found in stones, plants and in the sky.

(b) Dipping. This requires a larger quantity of slip but is probably easier. It is used to apply slip to the outside of a pot. The pot can be held by the foot, or your hand can be inserted inside it, depending on its shape. The bucket or bin containing the slip must be deeper than the pot and allowance must be made for the displacement of liquid when the pot is dipped. When the pot goes straight in, neck down, the air inside will prevent the slip rising inside the pot; if you are unprepared for the strong resistance set up by the air pressure, you will find you lose control (and possibly the pot). Should the pot enter the slip at an angle, the slip will go inside and you will find it difficult to complete covering the outside. If your hand is inside the pot you will have better control, but of course the base will be covered and will need cleaning up with a sponge.

Whichever way you work it is probably best not to immerse the last ½ in (13 mm) of the pot, then you will have a clean finish, the

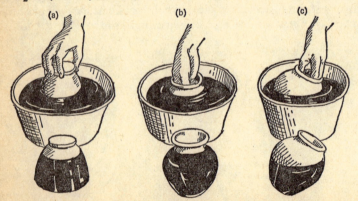

Fig. 66. (a) Dipping by holding the base; (b) dipping with the hand inside the neck; (c) part dipping (off-centre).

snag being that you may not get the line of slip exactly horizontal, which is irritating to the eye. Interesting divisions of the pot surface can be obtained by dipping the pot at a pronounced angle (base downwards of course) so that it is part-slipped.

Pouring slip is recommended for beginners, whereas dipping is difficult and it is best practised on small pots. There are other ways of covering the pot surface with slip by brush, sponge, or spray.

(c) **Brushing.** This needs skill in application. Use a broad brush and do not keep working over the surface or you will brush up the clay from underneath. White slip especially tends to dissolve in a clear glaze during firing, so it needs to be applied as a fully opaque covering. A second coat of slip may be required, but the first coat must be firm before a second coat is lightly brushed over it. Use the same slip as for pouring, or dipping.

(d) **Sponging.** With a fine plastic or natural sponge, and using thicker slip, this gives an even but textured surface. Start with a moist sponge and a modicum of slip. Pounce the slip onto the pot surface when it is firm. One coat gives a mottled finish when glazed, but two or three coats will give completely effective cover. The mottled effect can be emphasised by pouncing two coloured slips at the same time. Alternatively, sponge on one colour sparingly, wait until it dries firm and then sponge on the other, also sparingly. Try this out on flat clay before using it on a pot.

(e) **Spraying.** Spraying needs more sophisticated equipment (see Appendix One on page 260). Put the slip through a fine sieve (100 or 120 mesh) and add enough water for it to pass through the spray gun (electrically operated) or thumb spray. A good surface can be built up by degrees, one coat on another with a resting period for drying between coats. If the spray is held too near the pot, rivulets will form and the slip will be streaky. Spraying too long on one spot will have a similar effect. A turntable is essential for really even coverage. You will find that masks can be obtained quite cheaply (see the Ferro catalogue), and it is a good idea to wear one whenever you are spraying.

While there is a shine on the slip it is still too wet to apply a further coat so wait until it looks matt. If your spray nozzle is coarse enough to pass a thicker slip, this can give a pimply surface which is quite pleasant for a change. A fine, smooth sprayed surface is really good for brushwork, after biscuit firing. The pattern can be drawn clearly in pencil before painting (a technique which is explained in Chapter Eleven). If an electric spray is not available use a domestic hand spray, there are so many types it is not possible to specify—try yours, it may work. Of course it is rather slow and is less effective than a mechanical spray, but it is worth attempting.

Sgraffito

Sgraffito ('scratched' from the Italian verb *sgraffiare*) is a process in which the slip covering is cut away to expose parts of the body underneath. The Italians fully appreciated the decorative possibilities inherent in the accidental scratching of a recently slipped pot and they set about exploiting it, using a fine point to scratch out line drawings and lettering, occasionally removing whole areas of background with a broader tool. Tooth-picks, lino tools, modelling tools, screwdrivers, will all produce distinctive lines.

Practise first on flat clay. The cleanest line is cut when the slip is not too thick and is leather-hard—this is the true sgraffito! A rather blunt line is possible when the slip is still soft. Only trials will reveal the subtleties of scratching the slip at different stages of drying. Any burr which is produced on the line should be rubbed off with a modelling tool or sandpaper when the clay is quite dry. **Do not leave it on,** it will be rough and sharp when fired and glazed, and unpleasant to the touch if not dangerous! By now you should be interested in the different techniques of decoration. Doing detective work on the pottery you see when shopping will increase your awareness and on holiday there is bound to be at least one craft potter whose work will be worth analysing (and buying, perhaps). Many large seaside towns have museums containing local ware from the past, Brighton, for instance, has an excellent collection of English slip ware. Incidentally, there is a list of museums worth visiting in Appendix Four, on page 285.

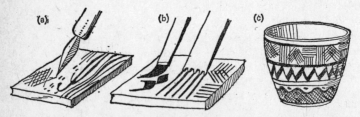

Fig. 67. Sgraffito: (a) with a stencil knife; (b) with bamboo tools; (c) sgraffito decoration.

A last word about sgraffito: if you try to scratch away the slip when it is over-dry you may succeed, but the line will chip on the edge and some slip will flake away. Patterns may be spontaneous or planned in detail and can be executed boldly and freely, or very carefully and precisely (see Plates 8 and 24). They should exploit the contrast between various thicknesses of line, and textures can be produced by stippling with a pointed tool, or dragging a hacksaw blade along the

Fig. 68. (a) Sgraffito tile; (b) pot with sgraffito lettering; (c) sgraffito decorated mug.

surface, etc. Experiment on flat clay or a tile first—sgraffito tiles for fireplaces were very popular once.

Brush and Slip

Use a well-shaped paint brush, which will draw to a good point, dip it in creamy slip and try making a series of natural brush marks, placing the head of the brush sideways on the clay to see the shape it makes. Then arrange these shapes in formal patterns, radially or facing alternate ways, in series, and so on. Go on to draw the fully charged brush swiftly across the clay so that it produces an elongated brush shape. When you can do this, combine the strokes to make patterns (see Plate 11).

Fig. 69. Brush marks using slip.

On the whole this direct painting with slip is most effective if done with the red slip on the lighter clays. It is difficult to obtain a thick enough brush mark with white slip, which tends to go transparent as has been explained before. As an alternative a pattern of simple shapes can be outlined in pencil or lightly impressed. The shapes are then filled in with slip, using the point of the brush, and given several coats so that a thick opaque colour results. This is a very deliberate process which lacks spontaneity but gives a clear pattern, especially

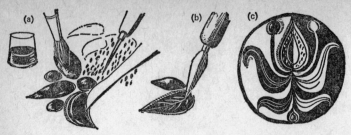

Fig. 70. (a) Outline emphasised by using modelling tool; (b) lines scratched through brush mark; (c) brush-painted pattern with scratched lines and textures.

if the outline is emphasised afterwards by indenting it with the narrow end of a modelling tool, or incising it with a sharp point.

Slip Trailing

The tool used is known as a **tracer** or **trailer**. It is basically a flexible container in which a hollow tube, drawn to a narrow end, is fitted, although the tube alone can be used if it is long enough. The old peasant potters used a clay vessel with a thumb hole in it. This controlled the flow of slip through the quill, which served as the nozzle. Rubber bulbs with an integral rubber nozzle can be purchased from the chemist (ostensibly an ear-syringe?) and used as trailers— they make almost too fine a line, but cutting off the end of the nozzle will enlarge the hole of course. The potters' merchant supplies a rubber bag, rather like a toy balloon, with plastic nozzles in several sizes of hole. Both rubber trailers are filled by sucking the slip into them, or the latter can be filled through a small funnel.

An improvised trailer can be made from a piece of bicycle inner tube, tied round a flat cork at one end and, after filling, closed at the other end by a bulldog clip. A nozzle is inserted through the cork. Nozzles can be made from large quills or glass tubing heated and drawn to a point. The very simplest trailer is glass tube alone, into which slip is drawn by sucking it (not too hard!); the flow is controlled by varying the slant of the tube between horizontal and vertical.

The slip used for trailing must be put through a fine sieve and should be creamier than the dipping slip. A little gum arabic improves its viscosity, so that it flows evenly and not too fast, and also ensures that it sticks to the pottery. If the slip is not perfectly smooth it will tend to come out in sudden spurts and ruin the decoration. Pressure on the bulb produces dots when the trailer is static and lines when it is moved (unsightly blobs if you lose control!). Fine and intricate work is untypical: a thick, fluid line, rhythmically applied and possibly punctuated by dots, is characteristic of the technique.

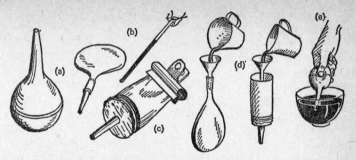

Fig. 71. (a) Slip trailer (bulb type); (b) glass tube trailer; (c) improvised trailer (inner tube, etc.); (d) filling a tube through a funnel; (e) sucking the slip into the rubber bulb.

Above all the trailer must be handled in an easy and relaxed way. Therefore, lots of practice on a sheet of clay is necessary and this can be wiped clean with a sponge time after time. Mistakes made when using the trailer are not put right easily, it is best to wipe the pot clean and start again. The decoration is most effective when the trailed slip stands up high in relief. Of course, as the water dries out the relief effect is diminished and the slip loses its gloss. However, the clear glaze, which is the standard finish for most forms of decoration on

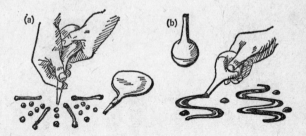

Fig. 72. (a) Using the nozzle-type trailer; (b) using the bulb-type trailer.

raw clay, brings back life and colour and restores its attractive appearance.

Trailed slip decoration contains a great deal of water and therefore should be applied sparingly. Apart from aesthetic considerations, too much slip can weaken the fabric of plates and dishes particularly and cause them to collapse. If you remember that when raw clay of no great thickness is allowed to stand loaded over-liberally with moisture of any sort (for instance covered by a really wet cloth, ostensibly to keep it damp) the water will penetrate right through it and cause cracking, then you will save yourself frustration and disappointment.

There are a number of fascinating tricks connected with the use of coloured slips all based on the natural way in which viscous liquids run together, but do not mix too quickly or easily. One simple gimmick is to drop a good fat blob of white slip onto the clay and then a blob of red into the middle of it: if you lift the board on which the clay stands and give it a gentle tap, the concentric blobs will spread, and a further white blob can be dropped in their centre. This process can be continued, providing an ever-widening series of concentric light and dark rings. Tipping the board in one, or in several directions, will change the shape of the rings accordingly, but if you play this fascinating game too long you will lose the clarity of your pattern and finish with confused streaks.

You could experiment further with slip decoration by combining some of the techniques—painting, trailing and sgraffito could be used together, if a very definite decorative conception suggested it. In general, over-elaboration is not good and should be avoided. Much depends on personal taste, there is no limit to the possibilities.

Fig. 73. Various types of slip decoration.

Finishing

Pots which have been coated with slip always need attention. The base and the collar will need careful **fettling** (trimming the surface), rough parts smoothing and blemishes repairing with a brushful of slip. There may be marks on the base or collar where they have been supported during pouring which need fettling with a modelling tool. Be particular and make sure that you remove any burr which has formed.

Further Work

Form objects from ropes and strips of clay welded together.

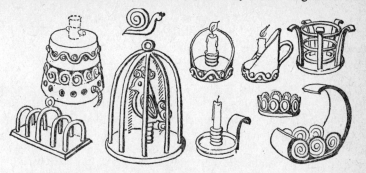

Fig. 74. Objects formed from or decorated with ropes and strips of clay.

Combine bent and flat clay shapes (see Plate 33).

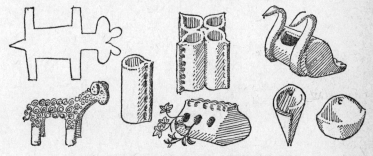

Fig. 75. Pottery formed from pliable flat clay.

CHAPTER FIVE

POTTERY WITHOUT THE WHEEL: SLAB BUILDING

In the majority of techniques raw clay is shaped while plastic and finished off in the rigid state. This chapter is concerned with those methods of building pottery which commence with leather-hard clay. Construction and design are based on box shapes made from sheets of rigid grogged clay, so a degree of precision is required. Thumbing and coiling are related to throwing on the wheel, but slab-building has an architectural or sculptural character.

Tools

The further tools which are introduced now would be difficult to improvise. They are simple mechanical cutters for mosaic squares and circular and square tiles. Additional requirements are a potter's knife especially designed for fettling, a hole cutter and a steel kidney or palette. Their use will be described with the practical work and they can all be obtained from a potters' supplier.

Preparation

Clay for sheets or slabs needs to be heavily grogged. Generally, the larger the work the heavier the grogging will need to be. Usually construction and function depend greatly on the clay remaining flat, so shrinking and warping must be avoided. It is important also to know how much your clay is going to shrink and tests for shrinkage could be made before starting to do the tasks.

As in Chapter Four you will need to cut clay and roll out sheets of $\frac{1}{4}$ in (6·5 mm) thickness or more. Look out for air-bubbles, and turn the clay over during rolling to ensure that both surfaces are compressed. This will reduce the likelihood of warping. When you are satisfied with your sheets of clay (you will need several) set them aside to dry in a draught-free place and turn them occasionally so that they dry on both sides. A way to keep them flat without slowing up the drying too much, is to place them between sheets of newspaper or kitchen paper when they are firm, with a thick board and a weight on top. Although air cannot circulate round the clay, the pressure will keep the clay flat and the paper will absorb some of the moisture. But do not use thin board such as plywood, because this will warp and do more harm than good. Several sheets of clay, interleaved with paper, can be dried at once provided there is sufficient weight on top. Take great care not to use paper with creases in it, as they would print on the clay: one piece of clay with a bad surface will affect others. Accurate placing is essential and, of course, the sheets must all be trimmed to exactly the same size. Use the clay when it is leather-hard and can be lifted without bending.

Practical Work Tasks

Task One: Making Tiles and Mosaic Squares

Tiles and mosaic pieces (known as *tesserae*) may be cut from rigid clay with a potter's knife guided by a steel ruler. It is best to mark out the rectangles first by scoring the clay with the end of a modelling tool. The sharp edge left by cutting must be fettled to a minimal chamfer and sponged to make a shaped edge which is comfortable to handle and neat in appearance. The tesserae are usually cut to $1\frac{1}{8}$ in (2·8 cm) from the raw clay, shrinking to 1 in (2·5 cm) when fired. Historically mosaic was used to make patterned and pictorial floor and wall coverings, as in the Roman baths and villas scattered about this country, though stone and glass tesserae were used in addition to clay. Their use now is limited and setting a mosaic in plaster or cement is a time-consuming craft. Mosaic was in vogue a few years ago with the home craftsman, as a heat-proof surface for coffee-tables and trays, but nowadays it is more popular in a mass-produced form, which is sold by the sheet for use in bathrooms.

Tiles can be formed in frames made from wood strips similar to those used as guides. These are filled with clay, trimmed with a wire cutter and finished off with a roller. The tile shrinks and is easily removed, when all it needs is chamfering around the edges. Make some 4 in (1 dm) tiles as a start and experiment on them with slip decoration—concentric circles look especially good. Later on you will need plain tiles with a white surface, for glaze and colour trials. Tesserae are easy to cut in large numbers, but they take a lot of care in fettling, firing and glazing. Unless you have a particular use planned for them there is little point in making them.

One of the craft potters' suppliers, Podmore's, has produced a range of semi-mechanical cutters for making square, round, hexagonal and mosaic tiles. Made of non-rusting metal the cutter is a rigid frame, which fills under hand pressure as it cuts through sheet clay. A spring-loaded back-plate attached to a rod ejects the tile which has been formed. There would be no point in purchasing any of these cutters unless you intended to make a large run of tiles of course. However, it is useful to have them available in a studio or classroom pottery.

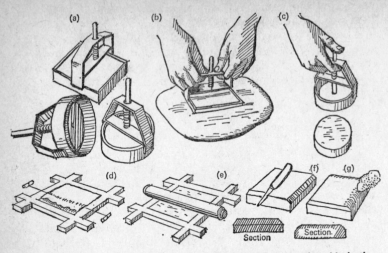

Fig. 76. (a) Disc and tile cutters; (b) pressing the cutter into the clay; (c) ejecting the clay; (d) clay pressed in a wooden frame for tiles and trimmed with a clay cutter; (e) clay rolled in a wooden frame; (f) cutting the chamfer with a knife; (g) rounding and smoothing the edge with a sponge.

Another tool we shall use is the **clay cutter**, a metal tube cut at an angle like a quill pen and set in a beechwood handle. The usual diameters are $\frac{1}{4}$ in (6·5 mm) and $\frac{1}{2}$ in (13 mm). The tapered piercer is a near relative, but it can be used to make any size hole up to its own maximum diameter. Holes are needed occasionally in pottery table lamps and teapots and also for hanging objects and decorative purposes. The Chinese decorated bowls by pressing seeds right into the clay to form a delicate pattern revealed as a series of small holes when the seeds burnt away during the first firing. The holes were filled with translucent glaze in the second firing. Such bowls can be seen in the Victoria and Albert Museum.

Fig. 77. Using the hole cutter and the tapered piercer.

Task Two: *Slab-built Boxes*

Before making clay boxes it is necessary to recapitulate the techniques of joining rigid clay at the edges and corners. These techniques have been introduced individually, but now they have to be
used in combination. As box forms are subject to stresses in drying
because the walls and base pull against each other as they shrink,
it is essential to work quickly and methodically to complete the box
in one operation. Sporadic work when assembling a box causes
uneven drying which leads to joins pulling and walls bowing. The
sides are butt-joined and the surfaces which make contact must be
scratched deeply and filled with viscous slip to form the bond. All
the seams are rounded on the inside, using a thin string of clay
which is slipped and moulded into the angle.

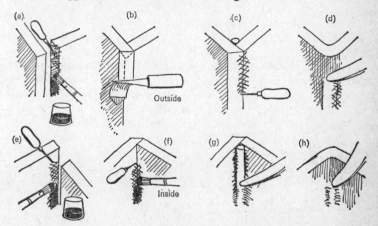

Fig. 78. Slab-built pottery: (a) preparing a butt join on the outside; (b) chamfering
the edge; (c) darning the join; (d) smoothing and rounding the join; (e) preparing
the butt join on the inside; (f) darning the join on the inside; (g) strengthening
the join with a string of clay; (h) modelling the clay string to form a rounded
surface.

The edges on the outside are trimmed by chamfering with a potter's
knife, then deeply scratched in a cross-hatch pattern and brushed
with slip. Pressure from the modelling tool will soon reconstitute the
surface and conceal the join. Softly-rounded corners are pleasant to
touch and are not as easily chipped as sharp ones.

You have seen in Figs. 62 and 63 how a clay box can be cut and
assembled from a single sheet of pliable clay. When using rigid clay
the base and the four sides are cut separately and joined, by the
scratch, slip, and darning techniques. When you have planned the
box you will have to consider whether to assemble the sides around,

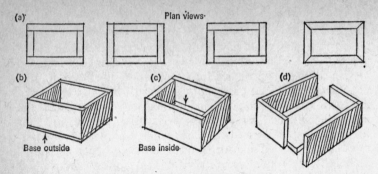

Fig. 79. (a) Four ways of assembling the walls for joining; (b) base assembled to show outside; (c) base assembled inside; (d) walls assembled first in pairs.

or on top of, the base: there is rather less likelihood of warping in the latter case. The sides can be assembled in any of the ways shown in Fig. 79.

Bowing or warping of the sides can be counteracted by using temporary struts to brace them internally. The third possibility is to mitre the corners, which looks good but is difficult to do because it calls for a steady downward cut at 45 degrees. Such a neat joint loses its point when the corners are darned and it is eliminated by the complete integration of the clay. If a lid for the box is intended it must be planned with care. You need a rectangle large enough to cover the box exactly, which must be cut from the same clay as the base and sides. A support to keep the lid in place on the box should

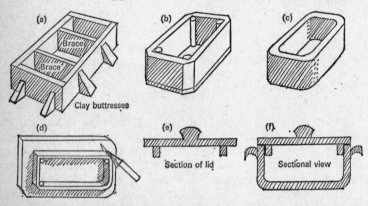

Fig. 80. (a) The box assembled with braces and buttresses in position; (b) first stage in trimming; (c) the final shape with corners rounded; (d) bird's-eye view of the box being trimmed; (e) section of lid; (f) sectional view showing the lid fitting loosely.

be $\frac{1}{2}$ in (13 mm) deep. Make it from strips of the same clay, $\frac{1}{4}$ in (6·5 mm) wide and $\frac{1}{2}$ in (13 mm) thick, joined to form a frame which fits on the underside of the lid. Stick it there temporarily with slip, try it for fit and make adjustments as necessary before making the join absolute by scratching and slipping.

A knob on the lid and handles on the inside can be improvised from remainders of clay.

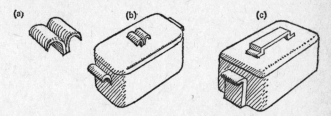

Fig. 81. (a) Knob formed from bent clay; (b) box and lid with bent clay knob and handles; (c) handles formed from flat clay strip.

A pyramidal lid formed from two pairs of triangles is an interesting variation.

Although the word 'box' sounds unexciting, box forms can be based on a number of geometric solids. For instance, hexagonal tiles fitted

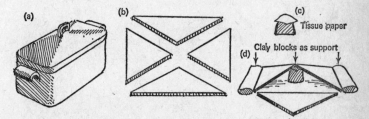

Fig. 82. (a) Box with pyramid-shaped lid; (b) pieces for the lid; (c) clay block for central support with tissue-paper guard; (d) method of assembly.

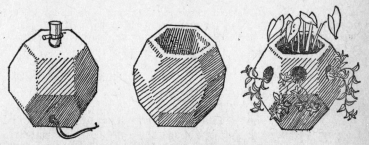

Fig. 83. Pottery made from hexagonal tiles.

together with small squares between, make an unusual shape which may be used as a weight, a pot or a lamp base.

Circular tiles are the basis for other decorative forms.

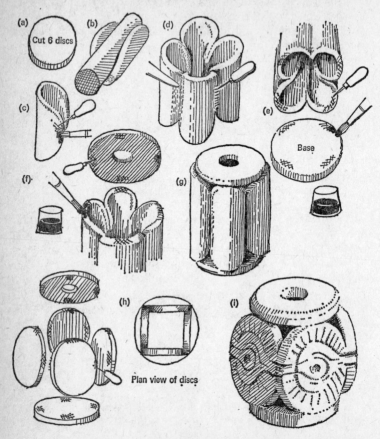

Fig. 84. (a) Flat disc of clay; (b) curving the disc; (c) preparing for joining; (d) assembling and joining; (e) preparing to attach the base; (f) preparing to attach the top; (g) pot completed; (h) six flat discs prepared for joining; (i) completed pot with tool decoration.

Such formal ideas require patience and accuracy. Nevertheless, leather-hard clay can be cut, scraped and filed into shape and small inaccuracies can be set right by dampening and softening the clay locally, and by coaxing it into shape. Of course one is not limited to strictly geometrical shapes, though these are easier to assemble than asymmetrical forms of no identifiable shape, which must be constructed first in flat card shapes, pinned and sellotaped together, and so calculated to ensure that the edges are chamfered at the correct angle to fit together.

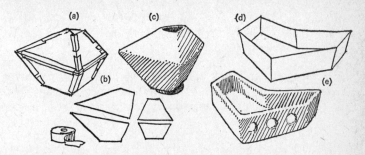

Fig. 85. (a) Cardboard trial model; (b) templates required; (c) assembled pot; (d) model for a trough; (e) clay trough.

Task Three: Making Other Shapes with Slabs

Flat pottery shapes, divided in various ways as containers for foods, are useful in the home and are easily constructed on bases cut from flat clay. To make the *hors d'œuvre* type of dish use clay strips, which are thicker where they join the base. They are usually about ¾ in (2 cm) high, and they are shaped by drawing finger and thumb along their length with a slight pinching action. These shaped strips are cut from the same clay as the base of course. They are

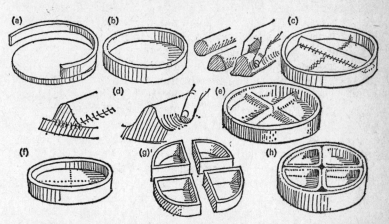

Fig. 86. *Hors d'œuvre dishes:* (a) bent clay strip and base; (b) basic dish; (c) forming the partitions and positioning them; (d) attaching and smoothing in a partition; (e) completed dish; (f) container dish; (g) four quarter-circle dishes; (h) completed dishes in their container.

scratched and slipped underneath and the positions, where they will be attached, receive the same treatment before they are pressed into place. Finger or tool is used to smooth the junction so that these dividing walls meet the base in a concave curve as in Fig. 86. Naturally there must be a perimeter wall also, so be particularly careful to make a really firm join where the divisions meet this wall because cracks are very apt to form.

Another project of a similar nature is to make a larger circular tray with 1 in (2·5 cm) raised walls, to contain four dishes shaped as equal segments which fit into it. All the parts must be made from sheet clay which has been prepared simultaneously.

Decoration

Slab pots have a number of flat surfaces which are suitable for most of the forms of decoration used so far such as slip trailing, finger and brush painting with slip, sgraffito, textures, carved and incised decoration, cut and rolled clay applied in relief, etc. (see Plate 31). However, carved and relief decorations, though very effective on box shapes, are not suitable perhaps for *hors d'œuvre* dishes. Conversely, slip decorations (which are both effective and practicable on these dishes) are difficult to apply successfully to all four sides of a box.

Inlaid and Stamped Patterns

Another way of decorating raw clay is inlays (see Plate 15): this was very popular in Mediaeval and later in Victorian times, in the form of inlaid tiles used in churches and homes. These are also known as **encaustic tiles**, implying that the inlaid clay is 'burnt in'. The inlay is produced either by scratching a pattern in the clay surface and brushing slip over it, or cutting into the clay with a wire-ended tool and filling the channels with clay of a different colour (this must not be wetter than the clay of the tile or shrinkage will cause the pattern to crack). The latter method is necessary where there are broad lines and solid shapes in the pattern. Alternatively a slip may be used which has a non-plastic additive such as china clay to counteract the shrinkage.

Clay stamps are used for impressed and relief decorations—simple forms such as printing sticks have been mentioned on page 39. Using lino-cutting tools of V- and U-section, patterns can be cut on the end of plaster or clay cylinders (the clay cylinders are fired before use). These stamps are used to press out 'seals' of clay (which are then applied to the pots with slip) or to impress patterns directly into the clay (see Plates 1 and 17). Impressed patterns brushed over with coloured slip become inlaid patterns. All such patterns are easily trimmed to a flat surface and a clear outline when dry, by shaving with a steel palette or kidney. It may be necessary to use a hacksaw blade in the first place to reduce the roughness of the surface.

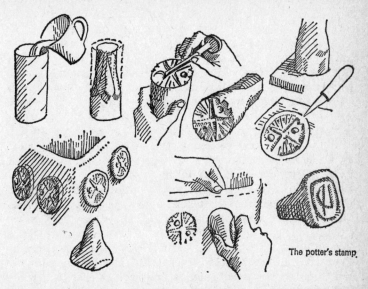

The potter's stamp

Fig. 87. Clay or plaster decorative stamps and a potter's clay stamp (for signature on base).

A further way of impressing patterns which can be used for inlay as well, is the use of an incised roller. The clay or plaster cylinder is engraved with patterns on its curved surface instead of its ends, and provided with a wire handle so that it looks like a miniature garden roller. Rolling this on clay produces a continuous pattern. (A similar device for decorating pastry can be bought in the shops. This is perfectly good for using on clay too.) Bands of pattern produced with the roller and filled in with slip are quite effective.

Fig. 88. Incised rollers for relief patterns on clay.

Resist Decoration on Raw Clay

Patterns are painted on leather-hard clay with liquefied wax. A contrasting slip is then painted, poured, dipped, sponged or sprayed over it, and it will run off the pattern like 'water off a duck's back'. The wax is burnt off in the kiln, exposing the natural colour of the clay underneath. Make some more tiles and experiment with this technique before embarking on pot decoration. Paraffin wax can be purchased by weight, or in the form of candles when only a small quantity is required. It must be melted in a double saucepan or glue pot, preferably diluted by adding paraffin (up to a third of the total volume).

Experiment with various paint brushes, soft or hard; you will find that brushes made from bristles, as used in oil painting, are good. They can be cleaned after use in warm paraffin to melt the wax and given a final wash and rinse in warm soapy water.

The paraffin jells very quickly, so your painting has to be done with the brush fresh from the melting-pot and there can be no hesitation. If the wax does not take then the clay is too damp. Resist painting is immediate, alive, and has an accidental quality. Some people dislike it for this reason and for the same reason it has its devotees. It will be introduced again in Chapter Eleven, when we discuss oxides and glazes. There is one firm which sells a ready emulsified wax which is easier to use, but gives a weaker effect. The address is in Appendix Five, on page 286.

An entirely different version of the resist is the old-fashioned paper stencil. Again try the idea on a 4 in (1 dm) flat tile. Cut a 4 in (1 dm) tissue paper square and fold it into four. Any shape you cut out with craft knife or scissors will be repeated around the four divisions of the square. When you have made a satisfactory pattern place it on the moistened surface of the clay and press it quite flat, smoothing out bubbles and wrinkles. Apply slip by any means you favour (spraying is effective, as the depth of colour can be controlled and varied). When the slip is firm the tissue paper is gently peeled off, and the pattern stands out in the body colour of the tile. Stencilled patterns are a good way of applying background shapes which can be embellished with detail from a slip trailer (see Fig. 89).

You will realise that cut paper gives a very sharp edge which may produce a rather mechanical looking decoration, whereas quite a different quality results if the shapes are torn, not cut, from the square of tissue paper. If you decorate a pot with tissue stencils, try folding a circle in four or eight parts as the basis of a pattern. Folded strips of paper with cut-out shapes are useful for applying decorative bands of slip.

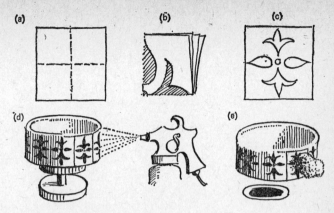

Fig. 89. (a) Folding paper square; (b) the cut pattern; (c) the pattern unfolded;
(d) applying the pattern by spraying; (e) sponging on the pattern.

Storage and Drying

As with all flat clay work, slab pots must be dried slowly and
evenly. Slatted shelves or narrow-gauge chicken wire frames, used as
supports during this final drying, allow air to circulate all round.
Remember to use spare pieces of clay as inside braces for the two
larger walls, to prevent bowing inwards, and remove them only
when the boxes have been fired. An excellent method of keeping
tiles flat during drying is to stack them between plaster slabs of the
same size and shape.

Making a Teapot by the Slab Technique

A cubic teapot is a good practical proposition. It contains more
tea than a spherical pot of similar overall dimensions, is not difficult
to clean, and although such pots occur in Chinese work of many
centuries past, it is somewhat novel (see Plate 21). The design suggested here is capable of many variations of proportion and detail
and is therefore as simple as possible, being based on a cube. There
are four principal parts and they must be prepared simultaneously:
they are the body, the lid, the handle and the spout. The construction
of the first three is nothing new but the spout is.

Spouts can be formed in a number of ways, the most direct of
which is to throw the basic shape on the wheel. However, as this
chapter is concerned particularly with slab construction, try assembling three or four wedge-shaped sections to make a funnel with
flat sides as the basis of a spout, then round the edges. The lip is
modelled carefully to ensure good pouring.

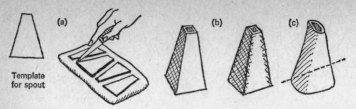

Fig. 90. A slab spout: (a) cutting the pieces; (b) the basic shape assembled; (c) the shape modified, with a pouring lip. The dotted line suggests the cutting angle for fitting it to the pot.

The hollow cube of clay for the body is assembled exactly as any other box. The finishing strings of clay, along the joins on the inside, are particularly important as they facilitate cleaning. The top surface will have an opening in it into which the lid fits, so before settling its shape one must know what form and size the lid is to be.

A square lid is not a good idea. It has been found from experience that sharp corners soon chip off. On the other hand a round lid is difficult to make at this stage and would not harmonise. The compromise shape is an octagon, having four longer sides parallel to the edges of the pot, and four short sides to replace the sharp corners of the square.

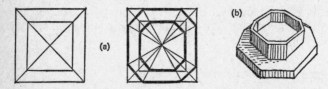

Fig. 91. (a) The geometric plan of lid; (b) the hexagonal lid.

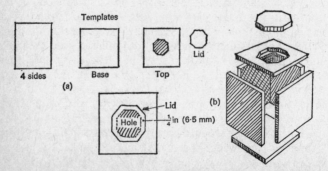

Fig. 92. (a) Templates for the pot; (b) the main parts of the pot.

The teapot must be planned carefully with all measurements exact, so card templates are prepared for the base, four sides, the top and the lid (Fig. 92). The latter is a flat octagon of clay supported on an octagonal collar $\frac{3}{4}$ in (2 cm) deep, which must be designed to fit loosely into, and rest on, the upper surface of the pot. The flat part of the lid should be $\frac{1}{4}$ in (6·5 mm) wider everywhere than the hole in the pot.

Assembly

1. First form the handle shape from strip clay $\frac{3}{8}$ in (1 cm) thick, round all edges, and then store it in a polythene bag.

2. Use a craft knife to cut the hexagonal opening for the lid; then form a low ledge to house the top of the lid using $\frac{1}{4}$ in (6·5 mm) square clay strip securely attached with slip, etc. The ledge will be $\frac{1}{4}$ in (6·5 mm) away from the hole all round.

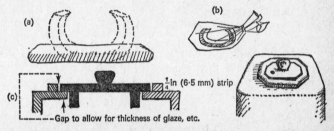

Fig. 93. (a) Basic handle shape from clay strip; (b) handle stored in a polythene bag; (c) sectional and perspective views of the lid in place.

3. The base should have a foot to keep the teapot off the table surface. This can be a duplicate (in reverse) of the ledge just described, or can be a little deeper. Weld together all six pieces of the cubic box which is the body of the teapot; then all joins are smoothed and rounded inside for cleaning, and outside for strength. Before the top goes on, stuff the inside with crumpled newspaper to support it against sagging. (The newspaper will burn to ash during the biscuit firing.) Remember to leave a depression into which the lid can fit.

4. Make the octagonal locating collar for the lid from eight clay strips 1 in (2·5 cm) deep, and try it for fit in the body of the pot. Attach it to the top part of the lid, try it again for fit and make any necessary adjustments. Pierce a small hole in the lid as an escape for steam.

5. Trim the spout, then flatten one of the top corners of the pot to make a seating for it and pierce it to provide straining holes. Next trim the spout to make a snug fit: it should be set at about 45 degrees, the opening for pouring must be above the tea level.

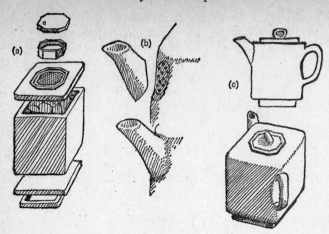

Fig. 94. (a) Details of the assembly of lid and pot; (b) placing the spout; (c) the assembled pot.

6. Before attaching the handle at the opposite corner, form a concave curve between the upper and lower points of attachment, to avoid the user's hand touching the hot surface of the pot.

CHAPTER SIX

POTTERY WITHOUT THE WHEEL: PLASTER MOULDS

You have used plaster only for drying purposes so far, such as making slip into plastic clay after refining locally-dug material, or reducing sloppy used clay to a more manageable condition, but you will have realised how quickly plaster absorbs water. Plaster is obtained from gypsum, a hard rock which is heated until the chemically combined water is driven off, then ground into a fine powder. It is sometimes known as Plaster of Paris because the original gypsum came from Paris. Clay which has been treated similarly produces the now familiar grog, which is quite insoluble, whereas powdered plaster is highly hygroscopic.

Because it seeks to combine with water every precaution must be taken to keep it dry. Keep it in an airtight bin—a strongly-made plastic dustbin with a tightly-fitting lid is ideal. In a dry atmosphere it will remain in good condition for months. When plaster is combined with the correct quantity of water there is another chemical reaction which gives off heat. In a short time it begins to stiffen and set, becoming hard in substance like the gypsum from which it derived. The time of setting varies with the grade of plaster. Solidified plaster is porous and absorbs water readily.

These inherent properties make it an ideal material for moulds which will support plastic clay, or slip, until a shell of clay is formed giving them a permanent, predetermined shape. Plaster moulds are used in industry to mass produce pottery articles. Although the amateur potter will not be likely to embark on mass production, moulds provide a ready way of forming simple shapes as a basis for improvisation and original design. Moulds are indispensable for producing the sets of pottery articles which are required in the home. Some shapes are best made in a mould, and there are forms of decoration which can be done on pottery only while supported in a mould. What should be avoided are the laziness and boring repetition which moulds may encourage, especially in school work.

Buying Plaster

There are several grades of plaster. The purest is fine white plaster ('superfine' or 'dental') which you may be able to obtain from a local

77

builders' merchant. However, he is more likely to stock the commoner forms of pink and grey plaster used in plastering walls and ceilings. This is adequate for making drying blocks though they wear rather quickly (it is excellent cast in boot-boxes, etc., to form blocks for children to carve, being attractive in texture and colour), but it is useless for moulds, being too coarse to take detail. Any potters' merchant will supply **potters' plaster** (remember the price of carriage increases the gross price considerably) and Podmore's sell a high-density plaster which is unusually tough but is mainly for industrial use where the moulds are subject to very hard wear. Adding a small quantity of salt to plaster will help to harden it. The larger chemists such as Boots often sell fine plaster in small quantities such as units of 7 lb (3·1 kg). Naturally the price is comparatively higher than buying in quantity, but it is economic if you require only a small amount.

Tools and Equipment

You will need two rigid plastic bowls, one for mixing plaster and one for cleaning hands and tools; a wooden spoon; a sandwich tin; machine oil; wood for casting frames and boxes; a plastic spatula; a soft rubber kidney; a measuring jug; a scoop and lots of newspaper. Knives, hacksaw blades, modelling tools, etc., as before, will also be required.

Mixing Plaster

You could easily become confused by the instructions concerning quantities given in the catalogues. One supplier recommends 2 lb (0·9 kg) plaster to 1 pint (0·6 litre) of water, another 5 lb (2·2 kg) of plaster to 3 pints (1·7 litre) of water, and a totally different authority states that the correct proportion for mould-making is 2¾ lb (1·2 kg) plaster to 1 quart of water. If you have a very high proportion of plaster it will be extra dense and therefore insufficiently porous for moulds, and too great a proportion of water will make the plaster weak and over-porous. Probably the most satisfactory is the traditional 'rule of thumb' method for arriving at a good proportion (you will be able to modify it yourself if it seems too strong or too weak). Before commencing to use plaster, cover the table and nearby floor with newspaper—it is easier to remove soiled newspaper than to clean off setting plaster! Another wise precaution is to use barrier cream or oil, or wear rubber gloves on your hands as plaster tends to crack most people's skin.

Practical Work Tasks

Task One: Making Batts

1. Half fill the mixing bowl (and fill the washing bowl) with water. Fill the scoop, or your hand, with plaster from the bin, and shake it slowly so that it drifts through the water to the bottom of the bowl. This way it absorbs water before it settles, whereas if the plaster were piled in, the water would not reach the centre and lumpiness would result. Continue to sprinkle plaster until a conical mound forms above the water which is absorbed only very slowly, stop sprinkling, allow the cone to subside, then leave it for another two minutes to slake.

2. Thorough mixing without forming air-bubbles is achieved by pushing your hand to the bottom of the bowl and paddling gently to promote the equivalent of a convection current in the solid–liquid combination. Mixing from above is bad because an air pocket is created and the air is pushed down into the mix, causing bubbles to form. Any dry lumps present in the mix should be removed or broken up with the fingers. (When a fine piece of modelling has to be cast the plaster should be sieved before use.) Mix for three minutes then leave the plaster to become creamy.

3. As a preliminary exercise mix enough plaster to fill the well-oiled or Vaselined sandwich tins. Fill the measuring jug with creamy plaster and pour it steadily into the tins: pouring too fast, or carelessly, causes splashing and, consequently, air-bubbles. The plaster should set in twenty minutes and be ready to drop out of the tins. The discs so formed are known as **batts.** They are used on the wheel as a removable base for throwing pots or to support coiled pots, etc., as they are being made. If they tend to stick in the tins soak them in a bowl of water. The water will find its way in and help to lift the batts.

4. As soon as pouring has finished, any tools or anything else soiled with plaster should be washed in the spare bowl of water. Never wash plaster down the sink as, if it finds its way into the waste pipe, some of it will set and cause a really difficult blockage which could spread to the drains. When work is finished empty the bowl outdoors. Remove the sludge by scraping it out with the steel kidney scraper and throw the sludge in the dustbin.

Task Two: Making a Press Mould

1. Preparation. A sample shape which is suitable for the first mould is a dish. The master shape (**prototype**) is solid. Dishes formed in moulds must slip out without catching anywhere: this has to be kept in mind when designing and modelling the prototype. There must be a slope on the sides, therefore, so that the base is narrower than the top. Paper or card templates are a help; a paper one for the base, and card patterns of two sections through the middle of the shape (or side and end elevations). A symmetrical shape is easiest to begin with. Build up the master shape on a smooth board preferably with a plastic surface, at least 3 in (7·5 cm) wider all round than the paper plan which you dampen and stick to it. Start to build the prototype with large lumps of plastic clay, pressing them together to cover the paper plan and roughly forming the height. Use the templates as guides and beat this rough shape with a paddle, adding smaller lumps of clay as required, until the true shape appears and needs only a good surface finish. Allow it to dry to a firm state and then rake over

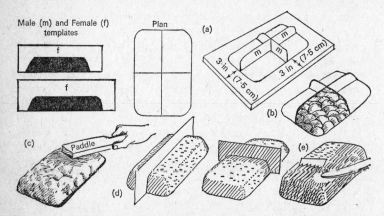

Fig. 95. Preparing the model: (a) templates, plan and method of assembly on a board; (b) commencing to form the shape; (c) further shaping with the paddle; (d) testing the contours; (e) finishing the surface.

the surface with a hacksaw blade, modelling it by working in many directions, and filling in any small depressions with the clay you have scraped away. Constantly use the card templates to check the outlines. Templates are sometimes cut in aluminium, when they can be used as scrapers and shapers themselves.

Compression and a wiping action with the broad end of a modelling tool will give a good surface, which will look polished as the clay hardens; plaster takes very well on such a surface.

2. Boxing-in. Preparation for mould making must start as soon as the solid model is finished. It is necessary to erect plaster-proof walls, which must be sufficiently high and wide to ensure a thickness of 1 in (2·5 cm) of plaster all round the model. The walls can be formed from lino strips, really thick card, hardboard, clay at least 1 in

(2·5 cm) thick, or plank wood. These need to be oiled or greased to prevent the plaster sticking. An adjustable casting box is the easiest and most convenient apparatus, consisting of four boards, with right-angle brackets of strip metal screwed to them to act as clips.

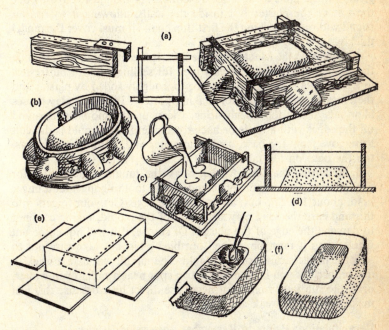

Fig. 96. (a) Model in assembled casting box; (b) alternative assembly in lino cottle; (c) pouring plaster for the mould; (d) section of the mould; (e) the box dismantled; (f) removing the clay and cleaning the mould.

Using lino, etc., the mould itself will be oval, while using wood it will be rectangular which is easier to store. In all instances the walls have to be sealed along the joins with wet clay, well smeared down, as plaster seeps out through the slightest opening. The sealing is done by running your thumb along the clay, then heavy lumps of clay are fixed against the walls to act as buttresses against the accumulating pressure of the plaster as it is poured in. Neglect this precaution and you may find yourself with a plaster flood on your hands (an experience which is better avoided). Clay walls are the most likely to give way because the water in the plaster weakens them.

3. Pouring the Plaster. Having completed the walls make a bowlful of plaster, which may be too much or too little. Unless you have a knack for judging quantities, you will learn how much you need by

D

experience. If a bowlful is insufficient you can make more or, conversely, if there is a surplus use it to make some more sandwich-tin batts. Take a jug full of plaster and pour it steadily over the model, completely covering it with a thin coating. Lift the base and tap it gently on the table to dislodge air-bubbles in the plaster. Now pour the rest of the plaster just inside the walls, allowing it to rise all round without disturbing the first thin coat—it must cover the model thickly.

4. Removing the Mould from the Box. In twenty minutes dismantle the box carefully. Keep the clay used for sealing, and for buttresses, in a special bin, as it is likely to be thoroughly soiled by plaster and therefore cannot be used for making pottery. **Plaster in clay causes blow-outs during the biscuit firing.** Clean up the mould and round off the edges with a knife or hacksaw blade. If the mould is difficult to remove from the base, soak it in water and, holding it sideways, tap the base on the table until it parts.

5. Removing the Clay Model. Soak the mould under water for five minutes, then use the open-ended wire tool to gouge out a finger hold, about 1 in (2·5 cm) away from the edge. Get your fingers into this and ease the solid clay shape out of the mould, taking care not to damage the edge of the plaster. Of course, if it will not come out whole, then it must be gouged out bit by bit, but take care not to scar the inside surface of the mould. The mould will take a week to dry properly if you keep it in a warm spot near a radiator in winter, or in the sun in summer, but never use direct heat because this will make the plaster weak and crumbly.

Recapitulation: Points to Remember when using Plaster

1. Slowly sprinkle plaster into the water until it forms an island above the water.

2. Allow the plaster to slake; complete water penetration takes about two minutes, pour off remaining water.

3. Agitate the plaster from the bottom using the hand as a paddle.

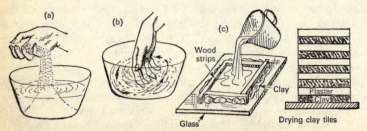

Fig. 97. (a) Shaking in plaster; (b) stirring plaster; (c) forming slabs from surplus plaster used to dry clay tiles.

4. Keep your plaster stock absolutely dry. Old plaster forms a scum on the surface and is of no use whatsoever.

5. Lumpy plaster requires sieving.

6. **Never run plaster water down your sink.**

A further use for surplus plaster is to make plaster tiles in a frame of hardwood strips. Assemble these on glass as shown in Fig. 97 and seal the gaps with soft clay, then keep it by you as a receptacle for excess plaster when mould making. Plaster tiles are excellent for drying clay tiles and keeping them flat.

Task Three: Using a Press Mould

1. Preparation. You have a hollow mould now, ready for shaping dishes from pliable sheet clay. Fix canvas or hessian to a board and roll out the clay sheet. The fabric texture will print onto the underside of the clay. The mould is perfectly clean, but when it has been used once it will need cleaning with a damp sponge before being used again. Never leave any dry clay on the upper (flat) surface of your mould, for if it flakes off it will spoil the surface of the dish being formed.

2. Filling the Mould. Cut the shape of the top of the dish from the clay sheet, but larger all round. Then either: (a) place the mould bottom up on the clay sheet, pick up the whole assembly and reverse it; remove the board, and the clay sheet will begin to sag into the hollow mould, or (b) if this is impossible because of the weight, lift the clay sheet from the board instead. Peel it back at one end and slip your forearm under it, then raise it draped over your forearm, and carefully transfer it onto the mould. If you have a turntable, place the mould on it if possible.

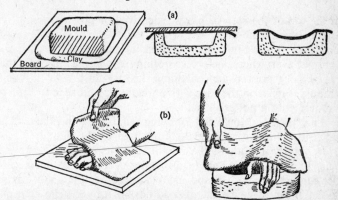

Fig. 98. (a) Positioning clay in the mould by reversing it; (b) lifting clay by hand onto the mould.

Ease the clay sheet down into the mould. Folds will have formed around the perimeter, so lift the edge a little at a time and shake the clay down, simultaneously easing it in with firm but gentle pressure, using a damp sponge rather than bare fingers which would mark the clay surface. The flat clay has to be moulded into the curve of the dish, but it must not be pressed too hard or thin spots will be formed; stroking with a sponge in all directions helps. Make sure no air pockets are formed between the mould and the clay. As soon as it is obvious that enough clay has been taken up to fill in the mould,

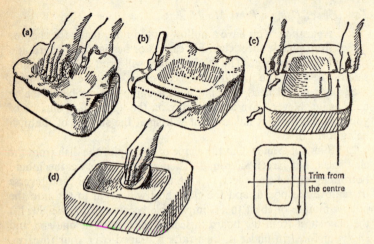

Fig. 99. (a) Smoothing clay sheet into the mould; (b) initial trimming of the top with a wire cutter; (c) trimming; (d) finishing the inside surface.

trim the top of the clay with a wooden tool or potter's needle very near the edge of the dish.

Continue pressing in the clay and ensure that it is in contact with the mould everywhere, before smoothing the inside surface with a rubber kidney presser, and trimming the clay flush with the top of the mould. Finish off the edge with a wet finger and then free it from the mould with a potter's needle.

3. Emptying the Mould and Finishing Off. By the time the clay has dried leather-hard it will have shrunk free of the mould. Place a board over the mouth of the mould, turn it over and remove it, leaving the dish on the board. In this position you can clean up the under-surface of the dish and make it smooth if the texture is not suitable. When reversing the dish do not lift it by the rim or it may break; slide it just over the edge of the board, get a supporting hand inside and then turn it over using both hands.

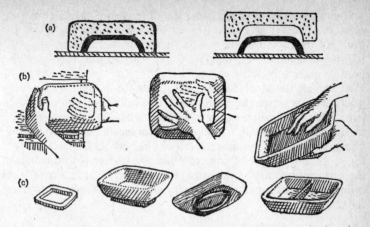

Fig. 100. (a) Removing the mould; (b) turning the clay dish over (c) adding a foot or partition.

A foot for the dish improves its appearance and can be made easily. However, it must be prepared at the time of filling the mould. Two strips on supports, or a simple ring formed from the trimmings, are allowed to dry leather-hard. They are then joined to the base as soon as the dish is turned out of the mould, using scratching and slip.

Task Four: Making a Hump Mould

1. Preparation. Whereas a hollow mould is used to form wide, shallow shapes from clay sheet pressed *into* it, a hump mould is used to produce similar shapes from clay sheet pressed *over* it.

The hump mould is a positive mould, so a negative (i.e. hollow) mould has to be made first, which is filled with plaster with which to duplicate the original clay shape. Plaster sticks to plaster, therefore to ensure the separation of the cast shape from the mould, the latter must be treated with a resist agent. The pores in the plaster need to be stopped up, which can be done effectively by brushing the surface with fairly thin ball clay slip, or with **size** made from soap. A third alternative is to treat the plaster with several coats of shellac followed by a coat of stearine, which is a good parting agent.

The **size** referred to is made by pouring boiling water on kitchen soap or liquid soap. This soapy solution stands for several hours until it has settled, then use the top off the liquid and brush a number of coats on the mould immediately before using it. Most suppliers sell a mouldmaker's size if you wish to buy a preparation.

If you use a ball clay slip, sieve it well to ensure absolute smoothness. In all cases take care to coat the top surface as well as the inside of the mould before you fill it with plaster. Ensure also that the mould stands level; wedges of clay inserted underneath can be used to make any adjustments.

2. Making the Mould and Handle. When the mould is full and the plaster begins to set insert wire loops or a cylindrical coil of chicken wire. This is the support, or armature, which when covered with plaster will form a stalk for this **mushroom mould** (as it is sometimes known) since when it is finished it looks like an old-fashioned darner for socks, only larger of course. When the plaster is firm, roughen the surface surrounding the armature and enclose it in a cardboard cylinder. Caulk the cylinder with clay and fill it with plaster to make the stalk.

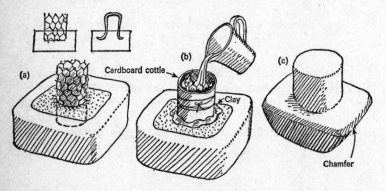

Fig. 101. (a) Forming the armature; (b) pouring plaster with the cottle in place; (c) the completed mould.

3. Removing the Hump Mould. Allow the plaster to dry for two days, then soak the complete assembly under water and after a while you will be able to part the two moulds. Fettle the edge of the hump mould to a 45-degree chamfer, as a sharp plaster edge does not permit satisfactory trimming and is too easily damaged. Clean up the moulding surface and allow your mushroom a week to dry thoroughly before using it.

Task Five: Using the Hump Mould

Roll out the clay on a board covered with cloth which has not been fixed down. Reverse the mould, handle upwards, and gently rock it around to estimate the area of clay required; trim it but allow a surplus all round. Reverse the board and the mould together and remove the board, leaving the cloth and clay draped over the

mould. If it is too heavy, however, drape the clay sheet over your
forearm and lay it over the mould with the cloth on top. Massage
the cloth and clay with your hands, but do not make finger marks.
Smooth it down so that all air is forced out leaving the clay in the
closest possible contact with the mould everywhere. Remove the
cloth and trim the clay flush with the edge of the mould, smooth it
with your forefinger and ease by running the potter's needle round.

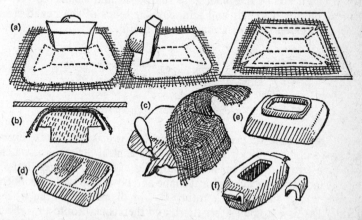

Fig. 102. (a) Using mould to estimate the area of sheet clay required; (b) board,
cloth, clay and mould reversed; (c) cloth removed and clay trimmed; (d) dish
with partition added; (e) dish with foot added; (f) container made from two
joined dishes.

Final trimming can be carried out when the pot is leather-hard,
and once again the addition of a foot could improve its appearance
and its function. Fixing the foot is made especially easy because the
hump mould constitutes a firm support; otherwise proceed as for the
press moulded dish. Bowls, dishes, or other shallow vessels formed
in either type of mould should be stored upside down on slatted
shelves, etc., for drying, so that the rim is under pressure from the
weight of the pot, which lessens the possibility of distortion—even
drying is most important.

Task Six: *Making and using a Circular Hump Mould*

Some shapes are suitable for reproduction by moulding alone, some
by throwing on the wheel and others can be made by either means.
However, as you will find out on page 219, throwing shallow forms
requires sophisticated skill. Therefore, they are a good subject for
moulding and will introduce you to one method of using the wheel,
i.e. for turning and fettling circular clay shapes. By now you are

familiar with two types of plaster one-piece moulds: the concave mould know as a hollow or press-in mould; and the convex mould known as a hump, mushroom or flop-over mould (the latter name derives from the way the clay is handled). A round, shallow bowl is a very versatile, basic shape from which more complex forms can be improvised with a little imagination.

Tools. Pottery turning tools are usually manufactured from strip steel. The heads of the blades are sharpened and shaped to give a variety of cuts. Circular and semi-circular loops of sharpened steel strip in wooden handles are also most useful.

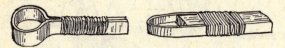

Fig. 103. Turning tools improvised from strip metal.

1. Preparation. Before making a mould for a bowl a useful exercise is to make a thick round batt with a central depression, which can be used for drying up small quantities of clay. Compress lumps of clay into a roughly cylindrical shape and beat them with a wooden paddle into a flat 'cheese', rather less in diameter than the wheel head. Let this become leather-hard, and then stick it onto the wheel and get it as central as possible. Use a curved turning tool to shave the clay. Practise this with the wheel spinning moderately fast. If the clay is in the right state it will pare off in long clean shavings. Plenty of clay must be removed before a convex curve is formed, so there is room for experimental error.

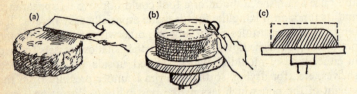

Fig. 104. Solid model for drying batts: (a) roughly shape by beating; (b) more accurately turned to shape; (c) section of shape indicating the mount of clay removed.

A strip of card or lino, somewhat higher than the apex of the curve is placed around the wheel head and joined, where it overlaps itself, with paper fasteners or staples and is finally tied with string. Caulk all gaps, etc., with soft clay and pour plaster to rise well above the model.

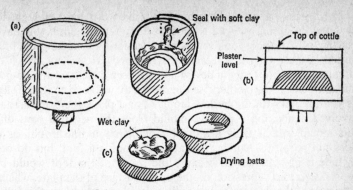

Fig. 105. (a) Cottle formed round wheel head and sealed; (b) sectional view showing the depth of plaster required; (c) drying batts.

Let the plaster set well before removing the retaining band (called a **cottle**) and pulling the batt off the model. If you wish you can repeat the process several times, because slight deterioration of the model is unimportant when you are making drying batts. Alternatively you could make a plaster reproduction of the model and make further moulds from this (for instance if you work in a school and need a good stock of batts). The advantage of batt making as a preliminary is that it need not be especially accurate, therefore you can learn to use the tools without any anxiety over the result.

2. Moulds for Deep Plates or Bowls. Moulds for plates and bowls are made similarly, but drawings are necessary to determine outlines and measurements in advance, from which card or aluminium templates can be cut and used for forming or checking. Build up the solid shape as before, and fix it to a circular slab of clay $\frac{1}{2}$ in (13 mm) thick, and equally greater than the maximum radius of your pattern. This will make a step in the mould to allow a surplus for trimming.

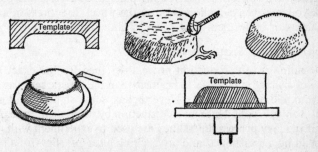

Fig. 106. Model for bowl similarly formed (Fig. 105) but using a template for accuracy.

The rough shape you build up is turned when hard enough, to give the exact outline and a good surface finish. Once you have mastered the turning tool, this is much easier than making the first mould because only one template is required for a shape which is circular in plan. When you design a bowl, keep it shallow and do not make the sides steep, otherwise the sheet clay will tend to form folds as you press it into the hollow mould. For a plate, the extra labour involved in making a positive mould from the negative pays off: this mould will be truly a 'hump' mould, not a mushroom, as it does not require a handle. A plate really needs a foot, but do not include it in your design because the shape of the foot would be reproduced as a depression on the upper surface of the plate, whichever type of mould you favour. Only a drawing can explain this fully.

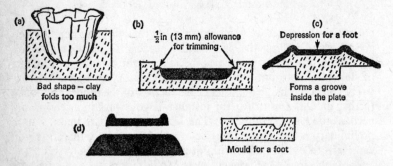

Fig. 107. (a) Too deep a shape causing folds in the clay sheet; (b) a step in the mould to form a ledge which can be trimmed; (c) if a depression is made for a foot this forms a groove on the top surface of the plate; (d) foot cast separately, to be joined onto the bowl.

A foot can be pressed out separately but simultaneously in a simple mould made by 'engraving' a ring in a plaster batt which is attached with slip to the base of the plate. However, if the plate is thick you can turn a shallow foot on the wheel (in a press-in mould the base can be formed extra thick to allow for trimming).

Using Moulds to Create New Shapes

Moulding is a reproduction process designed for the exact repetition of a shape and ceases to be creative in the artistic sense as soon as the mould has been made. Nevertheless, some children and many adults can gain confidence and satisfaction by using them once. After that it is a lazy process unless they are used to experiment with, both in building new shapes and in exciting uses of slip for all-over decoration. A bowl or dish supported inside a mould will not easily deteriorate under a weight of slip and furthermore the slip is best applied while the clay itself is soft and damp, because the two will integrate.

Suggestions are that you:

1. Use your press-in plate mould filled with a thick sheet of well-grogged clay and add a wall to it with ropes or strips coiled around the perimeter. Remove it from the mould when hard enough and darn the joins.

2. Use a press mould to make one bowl, remove it when firm and store it in polythene while a second bowl is formed. When they are equally firm, scratch and slip *both rims* (including the waste rims) and reverse the first to join it to the second. Cut a segment from the assembled bowls, which will allow you to stand the pot on its end: fill the gap with clay from the same sheet, thus making a flat base. This segment may be used to form a cup-shaped neck for the 'two-bowl' pot, or instead of making a neck pierce the pot in places on its shoulder, so that it can hold flowers.

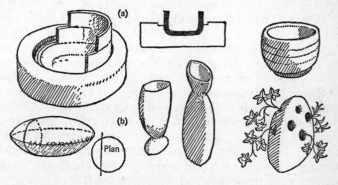

Fig. 108. (a) Height added to the bowl in the mould by building with strips; (b) shapes formed by joining bowls and sections of bowls.

3. Similarly two plates can be joined to make a horizontal pot with holes cut in it to a pattern, or quite arbitrarily. Add a foot to give it height (which can be made from clay strip or clay ropes) or use sections cut from another plate.

4. Try building a wall using strips of clay on a second bowl while still in the mould and add the first bowl to the top of the wall. Cut the base out of the second bowl to form a neck. Add feet to the pot so that it can stand as shown.

5. A mould for a pear- or almond-shaped dish (which is attractive in itself) when duplicated and cut and joined makes another interesting vase.

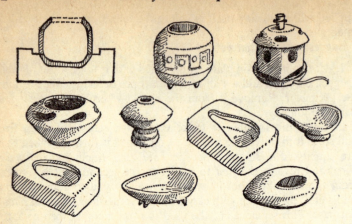

Fig. 109. More shapes formed from moulded dishes.

Pebble Mould

A different sort of hump mould altogether is a really large pebble such as those found on the beach at Kimmeridge bay in Dorset. Wrap it around (patiently) with firm but plastic sheet clay, or build up a covering by welding together clay patches. Roll it on a cloth to get a good surface, and at the same time the clay skin will expand and thus allow for shrinkage. Nevertheless you must cut around the pebble and release the two halves of the clay skin as soon as possible because of the shrinkage problem. If you find the clay tearing because it has stuck to the pebble then you must have used the clay too wet; either use the clay drier, or if you prefer wrap the pebble in damp tissue paper or grease it before covering it. Stuff the two halves with soft, crumpled newspaper and join them carefully. Then tap the pebble pot on the bench to flatten an area for a base and when it is really firm make an extra good job of darning the seam. Cut out a hole as soon as possible to allow the air to escape and to make an opening for flowers (see Plate 33).

If you like covering pebbles and feel confidence in your technique try covering an inflated balloon. It is difficult to lay down a method, but the general procedure is to make two sheets each large enough to cover one-half liberally. These have to be coaxed round the balloon very patiently and if unmanageable folds form the surplus clay has to be cut and rejoined until the two halves can be united. Joining is accomplished by wiping and smearing the clay together (the potter's needle cannot be used on a balloon!) assisted by rolling the balloon on the table. It is difficult, it may seem impossible, but be assured that it has been done many times. When the clay is firm it is pierced to collapse the balloon and release the air. The balloon is an evocative basic shape, which can serve as the body for pottery animals such as elephants, seals, mice, owls, etc., and a very good hedgehog if you stick short lengths of thick wire into it for spines. The wire blackens and burns a little in the kiln, but it is very firmly fixed because the clay shrinks onto it (Kanthal wire, as used for kiln elements, is best).

Fig. 110. (a) Covering a pebble with a clay sheet (the pebble should first be covered with moist tissue-paper squares or dusted with powdered flint); (b) a sectional drawing showing the pebble being loosened inside the covering clay by rolling; (c) animal figures made from pebble shapes.

Balloon Mould

To make a mould from a balloon fill it with water and mark the half-way line with a felt pen. Make a deep casting box and nearly half fill it with plaster. When the plaster is beginning to set push the balloon in, up to the marked line. Let the plaster set and remove the balloon which is very flexible and can be withdrawn easily. Make a second mould for the other half in the same way. A 'balloon' shape can be formed from the two moulded halves, joined in the usual way. Balloon shapes are excellent for cutting and reassembling as new pot forms. Such moulds *may* be difficult to fill with rolled clay, but patches of clay can be welded together if the inside is dampened a little first. Balloon shapes are suitable as hanging pots for growing plants. (See Fig. 111 on page 94.)

Decoration

Shallow pottery supported in moulds is ideal for some types of slip decoration. The slip can be applied as soon as the shape has been

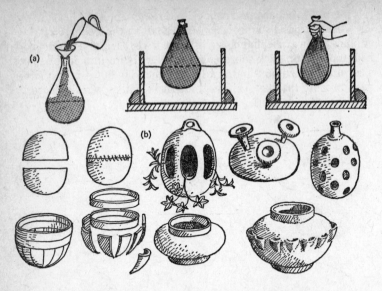

Fig. 111. (a) Filling a balloon with water and forming a mould from the bottom half; (b) pots formed from moulded balloon shapes and sections

formed and so a surface finish is unnecessary. Slip contains more water than clay, therefore it shrinks more, so it is best applied to damp clay for really good integration. Early English Slip Ware provides many good examples (and some bad ones!) of robust and energetic line drawings with a slip tracer, embellished with contrasting dots. An example is the earthenware candlestick in Plate 27. A fine coat of slip, possibly applied by spray, lends itself to delicate sgraffito patterns when it is firm. A thicker slip surface suitable for finger or comb drawn patterns, can be applied by swilling a quantity of slip around in the mould and emptying out the surplus—the fluid and slushy line which results is quite different from a crisp sgraffito line.

Marbling

(a) A liberal coat of slip having been applied to the inside of a dish or plate in a press-in mould, large drops of contrasting coloured slip are distributed over the surface from a trailer. Then the whole mould is shaken to make the slips move around till they form streaks and veins (as in marble). If the slips are too thick, or too thin, the results will be less satisfactory. A 'single cream' consistency is right for the best results.

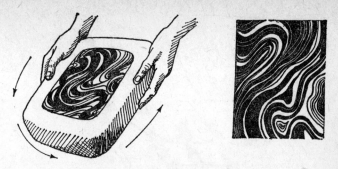

Fig. 112. Marbled slip pattern formed by agitating the mould.

(b) Alternatively, blobs of slip can be dropped into each other to form concentric circles which are then distorted by tipping the mould this way and that. If the tipping or shaking is continued too long the marbling will become blurred and confused (see page 60).

(c) Squeeze out coloured slip from points around the edge of the mould so that they fall in streams down the inside and meet in the centre; this effect can be shaken to change the pattern too, but it will soon spoil if restraint is not exercised.

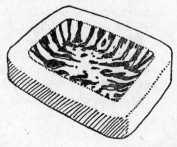

Fig. 113. Slip dribbled down the side of the dish in the mould.

Feathering

Without coating the dish first, use two slip trailers to lay alternate lines of different colours, so that they touch each other closely across the whole surface, from top to bottom or side to side. Strip a feather at the tip leaving the spine only (or use a finely-pointed brush) to drag lines at right angles across the bands of slip. This will draw one colour into the other in finely-shaped points and form little bracket shapes and, by dragging the feather in the reverse direction with each alternate line, the pattern becomes more complicated and

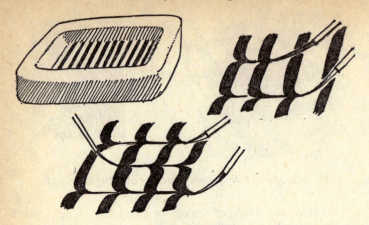

Fig. 114. Feathering.

fascinating. This is the pattern you will have seen on Battenberg cakes where a top coat of coloured icings has been treated similarly (see Plate 28).

Variations

Wax resist patterns are easy to manipulate in the mould. Could a marbled plus wax resist, or a marbled plus sgraffito pattern be a successful variation? There is a host of possibilities. For instance, a coat of white slip on a buff dish, painted when firm with a wax pattern, followed by a coat of red slip run in and the surplus drained off and, when leather-hard, sgraffito lines could then be cut through the wax (if it was not too thick). When fired there would be buff lines on white shapes against a red-brown background.

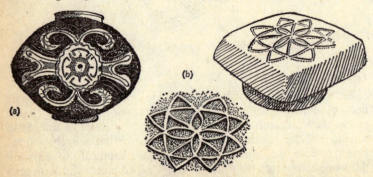

Fig. 115. (a) Wax resist and sgraffito pattern; (b) raised line pattern from engraved hump mould.

All these slip techniques are for pottery in hollow moulds. They are not suitable for mushroom moulds. However, there is one form of decoration which is viable only with the latter. If a line pattern is engraved with a gouge or sharp point on the plaster hump, it will print as raised lines on the inside of the clay. Use a V- or U-shaped lino cutter so that the raised clay lines will not break when the dish, . etc., is drawn off the mould. The lines enclose shapes which are filled in with colour later (see Plate 22).

CHAPTER SEVEN

PIECE MOULDS AND SLIP CASTING

Apart from throwing on the wheel, which requires special skill, the main methods of pottery making have been described with one exception. This last technique is **slip casting** and involves filling different types of mould with liquid clay and forming a shell through the absorption provided by the plaster, instead of using them as formers for clay which is pressed into them. Slip casting is important in industrial pottery as a mass-production technique which needs a minimum of final attention. However, assuming that you are interested in potting as a recreation, not as a business, it is unlikely that you will be content with much repetition work. Unfortunately, ready-made moulds are easily obtainable from the usual potters' suppliers, and all anyone need do is buy one or more, fill up with slip and then sit back and wait for the pots to make themselves. A process which makes for lazy potters rather than creative ones! The following pages, therefore, are devoted to the ways and means of preparing casting slip and of making one's own moulds.

Tools and Equipment

Extra jugs for pouring slips will be necessary. Mixing large quantities of slip is facilitated if you are able to use a mechanical mixer. For trimming the waste edge of the mould you will need a flexible knife bent at the end to a right angle.

Moulds for Slip Casting

When slip is dropped on plaster it dries rapidly so, if you hollow out a shape in a plaster block and fill it with slip, the plaster will absorb the water from the slip nearest to it first. This drying action will gradually penetrate through the whole of the slip, rendering it plastic first and finally drying it right out. Therefore, a hollow plaster shape can be used to dry slip (or wet clay), or it can be used as a mould. If the slip is emptied out as soon as a thick skin of clay has formed, this skin will retain the shape of the inside of the mould as it dries and shrinks. The thickness of the clay cast depends on three factors: (a) the density of the slip; (b) the porosity and dryness of the mould; and (c) the warmth and humidity of the atmosphere.

Provided there is no undercutting the shape will detach itself from the plaster by drying and shrinkage.

Practical Works Tasks

Task One: Casting from a One-piece Mould

Take one of the simple hollow moulds which you have made, one with an allowance around the lip for trimming is best, and clean it thoroughly. Set it on the table so that it is absolutely level and fill it by pouring slip slowly and carefully. Watch it, and when the level drops, top it up with more slip, or the top of your pot will be thinner than the lower part. (The level drops because the water is being absorbed by the plaster mould.) All the time a skin is being formed you must keep the level topped up and how long this takes depends on the three factors mentioned already. In general slip-cast pots are thinner and lighter than pressed-in ones, so if you aim at $\frac{3}{16}$ in (5 mm) this should be right. You may find by experience that this thickness tends to warp, or alternatively that it seems too thick and clumsy. The following exercise is an experiment to determine such points.

If there is a waste rim you can push the potter's needle into it to see how thick a skin has formed. When you are satisfied it is thick enough, pour out the surplus slip gently. Now wait for the gloss to disappear from the slip, and when it is no longer liquid, free the edge of the cast from the mould with the potter's needle, or it may hold fast in places and there will be consequent cracking as the pot shrinks. As soon as the clay appears to be firm enough to support itself place a board over the mould, reverse the whole thing and tap or shake the mould, removing it carefully so as not to scar the cast pot. Feel the pot to see if it is firm, and finish it off underneath with sponge and tool. Reverse it later when it is leather-hard (**don't** pick it up by the rim!). When your trial run has been completed you will have formed a pot from slip made from your normal potting clay in a press mould which was not really designed for slip casting.

What is special about a slip-casting mould? Does slip for casting need special preparation? The answer is that although you have managed quite well with the mould and the slip you have already, anybody who goes in for casting in a big way does make special preparations. When making a mould for casting, the plaster must not be too dense because the porousness is obviously very important. Of course, a slip mould gets gentler handling than a press-in mould, so it need not be especially tough. As slip contains more water than plastic clay it shrinks more (this has some bearing on which shapes are more satisfactory for slip casting than for press moulding) and so the pot you made from slip would be smaller than the original pot made in rolled clay from the same mould.

Because of the time factor and the high rate of shrinkage, slip used in industry has to be as dense as possible without losing fluidity. The mould is wet as little as possible, so that it can be used again as soon as possible (this is mass production!). The fluid and solid balance needs adjusting by measurement, so dry clay in powder form is necessary to mix a casting slip.

In a small studio clay can be pulverised manually or it can be purchased ready for making up as casting slip. In this case the water/clay content is reduced to 40/60 by adding chemicals which are termed **deflocculents.** There are two of these and they appear to break down the viscosity of the clay and free the particles so that they float easily in less water. The potter can add the deflocculents to his own clay by mixing them in some of the water which is to be added to it in powdered form, in a proportion of about three parts in a thousand. The two chemicals are soda ash and sodium silicate, sometimes known as **electrolytes.** They are alkalis which may reduce the static electrical attraction between the clay particles by making the water conductible.

Soda ash is a white powder which gives less fluidity and more surface tension; it easily becomes damp, when it would have the reverse effect causing the slip to jell. It tends to make the cast clay flaccid. On the other hand, sodium silicate gives a brittle cast and somewhat uneven flow, leaving tide marks when it is drained. Combined together they give optimum performance, but the proportion of combination is different for various clays so the potter must experiment if he wishes to do his own deflocculation. Known proportions of both chemicals must be added to part of the water, and by adding these in turn to a sticky mixture of water and dry clay, one will be discovered which produces fluidity. Whenever there is too much electrolyte apparent fluidity will end in jelling. The potters' merchants will supply either a powdered clay with the necessary deflocculent and the formula for its use, or powdered clay with the electrolyte already combined in the correct proportion for deflocculation. Grog added to deflocculated slip remains in suspension and does not show in the cast piece until it is sponged or scraped.

Simple Shapes for Casting

In slip casting there is no problem with the height of the sides. Suitable types of shapes are:

(a) A basically cubic shape, but chamfered or rounded along the edges and at the corners.

(b) A cylindrical shape with a round base and straight or curved sides.

(c) Sections of inverted cones. Lids for any of these shapes can be formed in separate moulds.

Fig. 116. Types of shapes (gradually narrowing to the base) for one-piece slip moulds.

Task Two: Making a Simple Mould

The prototype for a shape of the third type can be made from either clay or plaster. A similar shape, slightly larger, is formed in flexible card from a pattern based on two concentric circles.

Press soft clay into the card bucket shape and leave it until leather-hard, then remove the card and fix the shape to the wheel using slip. Centre it by the rings engraved on the wheel or if there are none draw pencil rings and check by marking a circle inside the top

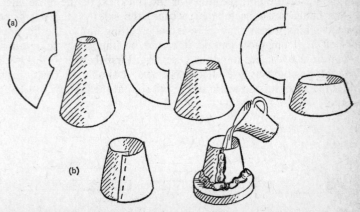

Fig. 117. (a) Three cut cones of different proportions and their templates; (b) forming a cut cone shape in plaster (truncated cone).

edge with a potter's needle as the clay rotates. If it is off centre push it towards the centre and check again. When you are satisfied that the clay is as truly centred as possible, press on it to fix it securely for turning, trimming and finishing with hack-saw blade, turning tools and modelling tools. A clay disc is necessary to provide a waste rim on the cast pot which can be trimmed. This disc should be slightly greater in radius than the model and fairly thick and can be shaped on the wheel. The model is then centred on it and the whole thing

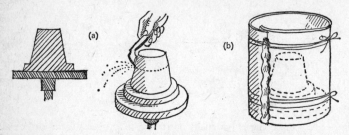

Fig. 118. (a) Finishing off a plaster shape by turning; (b) a lino cottle around the plaster shape on the wheel head.

enclosed in a wall of lino (keep the smooth surface inside and oil it), which is sealed with clay and tied with string. The mould is then formed in the usual way by pouring plaster.

Task Three: Making a Two-piece Mould for a Lid

Making a lid is slightly more complicated. A solid clay shape must be formed and the point to watch is that the flange fits loosely into the mouth of the pot, to allow for the thickness of the glaze later.

The flange must be tapered because the sides of the pot slope inwards. This means that there is undercutting and if the lid were formed in a one-piece mould it would be impossible to remove. Therefore a two-piece mould is necessary. First the rough shape for the lid top is built up with a convex curve: it should be fractionally wider than the outside width of the pot so that the lid may overhang a little.

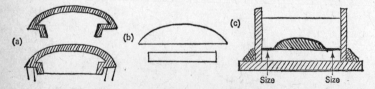

Fig. 119. (a) Section of a simple lid and its position in the neck; (b) the two parts of the lid; (c) making a mould for the top of the lid.

Secondly, a disc is prepared for the underneath part of the lid, i.e. the flange, which should be some ¾ in (20 mm) deep. Finish off the top and the flange by turning, etc., and stick them together temporarily in order to test them for fit in the mouth of the mould. Separate the top and the flange again. Prepare a lino cylinder or wooden casting box and pour in 1 in (2·5 cm) of plaster, which you allow to set before sizing it thoroughly. Place the top of the lid centrally on this batt. Mix plaster and cover the model to a depth of 1 in (2·5 cm). When the plaster has set remove the mould from the batt and reverse it so that the underneath surface of the lid top is exposed. **Natches**—semi-circular depressions—have to be made to provide locating positions for the next part of the mould. These are formed while the plaster is still tender by reaming out a hole with a coin such as a 2p piece.

Stick the flange in position, size the mould, and place it in the casting box again. Mix plaster and pour it in until it comes exactly

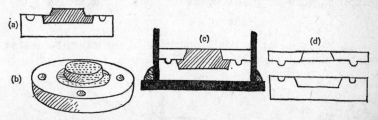

Fig. 120. (a) Sectional view of complete lid model; (b) perspective view of the same; (c) making the second part of the mould; (d) the two parts of the mould with locating natches.

level with the flange disc at the top (**do not** let plaster flow over the top surface). When this second mould has set hard, remove the casting box and prise out the solid-lid model. The first and second moulds, now parts of the same mould, are held together by the natches but can be separated easily. If there is any trouble at all in dismantling, soak the mould(s). Dry the moulds thoroughly (for up to a week) and all is ready to make both pot and lid by slip casting. Incidentally, no provision was made for a waste edge on the lid as this would have complicated the process unduly; the flange is deep enough to allow for at least ⅛ in (3·2 mm) to be trimmed off.

Casting

Ascertain that the moulds are dry by holding them against your cheek: if they are cold, they are still damp. They should be dried in a warm atmosphere but not on a hot surface. Assemble the lid mould and fill it at the same time as the main mould. Pour the slip from a jug for good control. If the slip proves to be full of air, then pour the slip from one jug to another several times until the bubbles have cleared. The slip should be poured in very steadily to avoid forming further air-bubbles. Keep both moulds well topped up until a sufficient thickness of clay has formed; the level in the lid mould should never drop. Any slip which dribbles onto the upper surfaces of the moulds must be sponged off, or it may dry up and fall back into the mould, remaining as a hard lump on the inside of the pot. For the same reason slip-casting moulds must be kept scrupulously clean at all times.

After emptying the moulds of surplus slip, be sure to free the casts around their rims before they shrink much. When the clay is approaching leather-hard the pot will slide out easily: the lid mould is dismantled as soon as possible. Try the lid for fit and if it seems altogether too loose you can scrape the mould a little to enlarge it and try casting again (but do remember that the lid will acquire an extra thickness when the glaze coat has been applied and fired).

Fettling

The waste rim for the pot is trimmed off at the leather-hard stage in the mould using a bent knife. If the clay is right for cutting it

Fig. 121. Bent knife used for trimming.

will come away very clean, but be sure not to trim while it is at all soft or wet. The trimmings can be rolled into a ball and formed into a knob for the lid. There may be pinholes formed by the release of air from the plaster mould and these will need filling with slip by brush, but the surface of the pot generally should be as good as the surface of the inside of the mould. There will be a slight ridge on the lid, where the two pieces of the mould joined, which should be removed.

Decoration

Slip for decoration is either purchased as such in pulverised form and water is added to it, or it is made up from your own clays, dried and powdered. It does not contain an electrolyte. An interesting experiment is to fill a mould with coloured slip, empty it almost immediately and then fill it with your normal casting slip. This provides a cast pot with a thin coloured coat which is ideal for sgraffito decoration. Similarly if a pattern is painted on the inside of the mould with coloured slips, and the mould is filled extra carefully with casting slip, the pot will shrink away from the mould with the pattern on it. Patterns can be engraved on the mould (provided that they are not so deep or intricate that they hold the slip and prevent it shrinking) and will register in relief on the surface of the pot.

Further Points Regarding the Use of Slip

1. Slip is prepared in the same way as plaster and should be stirred from the bottom to avoid air being drawn in.

2. Casting slip is best prepared with a mechanical mixer which will stir it continuously for some hours. It must stand for at least a day after mixing to ensure complete integration.

3. Slip should not be left uncovered as the water evaporates and chemical action from the air forms impurities, which can cause discoloration in the cast pottery.

4. **Flashing** is a fault in casting: if the slip splashes the sides of the mould as it is poured in it will dry immediately and form hard patches, which are then covered over by the remaining slip as it fills up the mould. These hard spots when fired are extra dense, and will not accept glaze because they are not sufficiently porous.

5. If the mould is too dry, literally bone-dry, it may absorb water from the slip too quickly, causing rapid shrinkage and subsequent cracks. A mould can be used several times in a day but the limit is about six, after which it is too wet to produce a firm cast.

6. If the slip is poured in too slowly, especially in a dry mould, or if it is poured in unevenly, casting rings will form round the pot.

7. Emptying a mould too rapidly can create a vacuum which sucks in the soft walls of the casting. Empty the mould steadily, disturbing the surface of the casting as little as possible.

8. Keep casting scraps when deflocculated slip has been used, and do not mix them with other clay, but mix them with the next batch of casting slip.

Task Four: A Mould for Casting a Vase

The truncated cone can be elongated and given gently-curving sides to make a wide-mouthed vase or beaker shape. A slightly different procedure is to make the prototype in plaster this time. A wheel is necessary with a head to which a plaster batt can be attached. Some wheel heads have holes into which lugs on the batt will fit, or there is a special cup head with sloping sides which can be fitted to the wheel. Plaster batts cast in the cup head can be used for throwing pots and then lifted out or pushed out if an ejection device is incorporated. One firm makes a wheel head which is a metal frame with a locating lug on which a wooden batt fits. As the prototype will be shaped on the wheel, a **chuck** or square peg is required to hold it in place. Cast this in the centre of the batt using the walls of a match-box to form it; if the batt is wooden, drive two screws into the centre and cast the chuck around them.

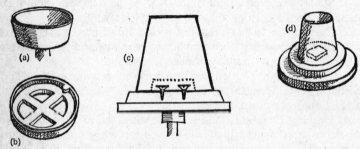

Fig. 122. (a) Cup head; (b) sectional view of plaster chuck secured to the batt; (c) section showing chuck held by screws; (d) cardboard shape in place over chuck.

Before forming the preliminary plaster shape over it, the chuck must be thoroughly sized. The proposed shape is based on a narrow, truncated cone (like a dunce's cap with the point cut off) which is first formed in card. A drawing of the shape will be necessary.

Oil the card inside, place it centrally over the chuck and seal all cracks, before filling it with plaster. Pour this carefully because you do not want air-bubbles. Remove the card when the plaster has set and give it a day or so to dry before shaping it finally.

Using a template as a guide the slightly-curved sides are shaped with a turning tool and quite a fine finish can be given to the plaster. Shaping a slight foot, which will affect the inside contour of the base, is in order this time as it will not be noticeable in a vase. The shape can be lifted off for inspection at any time and relocated by means of the chuck.

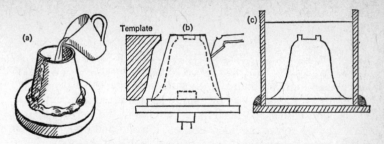

Fig. 123. (a) Pouring plaster; (b) turning plaster to the shape of the template; (c) plaster mould formed over the sized plaster model.

As this is still a one-piece mould the curve must be studied with care, for the slightest tendency to undercutting would make it impossible to remove the master shape from the mould. The casting should proceed as before, using a lino cottle around the batt and the master shape. The batt is cast into the mould as it will leave a recess for trimming. The mould should be thicker than the model-plus-batt in any direction.

When you cast pots from the dry mould in a week's time they should shrink and drop out very easily.

Two-piece Moulding

Task Five: A Horizontally-divided Mould

The only two-piece mould described so far (see page 102) was for a lid. There is, in fact, nothing particularly difficult about two-piece moulds. They are necessary, of course, wherever a shape has a return in it. The shape about to be cast, swells in the middle but has a shoulder and neck, and this is the reason why the second part of the mould is necessary.

Fig. 124 shows the two parts of the mould and you will see that, once again, a clay disc is included in order to form a step which allows for trimming the neck. Unless the prototype is turned on a lathe it is easier to make it in two halves, which are joined together

Fig. 124. Sectional view of a mould for a vase divided in two horizontally.

before making the mould. To set up for mould making, place a batt on the wheel and on that the prototype neck with the disc attached. Now make a lino cottle around the wheel head, higher than the model and take the usual precautions before pouring in plaster to half-way; the join in the two halves of the prototype will guide you. The plaster must be poured with care so as not to splash the top half of the prototype. When the plaster has hardened sufficiently take off the lino casing and make three natches in the top surface and then size it. Replace the lino case, seal it again and pour in plaster to the top well above the foot of the (upside-down) prototype. When set remove the case and the prototype.

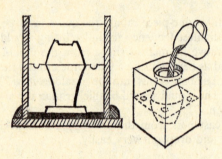

Fig. 125. Horizontally-divided mould.

When it has dried for a week the two-piece mould can be used for slip casting. The slip is poured in through the neck and should be level with the top of the mould. Empty the mould when a sufficiently thick cast has formed and let this shrink out which it could do in a couple of hours. It is possible to fill a two-piece mould of this type with rolled clay sheet. The two halves could be filled separately and their edges scratched and slipped for joining, assembled together, and left until the pressed-in pot dries leather-hard. When the pot has been removed the central join line should be darned, the surface cleaned up, and the neck trimmed. On the inside of the pot the join can be smoothed over by means of a sponge on a stick, or a profile.

Task Six: A Vertically-divided Mould

When the shape to be cast has an undulating outline, swelling, narrowing and swelling again, the two parts of the mould must part vertically along a centre line from top to bottom.

The procedure for making the prototype is as before and an extra piece, shaped like a cork, is added to make provision for trimming at the neck. The central, vertical dividing line on the prototype is found by resting a try-square against it and drawing perpendicular lines.

Make up a casting box (**don't seal it**) allowing for at least 1 in (2·5 cm) clearance, and make a bed of soft clay in it to a depth of the maximum radius of the pot plus 1 in (2·5 cm).

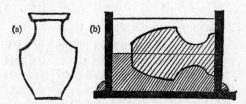

Fig. 126. (a) Pot with pronounced convex and concave curves; (b) solid clay model bedded in clay as far as the vertical centre line.

Hollow out the shape of the model approximately and bed the model up to the half-way line, filling in any gaps left in the bed. Remove the model and the box, press the clay bed flat with a board, trim the sides and replace the model and the casting box. The prototype model should be couched in a flat bed of clay up to its vertical middle line.

Seal the casting box and pour plaster to 1 in (2·5 cm) above the highest point on the prototype. When firm remove the plaster from the box and make four natches in it. Remove the clay bed, and

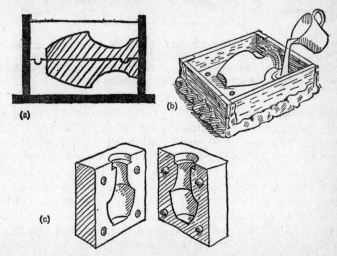

Fig. 127. (a) Section of a vertically-divided mould; (b) forming the second part of the mould; (c) perspective view of the half-moulds.

place the first half of the mould in the box with the model upwards of course.

Make sure the box is sealed, size the mould and pour the plaster for the second half of the mould. In a week you will be able to use it (be careful when taking the mould apart not to tear the cast pot in any way).

Task Seven: Moulds for Irregular Forms

A mould for an irregular shape such as the one in Fig. 128 can be made in two pieces. Shellac and size the model, then set it in a clay bed keeping the top level. Box it and pour in plaster. When the plaster has set, remove the plaster half-mould, and the solid model from the clay bed; make four natches. Remove the clay bed. Reverse the half-mould (with the model on it) and build a cylindrical clay stalk which will constitute a channel in the mould for the slip to enter by.

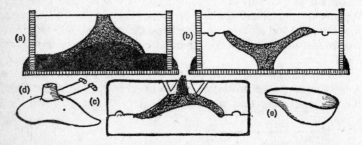

Fig. 128. Solid-casting an irregular shape: (a) upside-down model embedded in clay covered with plaster; (b) upright model with the two parts of the mould; (c) slip entering the mould forces air out through the escape passages; (d) cutting off the waste stem; (e) the finished bowl.

Size the half-mould and pour in plaster to cover the model to well above the highest point (and to the top, nearly, of the stalk). When set, open the mould and remove the model. Dry the mould for a week. Be very careful to pour the slip in slowly and fill the mould in all directions. The air has to come out as the slip goes in and it may be necessary to bore a hole in the mould for the air to escape. Keep topping up until the level ceases to drop. There is no surplus slip to empty out in this case.

Handles are difficult to cast in slip. A mug complete with handle can be cast in a two-piece vertically-divided mould. Air-bubbles are liable to form in the handle but again an escape hole can be made. Possibly a more satisfactory method is to make handles separately

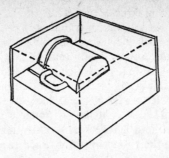

Fig. 129. Mould for a mug with a handle showing escape passage for air.

in a press mould. The press mould is a two-piece mould, which is filled with plastic clay and, of course, the halves have locating natches. There must be an escape channel for the inevitable surplus of clay which exudes from the handle—formed by the two halves when they are squeezed together. This escape channel can be cut free-hand with a U-shaped wire tool while the plaster is freshly set.

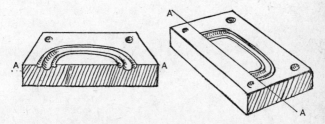

Fig. 130. Press mould for handle: section at AA shows the end view of the escape channels for surplus clay.

Fig. 131. Halving a mould by the use of a thread.

A quick way of making a two-piece mould where durability is unnecessary (as where it is known that only two or three casts will be required) is to mark the vertical dividing line down a clay model with button thread, pressed lightly onto the clay so that it adheres well. The model is cast in a box which is removed as soon as possible and, while the plaster is still tender, the button thread is drawn away from the model with a steady pull which cuts the mould in half (Fig. 131 on page 111). No natches are possible, so the mould would have to be tied to hold it together. Registration marks on the two halves help locate their exact position when reassembling them for casting.

CHAPTER EIGHT

POTTERY MODELLING AND CERAMIC SCULPTURE

A pottery model may be an interpretation of natural forms, a reinterpretation of man-made forms, or a construction arising from a completely personal concept. Whatever its inspiration, to be valid it must be characteristic of the techniques and materials used in its creation. If modelling is imitative and the material has been coerced unnaturally into presenting an effect, it is not pottery modelling, or ceramic sculpture (the word ceramic comes from the Greek *Keramos* which was used to describe all forms of pottery). The latter is a more erudite term, which if it has any further meaning could possibly imply greater scale, as in the larger coiled and slab-built pieces ranking as sculpture in the contemporary sense. Idea—Material—Technique are a unity. Clay, accidentally squeezed or otherwise shaped, may inspire a really lively idea; conversely a definite sculptural idea will suggest the appropriate technique. One potter found, for instance, that shooting soft clay with an air-gun produces coral-like forms which would be almost impossible to achieve by normal modelling methods. The exercises in modelling which follow are simple and practical. Clay can be pinched, punched, squeezed, pulled, rolled flat, made into ropes and shot at! Any of these methods of aggression can be used to form amusing and decorative forms.

Practical Work Tasks

Task One: Basic Shapes

This is a recapitulatory exercise in which the cubes, spheres, cones and pyramids in Chapter Two are united in a single abstract sculpture. Join them by scratching and slipping and, when they are firm, cut facets and gouge holes (try a potato peeler as a tool) to make the sculpture interesting.

Task Two: Punched, Pinched and Squeezed Clay

Punched Clay Models. Use a medium-size lump of grogged clay as a punch-bag and try a karate chop or two with the knuckles. The resulting shape will be rock like and if pierced with the potato peeler, can be used as an aquarium piece.

Pinched Clay Shapes. Everybody enjoys pinching! By pinching

E

alone a single clay shape can be formed of a fairly complex nature; the object of the exercise is to avoid adding or subtracting clay, and to develop smaller forms from larger ones without separating them from the parent mass. Such sculptures have some affinity with twigs, stones, shells, nuts, etc., they can be made more interesting by part decoration with glaze later on, so keep them for firing.

Squeezed Clay Shapes. Handfuls of soft clay squeezed vigorously produce interesting shapes too which may suggest ideas.

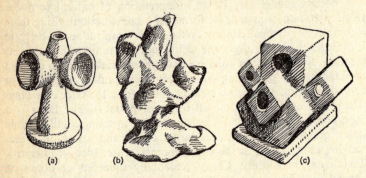

Fig. 132. (a) and (c) Sculptural forms from basic shapes; (b) punched and squeezed clay form.

Task Three: Pulled Clay Modelling

Pulling clay is a more controlled action: it is a combination of squeezing, and half pulling, half stroking. Take a lump of clay and hold it and pull it with moist hands.

When you have the feel of this action, try making an animal form (not necessarily any animal in particular: just a body, neck, head, legs). Use a fairly large sausage of clay and keeping the main part for the body pull and stroke out the neck, and with further stroking and squeezing shape a head (Fig. 133).

Pull out two ears and a nose; do not get them too thin. Now pull out the beginnings of four legs from the main lump, and fashion into stubby conical stumps. Again, do not attempt to make them too thin —this is pottery modelling; strength is more important than natural proportions (which is why it is suggested that you make a 'non-animal' for your first attempt). Support the figure on a base and use a lump of clay as a temporary prop.

Probably you will find that your 'animal' looks rather like those carved from bones by prehistoric man. Another good subject for pulled clay is a pair of wrestling figures: in wrestling the contestants' limbs intertwine in fantastic patterns—exposed roots of trees make rather similar patterns. Start off with this idea in your mind and see

Fig. 133. (a) Pulling clay with a moistened hand; (b) pulled clay models.

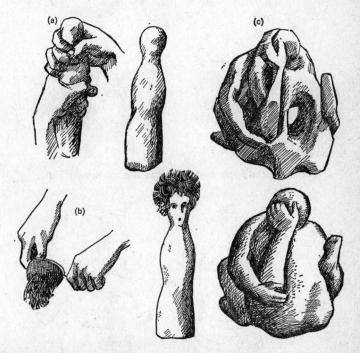

Fig. 134. (a) Squeezing a clay body; (b) pushing clay through a tea-strainer; (c) wrestling figures formed from clay rolls and, when leather-hard, hollowed from the outside and carved.

what you can create from pulled clay. Or take a sausage of clay and
by squeezing at the half-way mark make a waist, then move up and
squeeze a neck; by pulling and smoothing you will easily produce a
simplified female figure. You can shape smaller details by pinching or
by using a modelling tool; impressed patterns using keys and other
homely objects are suitable. The problem of hair can be overcome
by squeezing soft, ungrogged clay through a domestic strainer: a
tea-strainer gives fine filaments, and other strainers for sugar, flour,
etc., will give a variety of thicknesses. The filaments are removed
on a modelling tool and attached to the figure with slip (Fig. 134).

Fig. 135. Animal forms used rolled clay and 'tea-strainer' clay.

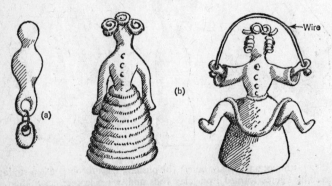

Fig. 136. Body with clapper assembled after firing and clay bells.

Once you have attempted such a figure and used the tea-strainer, this will suggest various simplified animal forms which can be made similarly; the first that springs to mind is a poodle (Fig. 135).

Now try pinching or coiling a shape for a bell. This will resemble a rather tall beehive and should not be thicker than necessary. Shape a head and body for a handle by pulling and stick it to the bell shape which serves as a skirt. Inside the bell a little loop of clay attached to the apex is necessary, from which a clay clapper can hang. Provided it is fired hard enough the clay bell will give a clear note (Fig. 136).

Task Four: Rolled Clay Models

A simple way of making animal shapes is to cut out their plan shape (like an animal skin) in fairly thin rolled clay. This is good practice in handling thin sheets of clay which can be formed into subtle curves and folds with practice; delicate handling is necessary for the clay has to be persuaded rather than forced into shape. The

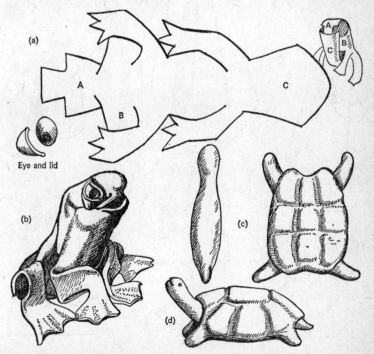

Fig. 137. (a) One-piece template for frog cut from thin sheet clay; (b) completed model with added eyes and lids; (c) rolled body and sheet clay shell with legs for tortoise; (d) tortoise completed.

plan shape is folded along the axis between nose and tail so that it can stand (see Fig. 75). Now it looks like any card or paper animal model, but by gentle pressure further modelling can be introduced to give it interest (you may have to introduce a temporary support beneath the stomach while the modelling is going on). Practise with paper templates first if you are unsure of the shape you want.

Now roll out some plastic clay (red will do) which is grogless, into

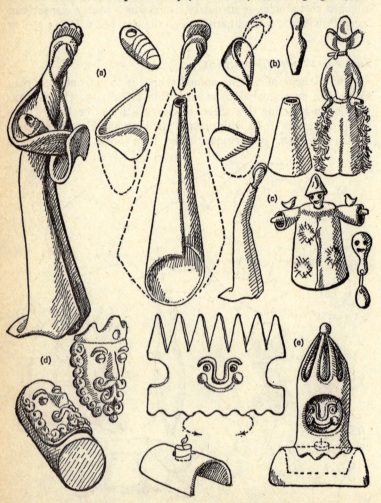

Fig. 138. (a) Thin sheet clay 'madonna' model with constructional details; (b) pottery cowboy; (c) scarecrow bell; (d) mask formed around a tube; (e) night-light holder with face inside.

a thinner sheet than usual and cut out as large a circle as possible. Halve this and bend it round until the edges overlap and attach them to each other by slip. Remove the pointed top of the cone, leaving a small hole, then make a torso which you insert into the cone.

This figure is somewhat similar to the bell you have made before, but this time the details such as arms, hat, sleeves, lapels, etc., are formed from the remaining rolled clay.

A male figure can be made by substituting two hollow cylinders of rolled clay for the cone, and adding appropriate details to create a pottery cowboy, sailor, or other figure, wearing baggy trousers.

Roll out well-grogged clay to make sheets of various thicknesses and let them stiffen before using them. To make an abstract structure cut strips of several widths and assemble them mainly by cutting slots; play around with all sorts of combinations and when you are satisfied make secure joints (scratching and slipping) at vital points (see Plate 34).

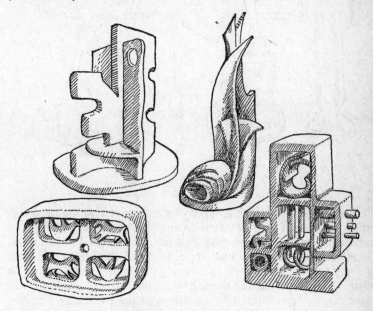

Fig. 139. Sculptures from clay sheet.

Task Five: Clay Rope Models

Roll clay ropes of three different thicknesses. Use these to form a simplified figure: a thick rope for the body, thin ropes for the arms and medium ropes for the legs. The head is a ball of clay pulled into a pear-drop shape, with a flat disc for the base. Bend the body and limbs into a flexible pose, and assemble them using scratching and slip. Temporary supports may be necessary if the body cannot support itself. Decorate the model with coloured slips when it is semi-hard. A group of such figures with an appropriate setting is fun to make. Why not start from the beginning with Adam, Eve and the Serpent; the latter, if not the former, is just right for slip decoration with the trailer.

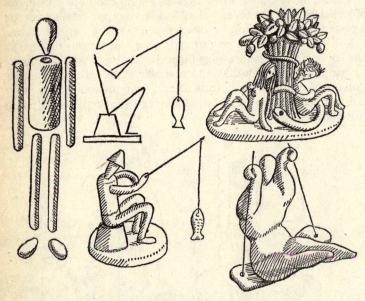

Fig. 140. Models from clay ropes.

Roll out thick ropes of grogged clay and build a hollow head with them, about half life size would be suitable. A coiled cylinder for the neck followed by two coiled bowl shapes integrated to form an ovoid is attached to the neck at an angle. Ears and other features can be formed from thinner ropes, with some gouging here and there to give extra depth and light and shade to the model. Hair on the head and face can be represented by clay strings or the usual clay filaments formed through a tea-strainer. A strainer for coarser filaments can be improvised from a small food tin (such as a Nestlé's cream tin) which has had holes punched or bored through the bottom. A giraffe-necked woman makes a good subject for caricature in this way of modelling. Animal heads as well as human are suitable.

With growing experience any or all of these techniques can be combined to produce quite large pieces of pottery sculpture. If they are too large for the available kiln, cut them up and introduce flanges, etc., so that the pieces can be interlocked after being fired separately. Highly stylised heads are suggested as subjects for coiled sculpture. However, more realistic modelling can be achieved by forming a thick rope coiled basic head shape, then beating and tooling to produce facial planes and the details of features. This saves either hollowing before firing, or casting in plaster.

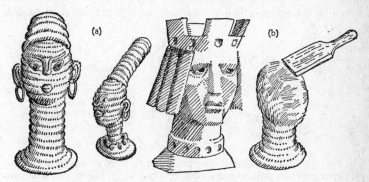

Fig. 141. (a) Coiled heads; (b) coiled and beaten head.

This concludes the initial exercises in pottery modelling techniques. There follows a more detailed description of some branches of the craft and the processes involved.

Ceramic Jewellery

Ceramic jewellery is a fringe branch of pottery requiring little knowledge of the ways of clay and only a very small kiln such as is used for testing glazes. Some potters make it when there is fashionable demand, but it is the province more usually of craftsmen who make a wider range of jewellery. Small things are easier to handle and organise on their own in a kiln; if you have access to one you may enjoy making some miniature objects for a change, which make acceptable presents. Of course small, precise work requires a fine clay such as white clay which is suitable for underglaze painting and also enhances the brilliance of a coloured glaze. Usually the shaping of pendants and brooches is done by hand methods such as pinching, rolling and cutting from clay sheet. Spherical beads are rolled in the palms, pierced with wire and strung on Kanthal wire (such as is used for elements of an electric kiln) supported by props, for firing.

Beads of circular shape and buttons may be sliced from a thick clay rope, but for shaped buttons use a concave plaster mould, and shape the inside with a plaster stamp (Fig. 142).

Cameos modelled in relief, or small figures of animals, birds, fish, flowers, etc., for use as brooches, are modelled very carefully in fine clay from which moulds are made. Sieve the plaster before mixing it. When the mould is firm and fairly dry, any fine relief lines which are necessary can be incised in the mould. The complexity of the modelling depends on your skill. Such jewellery must be carefully finished, but it need not be fiddly as broad and chunky designs often look more effective on modern clothes than finely detailed work. Form a cameo by flattening a ball of clay into a slightly moistened mould,

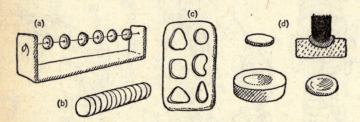

Fig. 142. (a) Beads on kanthal wire for firing; (b) bead or button shapes cut from clay rope; (c) pendant shapes cut from clay sheet; (d) forming a concave button.

making sure all the crevices are filled. Then remove it by pressing a piece of damper clay against it and pulling it away sharply. The first few pulls may not be perfect but with a little experience you will soon have good replicas every time (see Plate 3).

If the mould tears the clay anywhere it will be necessary to shave the offending spot on the mould. Pottery brooches, earrings and cuff-links are attached to metal fixtures called **findings**: flat, metal plates soldered to the appropriate pin, clip or catch, which can be obtained from firms specialising in jewellery. A good seating can be made for any particular plate by pressing it into the back of the clay in the mould and wiggling it around to enlarge it a little. This allows for shrinkage in firing and afterwards the plate can be fixed neatly and securely with Evo-stik or Araldite.

An interesting embellishment for a plain brooch shape is a pattern of relief lines enclosing separate areas all over which, after firing, are filled with coloured glazes. These are prevented from running into each other by the lines and give an effect very similar to cloisonne enamels. The raised lines are obtained by engraving the mould.

The small discs, which are used in earrings and cuff-links, can be stamped with a raised pattern using wooden printing sticks or brass leatherwork stamps. Alternatively, a small pattern incised in a flat,

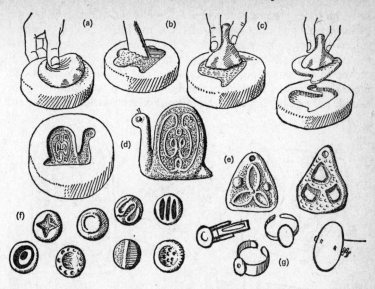

Fig. 143. (a) Filling a brooch mould; (b) trimming the surplus; (c) removing the clay shape with a wad of soft clay; (d) engraved mould and clay relief model for a brooch; (e) clay pendants; (f) clay shapes for cuff-links, rings, etc.; (g) findings (cuff-links, rings, brooch-plate).

smooth block of plaster can be transferred in relief by pressing the clay disc on it. Another effective form of decoration is to drop on concentric rings of different-coloured slips etc.

Flat clay cut to simple geometric shapes, or irregular shapes, are also suitable for pendants, brooches, and bracelets: for the latter they must be pierced right through using a needle to make two fine holes for threading. Thin, flat shapes can be rolled into the form of shells, suitable for beads and earrings, etc. Marbled clay (two or more colours mixed into each other) is another choice.

Ceramic Panels

Large and small panels (as distinct from tiles) are used externally and internally in architecture and are often an integral part of the architect's design. Small panels of a heraldic nature, connected with the brewery, are a common sight on pub-fronts. Shop-fronts (especially fishmongers) sometimes include a pottery panel. On a smaller scale there is the ceramic house name or number, which is a specialised sort of panel. There are three main ways of making panels:

1. A thick-grogged clay slab is set up, the thickness depending on the proposed depth of relief. A drawing is prepared, placed on the

slab and holes are pricked at intervals along the outlines. When the paper is removed the outlines will be seen clearly. Now by using a square-shaped, wire-ended tool the background is removed to the required depth. If degrees of depth are necessary these can be removed in the same way from the relief clay. Finally, textures and modelling are used to enhance the design, or slip decoration may be added. For a really large panel additions of grog, sand or fireclay are

Fig. 144. (a) Relief model with background carved away; (b) relief model built up in layers; (c) modelled relief for reproduction by press moulding. Note that there is no undercutting.

necessary to make a suitable body which will not crack, or crank mixture can be used.

2. In the second case the slab is the background, or base, on which the relief is built up in successive layers cut from flat sheets or slabs of clay. These may be used completely flat as silhouettes, or have modelled edges, impressed or incised line work on them, etc. They need not be stuck down flat, but bent into convex and concave shapes. Wherever they are attached to the background heavy slipping and scratching must, of course, be used.

3. A third way, especially if the panel needs duplicating, is to

make a one-piece mould from an original model, where all the relief must have chamfered edges and there can be no undercutting. Again relief lines (engraved in the mould) could be an important part of the design. The mould is filled with clay by hand (or cast in slip if the relief is low).

In all cases four holes must be made for attaching the panel to the wall.

Vinamold

Another method of making a mould is to use **Vinamold**. This is a rubbery type of plastic used in the moulds sold in craft shops for making plaster repeats of chess-sets and small figurines, not to mention concrete gnomes! It is expensive and has to be melted in a saucepan heated in a special jacket. The Vinamold and the heater are obtainable from Tirantis. It can be melted again and again for re-use but it gives off a vile smell, especially if overheated. It is extremely flexible and when plaster is cast in it, it is removed easily by peeling it away. It gives very fine detail time after time. It is useless for slip casting, but if clay is pressed in to form a thick shell and it is dried carefully in a warm atmosphere, a successful cast can be made. Even with Vinamold the modelling must not be too complicated, only light undercutting being possible since, although the mould is flexible, the drying clay is brittle and any great strain on edges as the mould is eased off would result in breakage. Concrete panels can be made very successfully in this type of mould.

Possibly the best application is for the small moulds required in ceramic jewellery, but do not try filling them with slip as the drying is too slow. Used as a press mould for cameos the casts are very easy to remove. Where a large kiln is not available relief panels can be made in sections, which are later set in plaster (indoors only), or cement. There is a large mural decoration assembled from a number of panels on Poole Quay advertising local pottery. Similar large mural panels take the form of huge mosaics made from hand-cut tiles, or walls covered with dishes, discs, ceramic stones, ceramic scrap, etc., set in concrete panels screwed to the wall. (Consult the local authority first before covering the front of your house in this way.)

Figurines or Statuettes

These are small figures, sculpture on a domestic scale, mantelpiece decorations. They are formed by pottery techniques such as using rolled clay or clay ropes, working directly and spontaneously (see Plate 35). There is another type of figurine which has been very carefully modelled in solid clay, either to be reproduced by piece-moulding, or to be hollowed out before firing if the original only is required (see Plate 32). Hollowing is effected from the base using a long, thin-bladed knife and a wire modelling tool. If the length is too great it must be cut cleanly in half with a thin wirecutter either horizontally or vertically (whichever seems most expedient) then hollowed and reassembled by scratching, slipping and darning. A figurine which could be cast in a one-piece mould, so that it slipped out via the base as it shrunk, would have to be very simple and of a generally conical shape.

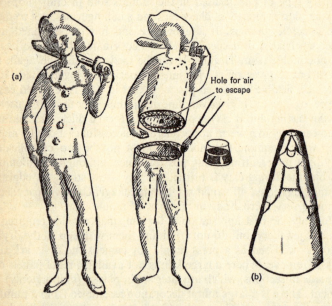

Hole for air
to escape

(a)

(b)

Fig. 145. (a) Cut modelled shape hollowed and joined; (b) simple modelled shape with details in low relief, based on the cone, for easy withdrawal from a one-piece mould.

Where there is only very slight undercutting (beneath the chin for instance) a two-piece mould parting vertically would suffice but, where there are complications such as a space between the legs or deep folds in the clothes, a carefully considered mould in several pieces would be necessary; the undercut parts require special attention. Wherever there is very deep undercutting it is best to form a small piece in the mould, which can be withdrawn separately when the slip is firm, otherwise the casting may tear as it shrinks.

Task Six: A Two-piece Press Mould

As a simple example of a two-piece press mould, use the uncomplicated almond shape of a fish: tail, fins, and eyes can be formed by hand or pressed in separate hollow moulds and added afterwards. The first step is to cut the fish exactly in half along a horizontal centre line and place one half on a piece of Formica or glass. Then make a wooden casting box and pour in sufficient plaster to make the first half of the mould. When set remove this half of the mould plus the half-fish, cut natches with a coin and size the surface plaster thoroughly, but do not leave surplus size in the natches. Replace the half-mould plus half-fish in the box just as it was, and stick the second half of the fish carefully onto the first half with slip. Mix

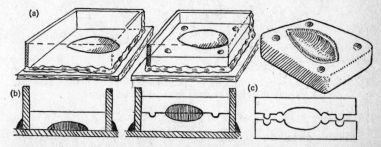

Fig. 146. (a) Stages in making a two-piece mould of a basic fish shape; (b) sectional diagrams of the process; (c) section of the completed mould showing escape channels for the surplus clay.

enough plaster, and pour the second half of the mould. When the completed mould is hard enough, dismantle it and remove the complete fish model.

Weigh this to find how much clay you need, then take a ball of fresh clay of fractionally greater weight and press it into one side of the mould. Place the second half of the mould over the first and attempt to press them together. You will probably find you have a slight excess of clay which prohibits this, so you take your wire tool and channel out grooves in the plaster (both halves of the mould) around the outline of the fish.

Try pressing the half-moulds together again and the excess clay will find its way into the grooves and allow the mould to shut tight. Once the mould has proved it works, allow it to dry and lose its tenderness before using it further. When it is used for casting you will have to trim the excess with a knife, after removing the leather-hard cast from the mould. Do not forget to make details such as tail and fins beforehand so that they are leather-hard when you attach them to the cast body (see Plate 35).

The mould will prove useful in turning out a basic shape which can be transformed into any number of differently shaped and decorated fish figures: try joining a group of fish together.

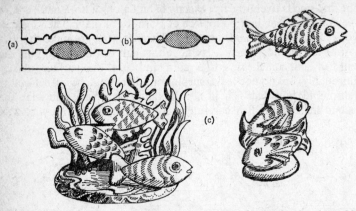

Fig. 147. Sectional view of: (a) clay in open mould; (b) clay in closed mould; (c) pottery models evolved from basic fish shapes.

Task Seven: A Mould in Several Pieces

Thinking ahead and visualising where best to locate the pieces of a complicated mould, so that they draw out easily without damaging the casting, requires experience. When there is really fussy detail the potter may have to make a mould for the model composed of a number of small parts which must then be held together in a plaster case. Where possible, difficult details like hats are cast separately and added later. A simple figure for a first attempt at multi-piece mould-ing could be dressed in trousers, have a simple back view, folded arms and a simple head with nothing more detailed than a *fez* on it.

A central line divides the figure into two halves, and a clay strip fixed in front of this line at the back (which is simpler in form) is to be cast first. This separating wall should incline inwards.

The front pieces will then fit into the rear like wedges. Use a piece of newspaper to work on, and place the figure face down on crumpled newspaper. Mix an adequate quantity of plaster in a jug and pour a thin skin of creamy plaster over the entire back (do not miss any-where). Now wait until the plaster is commencing to thicken before pouring again and covering the back. When the plaster is no longer fluid, shape the outside of this back piece of the mould with a knife by scraping, wiping or cutting. The mould should be $1\frac{1}{2}$ in (3·8 cm) thick all round.

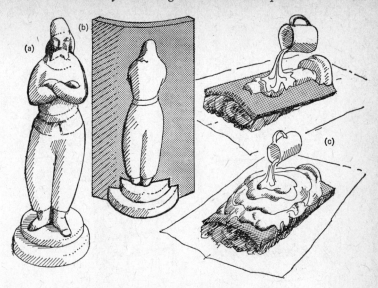

Fig. 148. Three-piece mould for (a) standing figure with base; (b) rear view with curved clay wall; (c) pouring plaster over the back. Note that the clay wall has been levelled using crumpled newspaper for support.

As soon as possible remove the clay wall and make locating natches. In order to cope with the undercutting on the folded arms the second piece of the mould is formed beneath them. Mark a line along the highest part of the arms and build a clay wall above it. Size the face of the plaster and cover the top of the model with moist newspaper. Mix plaster and apply it as before, using a spoon to throw in plaster where it cannot be poured (Fig. 149).

Put natches in the second piece when it has set, size it and remove the walls. A dividing wall is not required when you make the third piece.

This exercise illustrates the method of thinking when making multi-piece moulds for figurines. Each model will present its own problems and will have its own solution; there may be more than one solution. Multi-piece moulds are tied together and then tightened with a tourniquet to make a really close fit. Sometimes they are encased in plaster, especially where there are a great number of pieces. In this event, the piece mould itself must be shaped in such a way that it can be withdrawn easily from its case (Fig. 150).

In very finely modelled commercial work where an extra-smooth surface finish is sought after, a mould is used to make a replica of the original model in plaster. This plaster prototype can be scraped

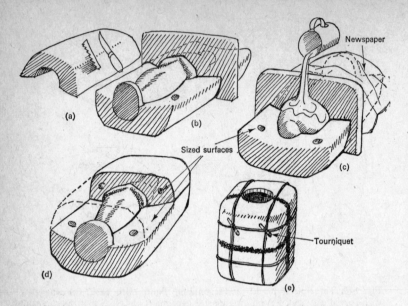

Fig. 149. (a) Trimming the mould for the back; (b) clay wall at the highest point of the front of the model; (c) pouring plaster over the torso, the lower half protected from splashing by newspaper; (d) forming the third part of the mould with the clay wall removed (note the natches); (e) the mould assembled and tied for slip casting, the seams sealed with clay.

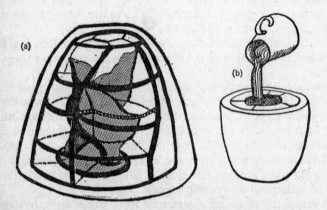

Fig. 150. (a) Diagrammatic representation of a multi-piece mould contained in a plaster case; (b) filling the mould with slip.

and sandpapered to a remarkable perfection of surface and, as moulds wear or break, fresh ones can be made from it. The production of clay copies of delicate examples of modelling became popular in the eighteenth and nineteenth centuries. Such collectors' pieces bore fragile lace decorations on their costumes, made from real lace dipped in slip and applied to the model when leather-hard (the lace burnt away but left its pattern in the biscuit slip).

Large Sculptures

Suitable methods for forming really large clay sculptures are coiling with thick clay ropes, and slab building with thick, heavily grogged and sanded clays. Coiling is more suitable for rounded sculptures and slab building for flatter, architectural type sculptures. The student, who possesses a relatively small electric kiln which will fire stoneware, can make garden sculpture in interlocking sections, or concrete can be used as a bridging material integrated into the design. Earthenware is useless out of doors as it soon disintegrates in winter. The enthusiast who builds his own solid-fuel kiln in the garden may be tempted to build a bigger one to match his sculptural ambitions. For a cut sculpture the seams can be joined on the inside with hessian soaked in cement, or dovetailed ledges on the inside of the pieces will lock them together sufficiently *in situ*. Ceramic sculptures in Renaissance churches were assembled in pieces which interlocked.

Coiled Sculpture

A large sculpture built from clay ropes is not difficult, provided it is planned carefully. The clay needs to be coarse and strong to match the scale of the sculpture. Mixtures of sand and grog should be tried with your usual clay. The addition of fireclay helps if your work is to be sited outdoors and a good preparation containing fireclay is known as **crank mixture**. One firm supplies buff modelling clay which will fire up to 1300°C. Experiment with clays and make a preliminary sketch model or maquette as well as drawings. This model can be sliced to provide you with a series of 'contour maps' which will guide you when building by coiling.

One section can be coiled at a time with a rest in between while it becomes firm enough to support the weight of a second section. Whether you join the sections depends on being able to fire the sculpture as a whole. The ropes must be very thick as you will want to modify the exterior when the whole of the main shape has been built. The modelling of such detail as is necessary will have to be done by scraping and cutting, as the clay will be too firm to yield much to pressure. Clay braces and props will have to be built in to the model

Fig. 151. (a) Maquette; (b) section from maquette; (c) parts of figure coiled for assembly; (d) clay brace in position; (e) sectional drawing of figure showing clay braces; (f) details of the figure showing coiled arm and slab-built hood; (g) completed figure of St. Francis.

to reinforce it from the inside. Of course the building must be carefully controlled and calculated; it is no good trusting to luck on a really large piece of work. Use string and callipers to get your measurements right.

Slab-built Sculpture

Use the same tough, rough clay as for coiling and make really thick slabs. Make an accurate maquette. Clay slabs can be flat, and assembled at various angles to each other, or they can be bent to concave and convex curves (these need supporting until the clay stiffens). Interesting concave forms can be shaped in ready-to-hand hollow moulds such as dustbin lids. The whole sculpture is assembled when the pieces are stiff enough to be self-supporting. The assembly can be effected by woodwork-type joints or by slipping and scratching, depending on the character of the design.

Decoration should be thought of as part of the sculpture *ab initio*. The most suitable types of surface decoration are applied relief ornaments related to the main shapes of the sculpture, or carved and impressed lines and textures to enhance the quality of the form. Colour is unlikely to be necessary; if it is, coloured slip brushed on vigorously with a 2 in (5 cm) brush could be used (see Plate 32).

CHAPTER NINE

KILNS AND FIRING

The Evolution of Kilns

In the beginning, perhaps as much as 10,000 years ago, there was no kiln but just a hole in the ground filled with raw pots, over the top of which was a bonfire of wood and grass to bake them so hard that they were unaffected by water. Firing is still done like this in some aboriginal tribes. Our modern, clean, super-efficient equivalent is the electric kiln, of very recent origin. In the years between, the eternal potter has invented many different types of kiln, more or less efficient, most of them burning some sort of solid fuel until the possibilities of gas and oil were discovered and exploited. Gas and oil continue to compete with electricity to heat the potter's kiln. All three have their good points, so which to use depends on your requirements, your situation and, of course, your purse. The solid-fuel-burning kiln has limitations in an industrial and urban society, but nevertheless it is used and ranks with digging and preparing one's own clay for personal satisfaction.

After a hole in the ground, the logical development was a hole above the ground. This was excavated from the side of a hill which gave natural insulation. A raised position for the fuel to burn also provided room for the ash to fall clear and for air to pass under the fuel to assist combustion—very much like the average domestic fire. The kilns which followed, though more elaborate, continued to be designed on the same broad principles. Modifications were introduced in the size and position of the combustion chamber; the chimney and the flues; the nature of the firing chamber; and the way the heat was distributed inside it by up- and down-draughts. Attention to particular factors produced distinct types of kiln such as Chinese and Japanese multi-chamber kilns climbing up the hillside, and the European beehive and bottle-neck kilns (which were replaced only with the advent of the Industrial Revolution). Whether the fuel is wood, oil or gas, the design of modern kilns is still the same in principle. Only the electric kiln is different in principle and performance and easier to control.

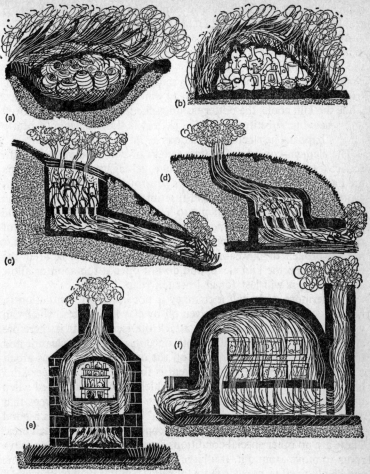

Fig. 152. Primitive bonfire kiln: (a) below ground; (b) above ground; (c) and (d) up-draught bank kilns; (e) brick up-draught kiln with ware enclosed in a muffle; (f) down-draught kiln with ware in saggars.

Electric Kilns

The basic difference from other types is that in the electric kiln combustion does not take place, so no chimney is necessary. The elements which are the source of heat are similar to those in an electric fire, except that they are made from nichrome wire or, for heavier duty, kanthal wire. They are set into grooves in the refractory insulating bricks of the walls and floor (and sometimes the door) and are partly exposed. It is said that in America sheathed elements (rather like those in bathroom heaters) are being introduced, which would prevent them being damaged.

As it is, elements should not be disturbed once they have been used. When it is obvious from their appearance that they have reached the end of their useful life they should be replaced. If just one element ceases to function in the middle of a firing the optimum temperature will never be reached; so time and electricity are wasted while the kiln cools, the pottery is unstacked, the element is removed and a new one substituted and the pottery is stacked again (it nearly always happens just before Christmas . . .).

The element consists of a great length of wire wound spirally (to reduce it to a workable length) without touching itself. If the elements are handled, or they collapse sideways through heating fatigue, contiguous loops may overheat and fuse into the insulating brick. The fused metal deposit is difficult to remove without damaging the groove in the brick. In time the colour and general appearance of the elements show that a protective coating has formed which must not be broken or a weakness will develop. If you look after the elements, keep the kiln clean, and do not open it too soon or allow draughts in, it will last for at least ten years.

Furthermore, although a chimney is not necessary ventilation is, because steam and gases are given off by clay and glazes, which can vitiate the kiln atmosphere and attack the elements. It is therefore a good thing to fire the kiln empty once in a while, to clean it and tone up the elements by burning off the deposits. Small kilns are at a disadvantage because the only vent is the spyhole, but larger kilns have a vent in the roof, with a bung which should be replaced when the firing has ceased so that no draught can enter. The fumes that escape from the vent are unpleasant and unhealthy which is a good reason for siting the kiln away from people in a well-ventilated area. There are no other special conditions for siting a kiln except to leave room to move around it. If a large kiln is sited upstairs a split frame can be obtained to make it more 'portable' (in this context 'portable' means the kiln is brought to the site, not built on it). Electric kilns have a metal frame and covering, and stand on 'skids'.

Kilns are supplied fitted with elements which are suitable for earthenware or stoneware firing. The latter is slightly more expensive and, as firing to 1300°C is a strain on even the heaviest element, the element life is shorter. Of course, the stoneware kiln can be used for the lower temperature ware, but if you try to fire to 1300°C in an earthenware-rated kiln you will probably succeed—once! After which you will need to replace the elements. In fact, all elements lose punch as they grow older and the firing time increases with each firing.

(a)

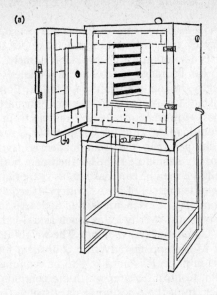

(b)

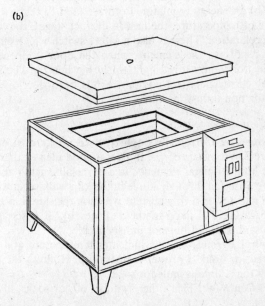

Fig. 153. (a) Front-loading electric kiln on a stand; (b) top-loading electric kiln.

There are front-loading and top-loading kilns: the latter do not
need elements in the door, which saves complications and therefore
money. It is easier to load from the top once you are used to it,
though a variety of different heights can make stacking difficult.
One firm markets a solution to this problem: namely, a fully-wired
extension which can be added to the basic top loader to increase its
height and capacity. Its top temperature is 1180°C. For some reason
the top loader is not very popular so they are difficult to find in the
glossy catalogues. However, to take an example from a catalogue,
of top- and front-loading kilns of comparable capacity, the top
loader is £25 cheaper than the front loader, a saving of 15%.
This sort of capacity should be right for the home potter who does
not want to fire more than he can make in his spare time and should
hold an average of ten pieces of mixed pottery. It requires a 30-amp
power supply (an electric oven needs this at least) and consumes
7 kw when flat out; just over twice as much as a 3-bar electric fire.
It reaches 1200°C in about twelve hours. The weight is about 5 cwt
(about 250 kg). Most suppliers advertise equivalent kilns and they
vary only a little in price. It is not likely to be economical to buy a
second-hand kiln. Control features which are common to this type
of kiln are either: (a) a three-position rotary switch (low, medium,
high), or (b) an energy regulator. Both are used to regulate the rate
of increase of temperature, the first in distinct stages, the second by
gradual acceleration. There is also a safety switch which cuts off the
electricity supply to the elements when the door is opened and a
mains indicator lamp—a red light to show when the kiln is 'alive'.
Other sophisticated control equipment has been developed and is
available for non-industrial kilns.

Optional Control Equipment

The Pyrometer. Universally popular, used on its own or in con-
junction with pyrometric cones, it gives a good idea of the temperature in the kiln. Bi-metal elements, in a porcelain sheath about 12 in
(3 dm) long, inserted through a hole in the kiln wall, react to the heat
in the kiln and set up a tiny current which is registered as a reading
on a temperature dial fixed to the wall nearby. It costs at present
about £35 and is useful but not indispensable.

The Control Pyrometer. This indicates temperature and can also
switch off at, or hold, a pre-set temperature. Holding the temperature steady for a time is called **a soak.**

The Dial Controller. This either switches off, or soaks, at a pre-set
temperature.

The Time-switch. Probably you are familiar with this device as it is
used with off-peak heating, and to 'time-control' heating in the home.

This is what it does for a kiln—switches it on and off at pre-set times. You could commence a firing in the middle of the night without disturbing your sleep, or in the middle of the day while you were at work and just in case you were not there at the right time it would switch off for you and ensure that your pottery was not over-fired! Of course you have to calculate the right time to switch off. The time-switch is a twenty-four-hour clock, so if you go away and leave it on, it will fire your pottery once every twenty-four hours until you return.

The Kiln Sitter. This switches off at a temperature which is determined by the bending of a pyrometric cone.

The Indicating Controller. This is a pyrometer and the final temperature is pre-set on the pyrometer scale. When the indicating needle reaches this temperature it holds the temperature indefinitely (type one); it switches off (type two); it switches off and can be switched on again by a reset button (type three); or it can be set either to soak or to switch off (type four).

The Programmed Controller. The most sophisticated device of all, it is motor driven and controls the programme by a cam, which you can cut yourself to give the time-temperature programme you require. This is an expensive instrument costing as much as the kiln recommended earlier, but it takes complete control and the firing can be done (using off-peak electricity) while the potter sleeps. However, it could be an economic proposition only for a large kiln which is fired frequently.

A Heat Fuse. This can be incorporated to cut off the power supply if the temperature exceeds a safe maximum. When a kiln over-fires—that is, continues heating beyond the safe maximum temperature—the elements bulge and spill out of their channels; the pottery melts as well as the glaze; and the shelves buckle and collapse. In fact, they can all fuse together and finally stick to the walls and floor. It has to be seen to be believed! No absent-minded potter should be without a heat fuse.

Pyrometric Cones

In conclusion there is a simple device which helps a potter to control the firing—**pyrometric cones** have been used for many years. They are composed of clay and fluxes in different proportions calculated to bend at certain temperatures. A number stamped on the cone indicates the temperature at which it will bend, provided it is fired at a prescribed rate. The softening of a cone depends on time as well as temperature, because it is due to the amount of heat-work done. Thus if the temperature rise is slower than the prescribed rate, the cone will bend at a lower temperature and *vice versa*. This makes them very useful as an indication of what is happening to the pottery.

There are different types of cone with different specifications. Traditional ones are Seger and Staffordshire cones, but a new American cone, the **Orton**, is favoured by some suppliers. There are two sizes of cone, standard and small, for different kilns and situations.

The cones are set up in a consecutive series of three, in a fireclay stand (purchased), or just in a lump of clay. The middle cone indicates the vital temperature and all three should lean slightly, to make their subsequent bending positive. The kiln is switched off when the first cone has collapsed and the second one is bending, but while the third one remains upright. Pyrometric cones cannot be used a second time. A small table of cones and temperatures can be found on page 144.

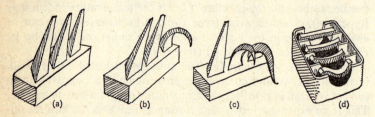

(a)   (b)   (c)   (d)

Fig. 154. Pyrometric cones: (a) three cones in fireclay stand; (b) approaching the desired temperature the first cone bends; (c) the second cone bends as the temperature is reached; (d) pyrometric bars in their stand.

A similar device is the **thermoscope** or **pyrometric bar,** which differs from the cone only in that it is laid horizontally in a supporting stand; otherwise it works in the same way.

Before installing an electric kiln check the cost of providing adequate power where you want the kiln to be—it may cost as much as the kiln. The suppliers of the kiln will deliver it and place it in position (which costs extra), but they will not make any sort of electrical connection.

Gas Kilns

Capacity for capacity a gas kiln is dearer initially than an electric kiln; in the small sizes about twice, and in the larger sizes about one and a half times as expensive. As for electric kilns there is also the cost of carriage, installation and connection. There is the added expense of building a large flue. However, the running cost is less especially now that natural gas has halved the consumption. Gas kilns can be operated using liquid petroleum gas (manufactured gas). The gas kiln is favoured by some potters and institutions because it is economical and also the kiln atmosphere is easily controlled; reduction in flow being achieved by the operation of a hand lever.

In this respect, as in others, gas kilns have improved since the author learnt to fire with one at Art School forty years ago, which was then at least ten years old. It was an up-draught kiln with a **muffle** (a large fireclay box which filled the kiln chamber, designed to protect the pottery from the gas flames). The muffle was cracked and had to be repaired with Pyruma before each firing, and even so the flames managed to penetrate the muffle. It had long burners beneath the muffle and theoretically the flames rose up the sides of the muffle and out through a flue. Naturally the floor was the hottest area and it had cracked the most. It is no wonder that when electric kilns came along they seemed very attractive.

However, gas is clean nowadays and gas-fired, down-draught kilns are popular. In these the heat comes from multiple burners on each side of the kiln, it strikes a **baffle** called a **bag wall** (which prevents the fierce flames contacting the pottery directly) and is deflected upwards and over the baffle. It is sucked downwards by the draught into a channel in the floor and then out through the chimney, passing through the pottery on its way. The rate of heating depends on the flow of gas and air and is controlled by a tap. Gas kilns need more attention and experience than electric kilns.

Oil Kilns

Generally oil rates as a cheap fuel though it is subject to sudden price changes. Its supply is fairly reliable (being interrupted only by the very occasional strike), but its use is not affected by power cuts or pressure reductions. It is, therefore, used by many craftsmen who make their living by potting. Building a kiln is fairly common too and the oil suppliers are keen to help and advise. The oil flame is used with a blower to attain a fierce, quick heat which is most intense near the source. This tends to localise the heat in the early stages of firing but it becomes evenly distributed as stoneware temperatures are approached. Oxidation and reduction atmospheres are easy to control. Oil kilns are therefore favoured by serious stoneware potters because controlled **reduction** is essential for them. (Reduction is explained on page 150.)

Oil kilns are similar in construction to gas kilns except that the spread of the flame, up to 6 ft (1·8 m) long, requires a larger combustion area. To accommodate this and achieve even heating the shape of the kiln is based on a Catenary arch in many cases (this is the shape formed by a uniform chain suspended freely from two points). Like the Gothic arch it is self-supporting and needs no metal reinforcement. Oil kilns are sited in the open, protected from the weather, because of the noise of the blower and the smell of oil and fumes. Various fuel oils can be used, but thick oils have to be thinned to pass through the burners. There are different ways of arranging combustion, but the rate of burning is controlled by regulating the air-oil mixture, and the forced draught from the blower. Naturally the potter must watch the firing and give it thought and skill.

Solid-fuel Kilns

Wood is the traditional fuel for kilns and its use continues where potters feel it is the best way. Wood prevailed in the past because it was a widely available fuel and the only rival was coal. Now, all that was learnt of the principles of firing, has been adapted to gas and oil. There are so many other uses for wood in our world that it has

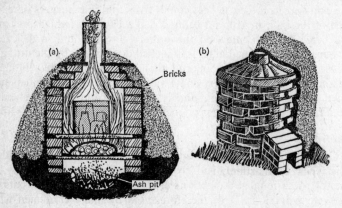

Fig. 155. Improvised kilns: (a) simple up-draught kiln; (b) Raku kiln.

become expensive, besides which there is an art in its use which depends on craftsmen born in the tradition.

Nowadays it is difficult to find a convenient site for anything but a small wood-burning kiln in an urban or suburban area because of the smoke. The country potter is better placed, because a wood kiln is less likely to cause offence or contravene bye-laws. An inexperienced potter, however enthusiastic, would not be advised to try building an ambitious oil or wood kiln until he had studied the subject thoroughly and seen many kilns at work. It is best to begin by building small experimental brick kilns (make a three-dimensional miniature one, to work out the details) constructed so that the combustion chamber and the chimney can be altered easily. The main problems are efficient combustion and even circulation of heat.

Figure 155(a) and (b) shows a simple up-draught kiln and a Raku kiln (Raku pottery is explained later in this chapter). Start with the latter because the temperature required is comparatively low. The principles of kiln building are simple but their application is so much a matter of experience that specialised reading is necessary before building a kiln of any size and complexity. Plans for an efficient coke kiln can be obtained by post; the address is in the back of the book, as is a list of books on this subject.

'Toy' Kilns

Baby electric kilns which are just portable are available with kiln chambers about 7 in × 9 in × 9 in (1·75 dm × 2·25 dm × 2·25 dm) which will fire to 1300°C maximum in six hours. They plug into the normal domestic 13-amp or 15-amp power sockets and consume 2 kW.

The normal use is for firing clay and glaze tests, but one or

Fig. 156. Bunsen burner kiln.

two 8 in (2 dm) pots (the first successful cylinders thrown?) can be accommodated.

The simplest kiln is a biscuit tin over a Bunsen burner. A more effective kiln can be made from insulating bricks heated underneath by a number of Bunsens or an outsize Primus blow-lamp. In fact, glazes can be melted on a piece of biscuit clay supported by asbestos-impregnated gauze over a Bunsen; a quick way of testing for colour, etc.

Kiln Furniture

Kiln furniture embraces a number of different supports used to stack pottery. Shelves or batts are a basic support for pottery and are used in creating storeys in the kiln chamber, in order to use it to full capacity. They are supported by props, generally tubular, hollow and castellated, though there are rectangular props, too, of various sizes, and extensions to give a range of heights. Care must be exercised to support the shelves adequately. Irregularities of surface quickly develop in the floor and shelves, so three props are more stable than four. If four must be used make sure they touch the shelves and the floor. Place the props an inch or two inside the batts, not on the edge. Where two or three batts are built up in tiers, place the props directly over each other.

Batts crack due to the stress of: (a) uneven or undue weight;

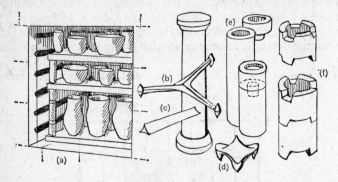

Fig. 157. (a) Ware stacked in kiln showing use and position of shelves and props; (b) stilt; (c) saddle; (d) spur; (e) props; (f) castellated props.

TEMPERATURE TABLE

Approximate comparisons between various cone numbers, kiln temperatures and kiln colours.

Seger cones	Staffordshire cones	Orton cones	Kiln colour	Temperature (°C)
—	021	—		650
018	—	—	dull	700
016	017	—	red	750
015a	015A	015	cherry	800
—	012	013	red	850
—	010	010		900
08a	08A	08	orange	950
05a	05	06		1000
03a	03A	04		1050
01a	1	03	yellow	1100
2a	3A	1		1150
4a	6	5		1200
7	8	7	white	1250
9	10	10		1300

Consult the manufacturers' tables for exact data

1

Plate 1. Early Egyptian pottery stamps.

Plate 2. Egyptian pre-dynastic vase (4000 B.C.). **Plate 3.** Earthenware mould for a relief-decorated bowl (Roman, from Arezzo, first century B.C.).

Plate 4. Earthenware cup with red figure painting (from Greece, about 520 B.C.). **Plate 5.** Eastern Persian bowl in red earthenware, with polychrome slip painting under a transparent glaze. **Plate 6.** Neck amphora with black figure painting (Greek, 520 B.C.).

Plate 7. Persian earthenware dish in white, with a blue glaze (mid-twelfth century).

Plate 8. Persian bowl, black slip on white earthenware with sgraffito decoration.

10

Plate 9. Two views of a Chinese porcelain stand for a bowl (twelft[h] thirteenth century). **Plate 10.** Chinese porcelain bowl, with pale cela[don] crackled glaze (Sung Dynasty, A.D. 960–1279).

Plate 11. Chinese porcelain vase, with carved decoration (Sung). **Plate 12.** Chinese porcelain bottle, with applied relief decoration under a 'Ch'ing-pai' glaze (mid-fourteenth century). **Plate 13.** Chinese bowls in buff stoneware, with brownish-black painting over a cream glaze (Sung).

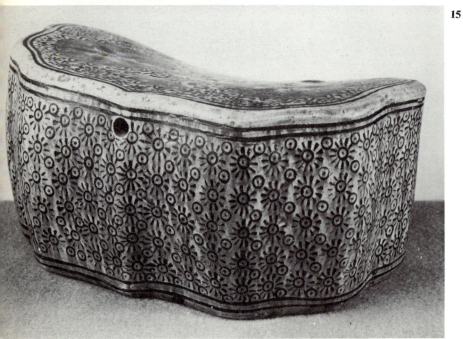

Plate 14. Chinese porcelain drinking bottle, painted in underglaze red (second half of the fourteenth century). **Plate 15.** Chinese pillow, in white earthenware with inlaid and marbled decoration in brown clay (T'ang Dynasty, A.D. 618–906).

16

Plate 16. Chinese porcelain bottle, painted in blue (Ming Dynasty, about 1400).

Plate 17. Chinese earthenware head-rest, with stamped patterns and coloured glazes (T'ang). **Plate 18.** Chinese porcelain vase of mallet form (Lung Ch'uan ware of the twelfth to thirteenth century).

19

20

Plate 19. Chinese painted, earthenware saddled horse. **Plate 20.** Chinese carved stoneware vase, with decoration incised through a brown glaze (Sung Dynasty, A.D. 960—1279).

Plate 21. Chinese red stoneware teapot, unglazed (late seventeenth or first half of the eighteenth century). **Plate 22.** Chinese stoneware bowl, with relief outline floral decoration filled in with coloured glazes (sixteenth century). **Plate 23.** Italian earthenware ewer, with a tin glaze painted with lustre colours (Majolica, about 1520). **Plate 24.** Italian jug, with sgraffito decoration (seventeenth century).

25

26

27

Plate 25. English salt-glaze jug in brown stoneware. The inscription reads, *Moses Froomes Livin in Chosley Parish Nottingham. June ye 26th 1759.* **Plate 26.** Spanish earthenware dish, painted in lustre (Valencia, fifteenth century). **Plate 27.** English earthenware candlestick, decorated with white slip (probably made at Wrotham, 1649).

28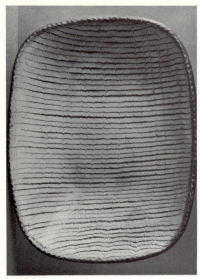

29

30

31

Plate 28. English earthenware dish, decorated with combed white slip (from Staffordshire, eighteenth century). **Plate 29.** Earthenware water pitcher, decorated in black and brown on a white tin glaze by Picasso. **Plate 30.** English salt-glazed stoneware basket (from Staffordshire, about 1760). **Plate 31.** *Left and centre*, slab-built vases with applied relief and textured decoration. *Right*, a strip-built vase (stoneware).

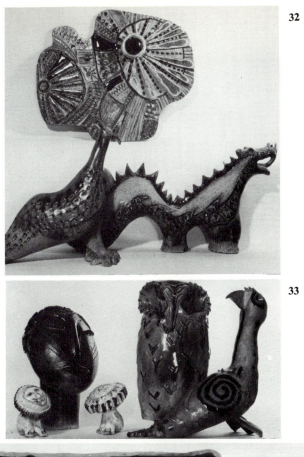

Plate 32. Slab-built wall sculpture: coiled bird form and modelled dragon cut, hollowed and reassembled. **Plate 33.** African head and owl, basically formed over pebbles using pliable sheet clay. The bird and lions are also formed from pliable sheet clay. **Plate 34.** Partly glazed wall sculpture from slab clay: standing sculpture of unglazed stoneware with coloured glass cullet inset.

Plate 35. Coiled and beaten pot, with metallic black glaze and red glazed neck formed separately and inserted after firing the pot. The figures were shaped from pliable sheet clay and the fish from a two-piece press mould.

(b) uneven support; and (c) uneven heating due to bad stacking or draughts (**do not open the kiln door at over 200°C**). **Stilts** are used extensively. They have three legs on which are upward and downward points. They are designed to stand on the shelves and support the pottery with the least possible contact, so that the glaze need not be cleaned off the foot. The points should support the rim of the foot. The points of a stilt often leave tiny splinters in the glaze which are exceedingly sharp and dangerous to the fingers. **Spurs** have a single upward point. **Saddles** are bars of triangular cross section with concave sides. Stilts, spurs and saddles are arbitrary alternatives. There are special batts and cranks for supporting tiles. **Saggars** are fireclay boxes used to protect the pottery from contamination (they were used mainly in English bottle-neck kilns). The name is probably a corruption of 'safeguard'. Remember that glaze accumulations and pieces of stilt stuck to the base of a pot can be removed by using a grinding wheel, or a carborundum stick.

Biscuit Firing

While the temperature in the kiln slowly rises to 200°C any remaining physically-combined water evaporates. Between 200°C and 350°C approximately, organic impurities disintegrate and commence burning, finally igniting. The crucial firing period is around 450°C. Steam escaping from the spyhole shows that the chemically-combined water is being driven off. Contraction and expansion take place so the temperature must be controlled carefully to ensure a slow, steady gain. After 600°C the firing rate can be increased until the maturing temperature of the clay is reached. At this stage certain elements in the clay begin to melt and vitrification would set in with further rises in temperature, until the clay melted eventually. However, the maturing temperature is the upper limit for biscuit (*bisque*) firing. The clay is as hard as it ever need be and if baked any harder it would become impermeable and distort. It is impossible to lay down a time for the biscuit firing as it depends on the size and type of kiln, and whether it is made of earthenware, stoneware or porcelain but a very rough average could be twelve hours. Within this broad classification approximate maturing temperature of clays are earthenware 1050°C, stoneware 1250°C, porcelain 1450°C. (This is a gross simplification.) There are soft and hard fired earthenwares and stoneware gradually merges into porcelain.

Maximum hardness is not necessarily a desirable factor in determining the ultimate temperature of a biscuit firing. It is quite possible and permissible to glaze raw clay and complete the pottery in one firing (this is known as **once-fired pottery**.) However, raw clay is both fragile and very absorbent which makes it difficult to handle. Again

F

not all clays will stand being dipped in liquid glaze and suitable glazes are limited, so the once-fired method is not often used for earthenware, although it is the basis of Raku pottery, and is suitable for stoneware which does not need a glaze to make it impermeable (not all stoneware is glazed, but unglazed stoneware would be porous unless fired to its full maturing temperature). Porcelain is once-fired. This underlines the main object of a biscuit firing which usually is to make the clay hard enough for free and easy handling when it is being glazed. (In the case of unglazed red clay such as bricks and flower-pots there are other factors, of course.)

The toughness of commercial domestic earthenware is due to being biscuit fired at the full maturing temperature of the clay, and subsequently dipped or sprayed to give a waterproof covering of glaze which melts at a lower temperature. This is to avoid a tendency of glazes to shrink more than the body in cooling, thus causing fine cracks known as 'crazing'. Durability and craze resistance are of paramount importance in commercial pottery and are the factors which determine the firing temperatures.

However, clay which has been biscuited to a temperature a little above the critical 600°C stage is reasonably safe to handle and, because the main chemical change has taken place, is unaffected by water. It is also very porous, so that it accepts the glaze easily, and makes a thick coating possible. The disadvantages of a low-temperature bisque are as follows:

(a) The increased likelihood of crazing because the glaze fires at a higher temperature.

(b) The fact that inherent defects in the clay due to inexpert handling, etc. do not show at lower temperatures, but develop nearer the maturing temperature.

(c) If the melting temperature of the glaze is less than the maturing temperature of the clay, then the clay will never mature fully, which means it will be softer than it should be. In certain cases this is acceptable, as when, for example, a school and an evening institute share facilities and, as a result, kilns are packed to capacity in order to cope with the volume of work. When a kiln is overloaded some of the pottery touches the walls (in the case of an electric kiln, the elements). The result is that pots on the outside are unevenly heated and often develop 'burnt' areas through being in direct contact with the elements. If fired to maturing temperatures, the areas may become so 'burnt' that they are impermeable and refuse to accept the glaze. With a lower firing temperature (800°C to 1000°C) this fault does not develop to the same extent and there is much less likelihood that pots will not accept glaze.

In packing a kiln, craftsmanship is as important as it is in making the pottery—the firing literally makes or breaks the pots. Great patience is necessary to sort out the pieces by thickness, size and shape, so that they can be placed strategically and supported adequately.

Points to Consider in Stacking a Biscuit Kiln

1. Pots can touch each other. Biscuit kilns fire most efficiently when they are loaded to capacity. The heat is held well amongst the pots and it is distributed evenly.

2. All pots must be bone dry (use the 'cheek test'). Any clay not containing sand, grog, sawdust, ashes, etc., over 1 in (2·5 cm) thick, is suspect, and should be rejected. It could explode and damage other pieces. In this respect examine modelled pieces carefully.

3. Really dry clay is particularly fragile. Get your hands underneath the pottery and handle it softly. With a top-loading kiln you cannot avoid placing your hands round the pottery. Do not squeeze it and never hold pots or bowls by the rim.

4. Pots may be stacked on each other, and in each other, with discretion; there is a sensible limit. After that use a shelf and stack on a new level. Make sure that the parts which bear the weight are designed to do so, and are adequate to take the load. Play for safety when you are unsure. The pottery at the bottom of a load takes most weight, so place the thickest ware there. **Clay softens at one point during the firing,** so curved shapes, stacked on their sides, will flatten. Wide bowls are best stacked upside down to avoid distortion of the rim and smaller pots can be stacked inside bowls or inside any larger pot.

Lids should be fired on their pots but if they are rather high because they are domed or have tall knobs, they can be placed upside down on the neck to save space. The temperature varies in kilns, so there is a danger of large pots being heated unevenly. Avoid this as far as possible by placing in the centre and surrounding with other pots: the smaller the kiln the more necessary this is.

5. Pottery decorated with coloured slip should not touch other pottery: oxides in the slip may melt or volatilise and make marks.

6. Large, flat pottery reliefs and slabs, or bowls and dishes with broad, flat bases, are best placed on a layer of grog, or flint, so that they can move freely when contracting or expanding during the firing.

7. Make sure your kiln shelves are clean.

Firing Procedure

1. The slower the firing the better: it cannot be too slow. In the initial stages, too sudden a rise in temperature can cause explosions.

Watch this also with grogged sculpture. The thick grogged clay may be dry on the outside, but can still contain moisture in the centre. This moisture becomes steam which will not cause damage if it is allowed to escape slowly, but with too fast a temperature rise, pockets of steam will form which 'blow out' and cause damage.

2. Having decided on the temperature at which your clay is to be biscuited, place cones for that temperature so that they can be seen through the spyhole (with a torch if necessary). Even if you have a pyrometer, use cones as well until you are experienced in firing with that particular kiln. Compare pyrometer and cone-melting temperatures, and note how hard and porous, etc., the biscuit is at the end of the firing. Make a written record.

3. Leave the stopper out of the spyhole until steam ceases to come from it. If there is a vent on top of the kiln remove the bung so that gases can escape.

4. Increase the rate of firing progressively after 600°C.

5. Hold the maximum temperature for a while if you have a variable control. This will ensure that all the biscuit is 'cooked' to the required temperature.

6. Allow the kiln to cool slowly. Push in the dampers if there are any, and do not open the door at all before 200°C, when it can be opened so that a tiny gap is left to assist the final cooling. It should take as long to cool as it took to heat. Do not remove the biscuit pottery until you can handle it with bare hands.

7. Biscuit pottery should be stored in a cupboard to keep it clean and free from dust. Handle it lightly and no more than necessary. Sweaty hands leave greasy marks.

Glaze Firing

Stacking a Glaze (Gloss or Glost) Kiln

1. Glazed pots should be dry before stacking.

2. Pots should not be placed too near each other. If they are too close radiation causes shiny spots. Also oxides like copper volatilise and 'fly' from one pot to another: copper will produce a turquoise blush on a white pot placed too close to it, and chrome a pink blush.

3. Keep pots at least 1 in (2·5 cm) away from the kiln walls. Take care pots do not touch the back wall and run your fingers round or use a mirror to check.

4. When stacking pots glazed with various colours be careful that your fingers do not transfer smudges of glaze from one to another. Once again look out for copper oxide! Beware also that you do not finger pots roughly and remove or knock off any glaze.

5. When you know the hotter and cooler areas in the kiln, place the glazes to suit their melting temperatures.

6. Coat one side of all shelves with a wash made from 50/50 flint and china clay (or purchase batt wash from the suppliers), mixed with water to a creamy consistency. Keep the edges clean and do not get any wash underneath (when dry the creamy wash would flake off and fall into pots below). Keep the kiln and shelves clean for the same reason.

7. Remove all glaze from the foot and from the foot rim to ensure pots cannot stick to the shelf. Bases without a foot should be cleaned of glaze (or only very thinly glazed) and placed on stilts. Never support stoneware on stilts because the clay softens and sags over the stilt; stand it on flint or sand.

8. Where a known or even suspected runny glaze has been used, stand the pot on a wafer of insulating brick, or on a scrap of kiln shelving heavily flinted.

9. As in the bisque kiln, lids are best fired on their pots to prevent warping and misfit (but clean the lid, and the pot, of glaze around the area of contact).

10. Avoid gaps in the kiln; a fully and evenly loaded kiln is necessary for even firing.

11. Where an electric kiln has floor elements the first shelf must be raised on props to allow heat to circulate. Do not place shelves too high in the kiln. Never use cracked shelves, they will disintegrate some time (usually near the end of a firing!).

12. Use cones to check temperatures.

Firing Procedure

1. Fire at low heat for one hour to ensure drying glaze.

2. Increase to a fairly rapid rate of firing, until about 900°C–1000°C, when the glaze begins to melt. Slow and steady then, while the chemical changes have time to develop satisfactorily. The shine on a melting glaze can be seen clearly through the spyhole.

3. Switch off or cease firing when the glazes have reached their maturing temperature. Leave the kiln to cool off. It takes about as long as it did to fire—maybe longer. **Do not** try to hasten it: any draught from open doors, etc., can ruin your pottery. **Do not** take the pottery out until it is cool, as, if it is hot, it may go 'ping' and fall to pieces. (This is a counsel of excellence: even the most experienced potters have been known to suffer from impatience.)

4. The firing rate of glaze averages about 100°C per hour. Some potters fire the glost in electric kilns at maximum rate from start to finish: this can speed the rate to 200°C per hour.

5. The firing procedure for mixed glazes and biscuit, and once-fired pottery is the same as for earthenware biscuit.

Raku Firing

The Japanese word *Raku* implies a contented frame of mind which is associated with the Zen Buddhism philosophy of living near to nature. The Raku ceremony includes making one's own tea-bowl, firing it, and drinking from it. The firing has to be, and is, immediate. To accomplish this the tea-bowl is formed with thick walls from a low-fire porous stoneware clay. Up to one-third of its weight consists of fireclay grog, so that it can withstand thermal shock. The glaze is of simple composition and contains some 60% flux, so that it melts around 850°C. The kiln is maintained at a slightly lower temperature and the glazed bowls are dried on top.

They are placed in the hot kiln using a long pair of tongs and watched while the temperature is boosted. In about twenty minutes the glaze melts and develops the tell-tale shine—the pots are removed from the kiln with the tongs, thrust into sawdust or cut grass and held there for two or three minutes. Then they are removed and plunged into water, which quickly cools them. This 'happening' is dramatic and breaks all the usual rules about firing. It is customary to build a small brick kiln out of doors especially for Raku. The pottery is soft and porous, the glaze is heavily crackled and often has surprising colour effects due to the 'reducing' atmosphere created by the smoking sawdust. In Japan you can hire a man to bring round a portable kiln for the afternoon.

Oxidation Firing

Combustion results from the union of carbon and oxygen. Normally the arrangement for burning fuel in a kiln produces complete combustion, ensuring a smokeless flame, which gives a pure atmosphere containing oxygen in the chamber where the pots are baking. In an electric kiln no fuel is burnt so no oxygen is consumed. In both cases there is an oxidation atmosphere.

Reduction Firing

If incomplete combustion occurs and smoke is formed, carbon and carbon monoxide may be released and find their way into the kiln chamber. When this happens the carbon monoxide goes in search of the oxygen it needs, and steals it from substances in the pots. Thus iron and copper oxides surrender their oxygen and are reduced to lower oxides, or back to pure metal suspended in the glaze.

This changes the colour of the melted glaze because there is a difference between the colour of the original oxides and the lower

oxides or pure metals. This reduction atmosphere is caused sometimes by smoke which gets into the kiln accidentally. Potters use
reduction deliberately to obtain unusual colours and metallic effects,
by cutting off the air supply or throwing wood, etc., into the kiln to
make the atmosphere smoky. Camphor balls can be used in an
electric kiln and will not damage the elements. The reduction of the
atmosphere is put into effect about the time that the glaze starts to
melt, but oxidation is restored later to even out faults which may
have developed in the surface.

Localised Reduction

If silicon carbide is introduced into a copper oxide glaze, red
speckles develop. The carbon reduces the green of copper oxide to
the red copper. This takes place in an ordinary oxidation firing.

Metallic and lustrous surfaces can be produced on a fired glaze by
using a combination of metallic salts, with oils and resins—the latter
burn and reduction is set up which gives the glaze a very fine coating
of metal. This takes place in an oxidation firing, reaching 700°–
750°C. Kiln vents are removed or the door is kept partly open to
allow pungent fumes to escape up to 400°C.

On-glaze Enamel Firing

The firing procedure is much the same as for lustres, etc., but they
should not be fired together. The firing rate recommended is a rise
of 150°C per hour, and there is no need for extra ventilation. A
thirty-minute soak (see page 138) will improve the quality of the
colours. Cooling can be a little faster than heating. You will find a
soak is recommended for some glazes by the manufacturers.

Salt-glaze Firing

Salt glazing is used with stoneware because it does not work at
lower temperatures. Salt is introduced into the kiln through the
burner openings, when the temperature is at its maximum. The great
heat turns the salt to vapour which fills the kiln chamber. This forms
a thin glaze wherever it finds and combines with silica and alumina.
Thus both the chamber and the pots are glazed, which means the
kiln can be used only for salt glazing. The texture of the glaze is
uneven, being permeated with tiny blobs which give an orange-peel
appearance. This is familiar to you though you may not realise it,
because the drainpipes under your house are of salt-glazed stoneware. It is cheap and efficient. Some contemporary potters are
experimenting with salt glazing because its full possibilities have not
been explored.

Assisted Firing

Fuel in the form of coke dust is mixed with the clay in bricks to give a local boost to the firing and to develop colour characteristics. Other readily-available fuels are used in peasant countries to assist the firing of pottery by mixing them with the clay.

CHAPTER TEN

GLAZING AND GLAZES

For most students glazing holds more fascination than any other process in pottery making. Nevertheless more pottery is ruined by clumsy glazing and unskilled firing than in any other way. The beginner should be cautious in his approach, not over-ambitious or in too much of a hurry. The main faults encountered among evening-class students and pupils at school are:

(a) Applying glaze too thick or too thin.
(b) Leaving glaze on the base so that it sticks to its support.
(c) Using an unsuitable glaze.

The first fault can be cured by experience gained from doing test firings (and from making mistakes), or by using one's imagination in looking at the coating of glaze as it has been applied in powder form and seeing it as a melted coating of glass. The second is a fault of laziness or ignorance. The third fault is due to lack of experience.

The main purpose of a glaze is to counteract the porous nature of the body by providing a hard, waterproof covering, and if the inside of the pot or bowl has been glazed this is sufficient for this purpose. It is also used to counteract a tendency for the pores of the body to fill with dirt, so that the outside can be either waxed and polished (and this is worth considering because it can be attractive to look at) or to make cleaning easier.

If the base and foot have been properly finished off in the making, there is no need for glaze because the operative area inside the pot has been waterproofed and the question of dirt on the foot can be disregarded. It is difficult not to cover the base and foot when glazing, but it is easy to remove the glaze with a knife or a stiff brush. If it is not removed it will melt and cannot avoid sticking to the stilt, or the shelf, whichever it stands on. If the glaze is thick, a stilt will be difficult to shift (stilts are not a good idea anyway because they have a tendency to get inside the foot which can cause tension when the pot cools and contracts). A situation can arise where the pot is stuck to the stilt, which is itself stuck to the shelf—this ruins the pot and the shelf. This has already been stated on page 149, but it cannot be over-emphasised because so much damage and disappointment results from neglecting a very simple precaution. Discourage glaze

153

adhering to the foot of a pot by dipping it in hot paraffin (but do not dip more than is necessary!), or alternatively in a wax resist.

The third fault is the result of using coloured and 'special effects' glazes without experience. It is for this reason that methods of decorating clay have been introduced before the biscuit firing throughout the practical chapters, in the hope that beginners will use only a simple clear glaze in the early stages. Having learnt to apply that successfully, they can then use coloured and other glazes with some assurance of success. The methods of getting the glaze onto the pot are similar to those used for coating pots with slip. To complete your introduction to glazing one point which has been made previously is worth repeating: the thickness of a coat of glaze when applied depends on the proportion of water in the glaze and on the temperature of the biscuit firing. If the clay has been fired to its maturing temperature it will be less absorbent than if it has been soft fired (if it has been fired beyond the maturing temperature you will have difficulty in glazing it at all!).

Pottery is usually glazed after the biscuit firing. Glazing raw pots was mentioned in the advice about firing kilns and, although it is not suitable for schools and institutions where the pottery is likely to receive rough treatment, it does have the advantage that it saves the time and cost of a second firing, which is a recommendation to the individual potter.

Preparation of Glazes

Fritts and raw materials for glazes will be mentioned on pages 160 and 167, but to start with assume that you purchase a quantity of a transparent glaze, recommended by your supplier for use with his clay. It comes to you already ground to a fine white powder so it needs mixing with water: for medium-fired biscuit pottery about ¾ pint to 1 lb (0·4 litre to 0·4 kg) glaze—more water if the biscuit is soft or if you are using a spray. After mixing, sieve it through an 80, 100 or 120 mesh sieve—use 100 mesh if you have it. It is then almost ready to use except that it is advisable to bind the glaze by adding gum, common size or carragheen moss size, etc., to improve the holding properties so that it adheres to the pot and has a firm rather than a powdery surface (easier to paint on and not so liable to get damaged in handling).

The powdered gum is steeped in water till it forms a mucilage: a teaspoonful of this added to 1 pint liquid glaze is sufficient. If the glaze is likely to be kept long enough for the gum to decompose, a few drops of carbolic acid should be included as a preservative. Prepared **Glaze Binders** can be purchased. The glaze can be used straightaway, but the mixture improves in a few days and becomes smoother. However, it needs constant stirring to prevent the more solid ingredients settling into a solid, unmanageable mass at the bottom of the plastic bucket (with lid to prevent evaporation) in which it should be kept. Two per cent of a very fine-particled volcanic clay called Bentonite will help to counteract this tendency to 'settle-out'. Mediaeval and peasant potters often glazed their pots by dusting them with powdered **galena** (lead sulphide), which is highly poisonous and even today could be a cause of injury or death. However, as our ancestors did not know this they may have died from lead rather than alcoholic poisoning! As you are using glaze in liquid form there is the following, rather arbitrary, choice of methods —dipping, pouring, spraying and brushing. As you have used all these methods with slip you are forearmed: careful planning and organisation is more important than which procedure you adopt. What is important is to get a satisfactory thickness of glaze first time —second attempts are rarely successful unless the glaze is all removed and the pot dried. To this end a piece of biscuit from the same firing should be dipped in glaze to judge the porosity of the clay and the viscosity, etc., of the glaze. Then the amount of water in the glaze can be adjusted before the glazing proper begins.

Preparation of Biscuit

1. The biscuit is cleaner and easier to glaze if it is glazed while still warm (not hot) from the kiln. If this is not possible, the pottery must be kept clean and dust free; sweaty fingers do most harm.

2. The biscuit, especially if low-fired, should be given a quick dip in water to clean off any dust and release the air from the pores. This decreases the porosity and prevents the glaze forming a thick coat too quickly. Do not get the ware too wet or the glaze will run and form an uneven coat, almost bare in parts.

3. If the ware is dense and non-porous do not wash it; warming it in the kiln may help the glaze to take, especially if it is sprayed and warmed alternately. Magnesium sulphate (Epsom-salts) thickens the glaze and assists adhesion.

4. Stir the glaze thoroughly, immediately prior to commencing the glazing.

Glazing Procedures

Dipping

Pour a pool of glaze into the pot and swill it around till an effective coat has formed. Alternatively, if a small bowl, cylinder or cup shape is to be glazed, it can be filled to the top and emptied quickly. Wipe the drips round the edge with the finger using them to glaze the rim. When the water has been absorbed the glaze will look matt. Hold it by the foot and immerse it in the glaze tub, then remove it and let it drip, holding it at an angle over the tub and, as the last drop is congealing, remove it with your finger. When the outside glaze has gone matt, touch up the finger marks with a brush. If you wish to avoid finger marks use tongs (which can be purchased or improvised with wire), so that touching up may not be necessary.

If, in spite of glazing tests, the pot comes out of the dip with a coat of glaze which is obviously too thin, wait for the gloss to disappear and immediately dip it again. If the inside glaze penetrates the biscuit and saturates it, the outer glaze will not cover satisfactorily and it will be some time before it is ready for a second dip. With confidence second dipping can be used deliberately to build up a more even coat of glaze on awkward shapes. It can be used, too, as a method of applying one glaze over another without resorting to spraying. But if the first coat is allowed to dry, a second dip will disturb it, causing blisters and flaking. Shave off any glaring irregularities in the glaze with a sharp blade, or rub them down with the finger. Any roughness will disappear when the glaze melts: clear glazes are very tolerant (especially if they are lead glazes) and smooth out more than other glazes. Clean the foot and ensure that at least $\frac{1}{4}$ in (6·5 mm) of the biscuit clay above the foot is clear of glaze, in order to allow for possible glaze runs. Finally look over the pot for pinholes (especially at ridges and junctions) which have been formed by escaping air-bubbles. Store it in a dust-free place to await firing.

Where the container is unsuitable or the quantity of glaze is insufficient a tall pot can be dipped from the top and then from the base, so that the half coats overlap slightly; the ridge formed should be rubbed down or shaved. Do not fill a tall pot with glaze because it will wet it too much. Double dipping is suitable for small pots with pronounced feet where the whole pot can be pushed into the glaze, almost withdrawn with a sharp twist, and then pushed down again, shaken and twisted back and forth. This, if done successfully, coats the pot inside and out in one action—it needs practice! Do not try it on a painted pot, but use a plain pot to get the knack. Small bowls can be held by the lip and double dipped with a scooping action, then shaken off (but only if they have been biscuit fired).

Pouring

Where there is insufficient glaze for dipping, or when the container is the wrong proportion, pouring is suitable. Glaze the inside of the pot first, allow the glaze surface to set, then reverse the pot and support it on chicken wire or a cake tray over a bowl. The glaze is poured over and round the pot from a jug (not too small a jug or the glaze will run out before you have finished!). If the whole arrangement is placed on a banding wheel or a throwing wheel, it can be rotated slowly while the glaze is poured steadily from one position. The outsides of large bowls usually have to be glazed by pouring because an undue amount of glaze would be needed for dipping.

Spraying

This can be done with a thumb spray or a power-operated spray. The latter is more efficient provided the glaze is well sieved, but blockages are a nuisance and can be difficult to clear. The main advantages of using a spray are that small quantities of glaze can be used, and the ease with which an even coat can be applied, which makes glazing rather less of a trial for the beginner. Other advantages are that the glaze falls lightly on painted ware without disturbing the colour, that coloured and plain glazes can be sprayed over each other, and that shading and blending are possible.

On the other hand, if an electric spray is being used a special booth with an extractor fan is an absolute necessity because spray must not be breathed in by the operator (face masks are a sensible additional precaution). Another disadvantage is that at least half the spray misses the pot and either settles on the walls of the booth or goes out through the fan (the reclaimable glaze from the booth can be used as a 'mystery' glaze—this 'waste' glaze can be modified by adding oxides to produce greys, browns, greens and blacks). Any attempt to counteract this by holding the spray gun nearer the pot is likely to build up the glaze too quickly, so that it becomes wet and is then blown off again by the force of the air from the spray. This leads to the point that there is an optimum distance for holding the spray so that the glaze falls on the pot, but is not shot at it, which is about 1 ft (3 dm) but varies with individual sprays.

Glaze can be too thick, when it will refuse to pass through the nozzle; or just thick, when it will build up a pimply surface; or too thin, when it will run down the pot without warning. It will be just right when it forms a fine-grained almost smooth surface, even so the pot should be turned round on a banding wheel as it is sprayed. If a thick glaze coat is required (this is not desirable with clear glaze as it tends to cloud if too thick) there should be a rest for drying between coats. If it does run, all the glaze must be removed before spraying is recommenced. Sprayed pots have to be handled very carefully when stacking the kiln.

The efficiency of spraying is one of its disadvantages because the glaze coat tends to be too all-over accurate and mechanical. This, of course, is from the studio potter's point of view—on commercial pottery tableware, for instance, a thin, even surface of glaze is desirable. Uneven glazing on factory wares labels them as 'seconds'. Nevertheless, spraying is used in industry only on intricate pieces because it is slower than dipping. In institutions where space and time are limited either one has large tubs and a severely limited number of glazes, or else a variety of glazes in small quantities which makes the use of a spray inevitable.

Brushing

Use a broad ox-hair brush or a 1 in (2·5 cm) house-painting brush to apply the glaze in slightly overlapping strokes. Work quickly so that the second coat is applied over the first before it is dry (as in dipping). The glaze should be a thin cream containing gum, size, etc.

Another method is to use a 'mop', a soft, floppy brush, and blob the glaze on quickly. Brushing is not easy and needs practice—there are occasions when it is the only way unless you try blobbing the glaze on with a piece of sponge.

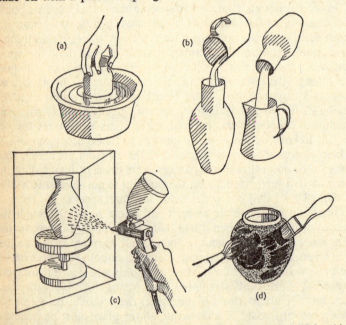

Fig. 158. Glaze application: (a) dipping; (b) pouring; (c) spraying; (d) brushing.

The Relationship between Clay and Glaze

As silica (silicon oxide) and alumina (aluminium oxide) constitute some two-thirds of the earth's surface, in the form of sand, soil or clay, it is not surprising that most clays are more than 80% silica and alumina, chemically combined with hydrogen oxide, i.e. water. 'Pure clay' is theoretical, but china clay (sometimes called **kaolin**) is 95% pure alumina and silica. As silica melts at 1715°C, alumina at 2050°C, and kaolin at about 1800°C, there is obviously another factor present in the clays which potters use, because even porcelain kilns rarely reach temperatures much over 1400°C. This other factor is known as a **flux**.

Fluxes are melting agents which promote vitrification, and they are present naturally in all clays. So great is the range of their performance that some clays will not melt at 1500°C while others collapse at about 1200°C. The latter are the more common clays, coloured by iron oxide which is itself a strong flux. They are classified, logically, as **fusible clays**, because they are fusible within the range of temperatures available to potters. Some of them form a shiny glass-like substance when they melt—they are called **slip clays.** In the parts of the world where they are found they are used to glaze **vitrifiable clays**, such as low-firing stonewares, to improve their impermeability and their looks. A glaze then is an **impermeable glossy coat,** closely related to clay, but necessarily melting at a lower temperature than the clay it covers.

The main point of difference between clays and glazes is their degree of fusibility, and this depends on the nature of the fluxing agent and the proportions of flux, silica and alumina. It may also help to understand the nature of glaze if the relationship to glass is examined: usually glaze is described as a 'glass-like' substance. Historically glass was used before glaze; it is fabled that it was discovered by chance in the ashes when sea-faring traders doused their camp fires on the sandy shores of the Mediterranean. The main ingredient in both instances is silica—thus glass is made from white sand, which is almost pure silica, and the melting point (around 1700°C) is lowered by adding a flux such as lead oxide. The characteristic difference is that glass is shaped independently by being melted rapidly and moulded or blown to give it form. It is heated and cooled fairly rapidly, compared with the glaze on a pot which is brought to maximum heat over a period of hours by a steady firing cycle. The glaze plays a secondary role in a sense, because it must fit and adhere to a clay shape. Therefore, although both glaze and glass consist of silica and a flux, something else is necessary in a glaze to ensure its adhesion to the pot at all stages, and especially during the firing. This is the alumina which is found naturally in clay (in combination with silica and a flux). It is rare to find alumina in anything like a pure form (**bauxite** is the nearest and this is not a common mineral) which is another reason for using clay in glazes. Alumina stabilises the runny glaze and promotes adhesion, whilst silica gives glassiness and hardness, and the flux assists fusion and promotes fluidity.

Glass—Silica   flux
Glaze—Silica   flux   alumina
Clay—Alumina   silica   flux

In short, without alumina the 'glass' would run off the pot. If an ordinary clear glass bottle were crushed under a steam-roller the result would be a fine white powder. Heated in crucible or furnace this would rapidly fuse and cool to become clear glass again. If the finely-powdered glass were mixed up as a liquid with water and gum it could be applied to the surface of a pot and heated till it melted. Unfortunately it would be almost certain to drip off the pot because it contained no alumina. However, coloured bottle glass and coloured glass chunks (known as **cullet**) can be used in flat shapes, such as ash trays, because there it is contained and cannot run away when it melts. This is a very popular contemporary technique: enough glass is placed in the pottery to make a deep pool when it melts—on cooling it crazes and produces an attractive crackle (fine lines in a crazy-paving pattern). The cullet can be bought from your usual suppliers or from a local glass works. Materials which have been melted together into a glassy substance, cooled and ground to a powder are known as **fritts.**

Fritts and Glazes

Glazes are made up from natural materials such as clay and sand, or from oxides which have been isolated such as lead oxide, boracic oxide, tin oxide, etc. All materials used in glazes behave as oxides once they melt into the fritt. Some of these materials are highly poisonous, such as lead, and some, such as borax, are highly soluble. Soluble materials combine too readily with water and are easily lost during grinding, sieving and application, or by absorption into the pores of the clay. To counteract the poisonous character of some materials and the soluble nature of others, they are fired with other basic ingredients such as silica and alumina, and ground to a powder to form a fritt. A fritt is a simple glass or glaze which can be used on its own in some circumstances or which can have further non-toxic and insoluble ingredients added to it (including colouring oxides, or stains, of course). Fritts are uniform and dependable but need Bentonite, etc., to prevent them forming a hard deposit, known as a **pan**, at the bottom of the container. It is too difficult to make your own fritts and would not be worth the time and trouble. They are classified by the following types of flux.

Lead Fritts

  (a) Lead bisilicate (1 of lead to 2 of silica).
  (b) Lead monosilicate (1 of lead to 1 of silica).
  (c) Lead sesquisilicate (1 of lead to 1½ of silica).

It will be seen that these are all 'glasses' containing no alumina. Because lead is a strong flux with a low melting point, the lead fritts fire in the low temperature range. At high temperatures, around 1200°C, lead tends to volatilise. Lead bisilicate is a widely-used base for earthenware glazes. Physically it is heavy and easily pans. It can be used for Raku where it is applied to the raw clay and combines with the alumina in it to form a clear glaze. There are other examples of this sort of practice such as the use of raw galena (a native lead oxide) or red lead to produce a glazed surface. These used to be applied in powder form to the raw pottery by peasant potters: the lead flux combined with the silica and the alumina in the raw clay to form a glaze during the firing.

Lead Glazes

You will have realised that the lead fritts are glass rather than glaze and that they need the addition of alumina. In the case of lead bisilicate there is a high silica content and only a small proportion of other materials can be added. Ten per cent of china clay will convert the fritt to a glaze, and there are other simple additions which can be made to improvise a small range of lead glazes. Often the manufacturers' catalogues are helpful on this point. Again lead bisilicate can be combined in various proportions with pottery clays or local clays to make clear and amber (transparent) glazes. Lead glazes have richness and depth but they are comparatively soft; because small errors smooth out in the firing and because they are clear, shiny and add a bright colour, they are the easiest glazes to commence with.

Borax Fritts

They have different characteristics from lead, but they are also the basis for low-firing earthenware glazes. Borax is very soluble (not poisonous) and is difficult to handle directly in glazes.

  (a) Soft, standard and hard borax fritts differ slightly in composition and firing range. Not all manufacturers offer the three types.
  (b) Calcium borate fritt is based on **Colemanite** (which is calcium borate), a by-product in the manufacture of borax. The fritt as sold contains boric oxide combined with silica and alumina, so it provides a glaze in itself.

Borax Glazes

Borax glazes can be made by combining the fritts with pottery clays, as for lead fritts. In both cases the accepted practice is to make a **line blend**—at one end of the line 90% clay plus 10% fritt and, at the other, 10% clay and 90% fritt. These can be fired in a test kiln. Tests can be made on small, flat tiles, but upright tiles with feet, or small bowls give a better idea of the performance of the glaze on upright and curved surfaces. Borax glazes are harder than lead glazes. They have a different colour response and because of their low expansion they are less elastic. They are often opalescent or milky at low temperatures, especially on red clay.

Alkaline Fritts

They contain **soda** and **potash** as well as borax (which is also alkaline). Unlike borax fritts they have high expansion which makes them craze easily, therefore they are used for crackle glazes. The colour response is brighter than from borax fritt.

Zircon Fritts

Zircon fritts contain **zirconium**, an opacifying agent, which makes it a basis for opaque glazes. It has a wide firing range and remains opaque up to 1100°C.

To Recapitulate: fritts are mixtures of ingredients which have been melted to a glass and then reground; with or without additional materials they function as glazes.

The distinction between fritt and glaze is that a glaze has not necessarily been fritted, but may be a direct mixture of ingredients. All materials were molten before the earth cooled down, so it is not surprising that 'natural fritts' exist, e.g. **feldspar**, a natural rock with many varieties some of which can act as glazes at about 1300°C.

Simple Glazes

Transparent

We have already seen some of the ways of preparing a clear glaze; a transparent fritt is combined with pottery clays (satisfactory proportions are arrived at by a line blend). The alternative is to buy a prepared glaze to fit your clay (from the same manufacturer). When you have learnt to use this glaze efficiently you can introduce variations gradually, making tests and keeping a careful record.

Opaque

Oxides such as tin oxide (10%) or zirconium oxide (15%), which remain in suspension and do not melt, unless the glaze is over-fired, make a glaze cloudy (similar in effect to powdered chalk in water or the globules of fat in milk). An opaque white earthenware glaze can be obtained:

(a) By adding 10% of tin oxide to a glaze compounded from a transparent fritt (plus a suitable quantity of clay).

(b) By using a prepared white opaque fritt plus a suitable percentage of clay.

(c) By using a prepared transparent glaze plus 10% tin oxide.

(d) By using a prepared white opaque earthenware glaze (matt or gloss).

In (a) and (c) 15% zirconium oxide can replace the tin oxide. Clear and opaque glazes can be coloured by the oxides (remember that the white in opaque glazes gives what are sometimes called 'pastel' tints because of their chalky quality). The colours are affected decisively by the type of flux and the type of flux varies with the firing temperature. Broadly speaking, as the melting temperature is increased the proportion of fluxes is decreased and the proportion of **refractory** materials (those which resist melting) is increased. The nature of the fluxes changes also: whereas lead and borax predominate in the low firing glazes, other materials such as calcium carbonate (whiting), zinc, magnesium, potash and soda displace them in stoneware and porcelain glazes.

Glaze Colours from Oxides

Colouring Oxides

Copper. The carbonate form is easier to use. Use up to 5%. It is a flux and over 5% increases fluidity and its use in lead glazes gives fresh yellow-greens; in alkaline glazes gives forms of turquoise (blue-green to green-blue). In the presence of potassium it develops yellow; with barium and zinc, blue; 10% of copper carbonate gives a metallic black because the glaze is 'overloaded' with metal (see Plate 35). There is a dull metallic finish when it is under-fired, rather like pewter and when over-fired green and black break into each other. At the optimum temperature it can give almost lustrous black. Copper in alkaline opaque glazes gives a soft turquoise blue. In a reduction kiln copper reverts to red.

Cobalt. The carbonate form is best. Use $\frac{1}{2}$%–3%. Inky blue in lead glazes and brilliant blue in alkaline glazes: in the presence of zinc the blue is more intense. In the presence of magnesium, pink-to-purple especially if manganese is introduced. It is used in minute quantities to counteract any tendency to yellow in white glazes. It is a base for black.

Iron. Three to eight per cent. It has many forms. The red and yellow oxides give browny-yellows to amber, tan and red-brown, particularly in lead glazes. Black iron and *crocus martis*, which is a form of iron oxide, give brown with speckles; and iron oxide spangles gives black with speckled highlights. Iron chromate gives grey.

Manganese. Two to five per cent gives brown, but in an alkaline tin glaze gives purple. In magnesium and barium, high-temperature glazes, it gives pale to deep violet. The oxide produces spots in the glaze; so the carbonate is better for even colour. Large quantities cause blistering and there is a tendency for glazes containing manganese to bubble violently during firing. It is a strong flux.

Chromium. One to three per cent generally produces an opaque, rather lifeless, green. In highly alkaline tin glazes it gives pink and, in the presence of zinc, brown. In low-temperature (900°C) high-lead glazes, orange to vermilion, turning to brown at 100°C, and to a brown-green at 1100°C. In a reducing kiln it turns black. (Keep chromium-glazed pots away from other pots as it can affect their colour.) Chromium oxide is **poisonous**, so wash your hands after using it. Potassium bichromate can be used for red in low-fired lead glazes.

Uranium. Two to seven per cent produces orange and red, in soft lead glazes at 900°C, and yellow in higher-fired glazes.

Nickel. One to five per cent gives a grey colour in lead glazes and, in higher-fired glazes containing magnesium, bright green; barium gives brown. It is used to modify other colours.

Antimony. Ten to twenty per cent can give a weak white or, in a high lead glaze, yellow. This is also **poisonous**.

Antimoniate of lead. Five to ten per cent gives a stable yellow, known to painters as Naples yellow, in a lead glaze. This again is **poisonous** and you should take care in using it.

Vanadium pentoxide. Five to ten per cent gives yellow in tin glazes.

These metals can be used to stain clays and slips. The colours and tints which the metal oxides, carbonates, etc., produce are not entirely predictable because they are the result of chemical action and reaction. The final colour depends upon such factors as the acidity or alkalinity of a slip or glaze; the presence of certain materials which produce a strong reaction in some oxides; and the physical characteristics such as opacity. This colour also depends on the firing temperature and the kiln atmosphere, as the notes about the individual colours indicate. The percentage of colour (by weight) added to the glaze is critical especially in the case of the very strong stains, such as cobalt. The only way to learn is to mix the oxides or carbonates in a series of percentages with your standard basic transparent and opaque glazes. This will take quite a time, even if you use only the more obvious metals.

Your range of colours can be further extended by mixing metals such as cobalt and copper, iron and manganese, or copper and nickel, etc., in various percentages, for example:

Copper (max. 6) $\frac{1}{2}$ $\frac{1}{2}$ 1 1 1$\frac{1}{2}$ 1$\frac{1}{2}$ 2 2$\frac{1}{2}$ 3 2 1 %
Cobalt (max. 3) $\frac{1}{2}$ 1 $\frac{1}{2}$ 1 $\frac{1}{2}$ 1 $\frac{1}{2}$ 1 1$\frac{1}{2}$ 2 2$\frac{1}{2}$ %

Blacks are obtained from mixtures of cobalt, copper, iron and manganese; the range of blacks, from warm to cold to metallic, is fascinating.

To recapitulate:

Blues are mainly from cobalt
Warm browns are mainly from iron
Cold browns and purples from manganese
Bright greens and turquoise from copper
Opaque green from chromium
Reds from chromium or uranium
Yellows from iron, antimony, antimoniate of lead, vanadium pentoxide

The addition of these stains, in the percentages given should not have much effect on the behaviour of the simple glazes we have used so far.

Glaze Stains

Predictable colouring can be introduced by purchasing prepared glaze stains from the manufacturers such as Podmore's, Wengers, Fulham Pottery, etc., whose addresses are listed on page 225. These should be used as recommended, but again it is a good idea to make percentage tests. Apart from transparency, opacity and colour, glazes can be classified by other physical characteristics.

The Physical Appearance of Glazes

(a) *Transparent:* the effect of glaze on the clay is like water on a stone.

(b) *Opaque:* the glaze hides the clay body.

(c) *Semi-opaque:* the clay body is seen as through a cloud or mist.

(d) *Matt:* a non-reflecting surface having a waxy or vellum appearance, or even a sand-blasted look. Matt glazes can be clear or opaque.

(e) *Crystalline:* crystals in the glaze sparkle and tend to obscure the body.

Opacity and colour are introduced into glazes by adding metals as oxides, carbonates, etc., which are not part of the structure of the glaze. Most of the above physical characteristics are due to the presence of certain materials in the glaze. If they are not part of the original composition of the glaze but are added, other materials may need to be added also to restore the chemical balance.

Ceramic materials used to promote opacity and mattness in glazes:

(a) Tin oxide; zirconium oxide and silicate; titanium oxide; and antimony oxide are used as opacifiers.

(b) Zinc oxide is a flux and opacifies in large amounts (10–20%); it gives a frosty surface.

(c) Magnesium silicate (talc or french chalk) is a flux and in large quantities gives an opaque glaze with a vellum surface.

(d) Whiting (chalk or calcium carbonate) is a high-temperature flux and in large quantities gives a dull matt surface.

(e) Rutile is an impure source of titanium oxide, containing iron. It gives opacity, streaks and spots and interesting, but unpredictable, textures generally. It is known as **break-up** because it has this effect on other colours.

(f) China clay which is used as a source of alumina in glazes can also be used to produce a matt finish. Try this with lead and borax fritts.

Additions can be made by trial and error, as they were in the days of rule-of-thumb pottery. It is fairly safe to try additions of rutile for instance, and suggested proportions of materials to produce matt surfaces in earthenware glazes are:

Whiting up to 20% in all the glazes.
Rutile and zinc oxide in equal parts up to 20% in a lead glaze.
Magnesium carbonate and zinc oxide in equal parts: up to 15% in a non-lead glaze.

By using clear and opaque fritts/glazes with lead or alkaline fluxes, and varying the surface (shiny or matt) and the colour, a whole range of glazes can be produced which are perfectly satisfactory for most earthenware pottery.

Batch Recipes

These are used in making glazes from raw materials. The latter were ground before you purchased them and only if they have become caked through exposure will they need further grinding. Materials such as sand which have been dug up locally should be ground, with water, in a fairly large mortar. Most batch materials are insoluble except for borax and similar materials which are used to obtain brilliant turquoise colours. Where such soluble materials are used they have to be applied immediately on well-fired clay to prevent absorption and loss. After using prepared fritts and glazes, if the student wishes to go further the next step is to study glaze recipes, and acquire some knowledge of further common ingredients and their functions in the glaze. He will then have to rely on other people's recipes, experimenting with them and gradually altering them by trial and error, until he has the courage to try out ideas of his own. Recipes are sometimes expressed as parts by weight and sometimes as percentages.

A recipe for transparent glaze stained green could look like this:

Parts by weight			*Percentage*	
White lead	60	or this	White lead	63·8
Flint	18		Flint	19·1
Clay	12		Clay	12·8
Copper carbonate	4		Copper carbonate	4·3
				100·0

In either instance you need a good pair of scales with metric weights. Materials mostly look the same so weigh them separately and make sure they are all there before adding water to them and mixing them. The recipe includes lead oxide. As its use is discouraged in educational establishments in England (because of the risk of poisoning) it may be necessary to include a lead fritt in your batch recipe because lead is such a useful flux. (**Care should be exercised not to allow any glaze materials near the mouth, and hands should be washed frequently when preparing glazes. Never breathe in glaze dust.**) Record all your recipe experiments and materials used and results, for future reference. It is a good idea to write the recipe on the container with a chinagraph pencil.

Ceramic Materials used in Glaze Recipes

Alumina	Increases viscocity and is useful as a batt wash also. Alumina hydrate is also used to introduce alumina in glazes.
Ball clay	Used to introduce alumina and silica and to aid adhesion and suspension.
Barium carbonate	Used as an auxiliary flux in stoneware glazes. It gives alkaline colour response (i.e. turquoise from copper).
Bentonite	A very plastic volcanic clay which is colloidal and is therefore used as a suspending agent (it also improves the plasticity of clays when added to them).
Bone ash (calcium phosphate)	Calcined bone is a secondary flux in glazes and an essential part of bone china. **Calcining** is defined as **heating to red heat in order to drive off volatile material!**

Borax (sodium borate)	A low-temperature flux which, added in small quantities, reduces the melting temperature of a glaze. It brightens the colours from oxides. It is soluble and is usually fritted.
Boric (boracic) acid	Like borax, a low-temperature flux, but without the sodium.
China clay or kaolin	Decomposed granite. Being refractory it raises the maturing temperature and introduces alumina and silica and is also useful as a suspending agent. Calcined china clay is pure clay.
Colemanite (calcium borate)	A strong flux in low-temperature glazes. As it contains boric oxide in an insoluble form it is a natural fritt.
Cornish stone (pegmatite)	Used as a high-temperature flux or as a secondary flux in low-temperature glazes. It is partly decomposed granite, is often purplish in colour and known as **purple stone**, or as **china stone.**
Cristobalite	A form of silica, it increases thermal expansion and can be used to cure crazing.
Cryolite (sodium aluminium fluoride)	A natural source of sodium which produces the characteristic alkaline colours (e.g. copper-turquoise): the fluorine volatilises and can cause the glaze to boil, thus producing pinholes.
Dolomite (calcium magnesium carbonate)	Used in stoneware glazes as a flux.
Feldspar	A secondary flux in low-temperature glazes. The principal material and flux in high-temperature stoneware glazes.
Flint (silica)	Highly refractory and non-plastic. Used in glazes as main source of silica.
Fluorspar or Fluorite (calcium fluoride)	Combined fluorine and calcium; the latter is a strong flux, the former tends to cause bubbling at low temperatures.
Galena (lead sulphide)	The original source of lead especially in mediaeval pottery, where it was used to make a simple slip glaze. **Poisonous:** its use is not recommended.
Ilmenite (ferrous titanate)	Two per cent used with rutile develops interesting textural effects in glazes. Coarse ilmenite produces specks.

(lead carbonate)	White lead	Powerful fluxes
(lead oxide)	Red lead	in earthenware
(litharge)	Yellow lead	glazes. **Poisonous.**

Lepidolite A lithium-based mineral used as a secondary flux in medium to high temperature glazes. It can cause pinholes.

Lithium carbonate An alkaline flux similar to sodium and potassium. It increases the firing range and adds brightness to the colour.

Magnesium carbonate Used as a source of magnesium oxide, it is a high-temperature flux. Quantities up to 10% produce a buttery, semi-matt surface. Magnesium is recommended in its carbonate rather than oxide form because it is more stable.

Nepheline syenite A feldspar containing a high proportion of sodium and potassium in relation to silica. This makes it a useful flux in lower-temperature glazes.

Pearl ash
(potassium carbonate) A source of potassium, it is soluble and therefore generally used as a constituent of a fritt.

Quartz Like flint, is mainly silica and is used as a source of silica.

Saltpetre
(sodium nitrate) A highly soluble source of sodium.

Silica Quartz or flint.
Sand (white sand) Almost pure silica and used for making glass.

Soda ash
(sodium carbonate) Provides sodium in alkaline glazes, it is very soluble and therefore is used as fritt constituent. Gives a brilliant colour response.

Talc or french chalk
(magnesium silicate) A secondary flux in high- and low-temperature glazes (gives an opaque semi-matt or 'vellum' surface).

Whiting, chalk
(calcium carbonate) The main source of lime (calcium) in glazes and the most common high-temperature flux. Also known as carbonate of lime.

Wood ash Used in high-temperature glazes. Can be purchased from some potters' suppliers.

| Zinc oxide | Useful as flux in middle- to high-temperature glazes. Small amounts used as a secondary flux can contribute to smoothness and reliability. |

Ash Glazes

All vegetable matter when it burns away leaves a deposit which consists of the six more important ceramic oxides—alumina, silica, lime, soda, magnesia and potash. Ash compositions vary according to the nature and condition of the plants they came from. However, if they are soaked in water and sieved they can be used as fluxes in high-temperature glazes, formed by the addition of clay or feldspar, etc., which are applied to raw stoneware and once-fired. (Wood ash can be purchased from some potters' suppliers.)

Ceramic Chemicals and Minerals

In reading through the list of materials used to make up glazes you may find it a little confusing to come across so many different sorts of descriptions. Common-usage names are mixed up with more scientific names, and the materials vary from rocks to oxides, carbonates, nitrates and sulphides. The fact is, of course, that nearly all the oxides used in pottery originate from rocks of one sort or another because few of them exist in a pure form in nature. But, whereas clay, flint (almost pure silica) feldspar and Cornish stone are natural materials, boric acid is not—it is a chemical which has been extracted and prepared for use. In reading American books on pottery (there are some very good ones) you will come across materials which you cannot find in the English catalogues, either because it is a natural material available over there but not here, or because they use a different name.

To overcome this sort of problem and provide a language with universal significance, the chemists define all substances in terms of the 104 known elements. About 30 of them are involved in glaze making. All the elements are known by symbols; the main elements and symbols concerned in glaze making are:

Aluminium Al	Antimony Sb (Stibium)	Barium Ba
Boron B	Cadmium Cd	Calcium Ca
Carbon C	Chlorine Cl	Chromium Cr
Cobalt Co	Copper (Cuprum) Cu	Hydrogen H
Iron (Ferrum) Fe	Lead (Plumbum) Pb	Magnesium Mg
Manganese Mn	Nickel Ni	Nitrogen N
Oxygen O	Phosphorus P	Potassium (Kalium) K
Selenium Se	Silicon Si	Sodium (Natrium) Na
Strontium Sr	Sulphur S	Tin (Stannum) Sn
Titanium Ti	Uranium U	Zinc Zn
Zirconium Zr		

Atoms of two or more elements form larger particles, 'compound atoms', known as 'compounds'. An example is soda ash—sodium carbonate which is a compound of sodium (Na), carbon (C) and oxygen (O). Molecules are combinations of atoms (atoms usually exist in small or large clusters) and therefore compounds consist of molecules.

The notation employed by the chemist is used not only for elements but also for compounds (which consist of molecules). So, the notation informs us of the number of atoms in any particular cluster or molecule. If a molecule contains two (or more) identical atoms their number is placed after the element symbol, e.g. O_2, which means that a molecule of oxygen normally contains two oxygen atoms. A molecule of water is a compound of one oxygen atom and two hydrogen atoms; therefore the chemical language for water is H_2O. This is a simple compound, but some compounds are very complex. Sodium carbonate, mentioned above, is Na_2CO_3—two atoms of sodium (which is natrium to the chemist!) one atom of carbon and three atoms of oxygen. To take another example, with which you are probably familiar, pure clay is a combination of alumina, silica and water:

Alumina — aluminium oxide — aluminium and oxygen
Silica   — silicon oxide   — silicon and oxygen
Water   — hydrogen oxide   — hydrogen and oxygen

The clay molecule consists of two atoms of aluminium, two of silicon, four of hydrogen and nine of oxygen. Its notation is:

$$Al_2O_3 \cdot 2SiO_2 \cdot 2H_2O$$

One molecule of alumina (containing three atoms of oxygen—3) combines with two molecules of silica (each containing two atoms of oxygen—4) and two molecules of water (each containing one atom of oxygen—2): so there are $3 + 4 + 2 = 9$ atoms of oxygen.

The substances used in glazes all combine in some way with oxygen. Although they may not be oxides before they are fired, they become oxides in the glaze. Some of the materials listed earlier add several oxides. The following are a few typical examples:

Bentonite—$Al_2O_3 \cdot 5SiO_2 \cdot 7H_2O$
Cobalt oxide—Co_3O_4
Cornish stone—$K_2O \cdot Al_2O_3 \cdot 8SiO_2$
Dolomite (calcium magnesium carbonate)—$CaCO_3 \cdot MgCO_3$
Litharge (yellow lead)—PbO
Nepheline syenite—$K_2O \cdot 3Na_2O \cdot 4Al_2O_3 \cdot 8SiO_2$
Tin (stannic) oxide—SNO_2
Whiting (calcium carbonate)—$CaCO_3$

The Molecular Glaze Formula

This is an empirical formula deduced from the way successful glazes act. The ceramic chemist divides the oxides into three classes according to their functions and they are listed according to their molecular nature. In the first column are the elements which combine one-to-one or two-to-one with oxygen. In the second column the ratio is two-to-three and, in the third, one-to-two. A convenient symbol is used to represent an atom of any of the elements which form oxides. The three columns are therefore known as RO or R_2O, R_2O_3 and RO_2. The three columns give the basic pattern for glazes. The usual oxides are therefore arranged in this manner with the essential ingredients alumina and silica in the second and third columns. The symbol **R** represents an atom of the elements which combine with oxygen to form oxides.

	Base		Amphoteric	Acid
The pattern of combination with oxygen	RO	R_2O	R_2O_3	RO_2
Lead oxide	PbO		Aluminium oxide (Alumina) Al_2O_3	Silicon oxide (Silica) SiO_2
Zinc oxide	ZnO			
Calcium oxide (lime)	CaO			
Magnesium oxide (Magnesia)	MgO			
Barium oxide	BaO		Boric oxide B_2O_3 (is an exception because it acts as a flux)	Titanium oxide TiO_2 Tin oxide SnO_2 Zirconium oxide ZrO_2 Do not affect the formula but change the glaze appearance
Potassium oxide (Potash)		K_2O		
Sodium oxide (Soda)		Na_2O		
These are all fluxes				

The terms base, amphoteric and acid are used to describe the materials in the three columns:
Base—basic oxides are fluxes which neutralise the acid.
Acid—silica, an acid which is neutralised by the basic oxides.
Amphoteric—aids the interaction of base and acid.

By experience it is known that by changing the substances used as main and subsidiary fluxes (bases) and by varying the proportion between base to amphoteric and acid (alumina and silica), glazes with different physical characteristics (matt, glossy, opaque, etc.), which melt and mature at particular temperature ranges (low, medium, high—earthenware, stoneware, porcelain), can be obtained. The expansion of a glaze, which is the important factor in making it fit the clay it covers, can also be adjusted by slight changes in the proportion of acid. The molecular formula analyses the fired glaze. It states the proportions of the oxides in the glaze in terms of molecules of those oxides. So that there is a standard by which any glaze can be compared with any other glaze, the base oxides are expressed as decimal fractions, which added together always make a total of one. The base then adds up to one; the amphoteric is less than one; and the acid is more than one (usually three times the alumina plus one). The last two proportions depend on the bases used and the firing temperature. There is a table of limits for each type of glaze which gives the range of proportions viable at particular temperatures. These limits are expressed for convenience as fractions of molecules (fractions of molecules exist only in theory), which is necessary for the assessment and comparison of glazes as explained before.

The molecular formula for a glaze must, however, be interpreted as a recipe, in terms of quantities of ceramic materials which can be weighed, mixed and applied to pottery. To do this a table of **molecular weights** is necessary. The molecular weight is obtained by adding together the weights of the atoms which make up one molecule of any substance. The atom of each element has its own particular weight and no two elements have the same atomic weight. The lightest element is hydrogen with a weight rating of one: by comparison oxygen is rated at 16, calcium 40 and lead 207. Therefore lead oxide— PbO (lead oxygen) is $207 + 16 = 223$, i.e. The weight of one molecule of lead is 223 (compared with hydrogen: molecular weight $= 1$).

So there is another table—a table giving the molecular weight of the ceramic raw materials with which you are now familiar. Examples from it are:

Clay ($Al_2O_3 \cdot 2SiO_2 \cdot 2H_2O$)   258
Borax ($Na_2O \cdot 2B_2O_3 \cdot 10H_2O$)   382
Flint (SiO_2)   60
Tin oxide (SnO_2)   151

Also in this table there is a second figure known as the **equivalent weight**. In most cases it is the same as the molecular weight, but sometimes it is different. For example, the molecular weight of red lead, Pb_3O_4, is 684 and its equivalent weight is 228 (exactly one-third), because after it is fired it becomes PbO (lead oxide), the molecular weight of which is 228.

The batch recipe is derived from the molecular formula, by multiplying the amounts of oxides in the formula by the equivalent weights,

giving quantities of materials. If there were 0·5 of lead oxide in
a formula this would be 0·5 × 228 (equivalent weight of red lead) =
114 of red lead. In this way quantities of ingredient materials are
arrived at, but the oxides in the materials should satisfy the requirements of the molecular formula within the limits suggested for the
particular type of glaze being prepared. The materials therefore must
be chosen to satisfy these requirements, so the oxides in them are
listed under the base, amphoteric and acid columns. This process can
operate either way: a molecular formula for a glaze can be translated
into a batch recipe, or a recipe can be converted to a formula for
comparison and checking.

Devising recipes by trial and error or by molecular formulae calls
for specialised reading, so please consult the Recommended Reading
List (Appendix Three) at the back of this book if you are interested
in a full understanding of glaze formulation, the principles of which
have been broadly sketched in this chapter.

Glaze Defects

(a) **Crazing** is the appearance of fine cracks in the glaze. It is
sometimes used deliberately for its decorative effect, but it is a technical defect in vessels intended to hold liquids because seepage
occurs. Crazing is sometimes delayed; the characteristic sharp
'ping' of a cracking glaze may be heard months after firing. The cause
is a bad fit of glaze on clay, so the glaze contracts more than the body
and therefore cracks. To cure it the contraction of the clay body must
be increased or the contraction of the glaze must be decreased. The
addition of flint to the body or to the glaze may have the desired
effect. If the body has been deliberately soft-fired, try re-firing to the
maturing temperature of the clay, and when this glaze and body are
used together again hard fire the biscuit. In ware which does not hold
liquid, crazing is only a matter of appearance.

(b) **Shivering, chipping and peeling** of the glaze are the opposite of
crazing, being due to a glaze which fits too loosely and therefore
comes away. Again, firing to full maturing temperature may be the
answer to the problem but, if not, add ball clay to reduce the silica
in the body or add flint to the glaze.

(c) **Crawling** describes an irregular glaze finish with bare patches
usually due to the glaze layer cracking before or during the early
stages of the glost firing, which may be the result of insufficient gum
in the glaze. Crawling is caused also by glazing over dirty or dusty
biscuit.

(d) **Blistering** may be due to oxides like manganese in the glaze
which cause bubbles, or to a very thick glaze coat. If a glaze which
bubbles is under-fired, the bubbles will not have had a chance to

flatten out. Over-firing can cause blisters because some constituent substances start to form gases which bubble.

(e) Running and stuck ware are either the result of too much flux in the glaze or too high a firing temperature. If the foot, etc., have been glazed, the glaze will flow down onto the stilt or shelf (or both) and the ware will be well and truly stuck! (See pages 149 and 153.)

(f) Dryness. A dry, 'sandpaper' or starved-looking surface can result from soluble materials in the glaze being absorbed from under-firing, or from too thin a glaze coating.

(g) **Dunting** describes chips and holes due to air, stones, plaster, etc., in the clay, which cause small local explosions during firing.

(h) Pinholes are caused by air in the clay, especially minute air-bubbles from the slip used in casting a pot. Painting a fresh glaze over a dried coat of glaze, too rapid firing of a damp glaze, or too rapid cooling are other causes.

(i) Discoloration can be caused by volatile oxides which 'fly' from one pot to another if they are too close, or by the presence of chromium in the kiln.

CHAPTER ELEVEN

COLOUR AND DECORATION

Many ways of decorating pottery have been detailed already. These were not described independently but in association with the appropriate techniques. Because making pottery precedes baking it, naturally all these decorative processes were involved with raw pottery, which when fired needed coating with a clear glaze only. A further range of decoration is applied after the biscuit firing and much of this is also enhanced by a simple clear glaze. However, other methods depend on special glazes, such as opaque and coloured glazes. It will be convenient, therefore, before describing ceramic decoration generally, to divide it into four categories: (a) decoration of biscuit ware under the glaze; (b) decoration on the glaze; (c) decoration by coloured glazes; and (d) decoration on the raw clay. The first three are types of applied decoration, the fourth includes both applied and integral methods. Decoration can be part of the conception of the pot, but 'applied' after it is made, or can arise without affectation from the making process. It is sometimes misapplied, as an afterthought, by the amateur dissatisfied with his pottery as it is. Before any description of decoration is undertaken the nature of colour in ceramic work needs further explanation.

Colour

There are cheap forms of pottery which have been decorated with ordinary paint, but they have a very short life because moisture and abrasion soon attack. Colours which have to withstand the intense heat of the kiln must derive from metals with high melting points and therefore they are very tough. In order to make a metal into a pottery paint or stain it must be in a convenient form, i.e. a liquid or a reasonably fine powder, such as the oxide or carbonate, which can be mixed with water.

Beginners generally find this sufficient, but please remember that the facing tables are very much **generalisations**. The oxides introduced are those with the widest application, but there are other colouring oxides.

Carbonates and oxides can be used as colours for:

(a) Underglaze painting and onglaze painting (pigments).
(b) Decoration by coloured glazes (stains).
(c) Decoration using coloured clay and slips (stains).

176

TABLE OF OXIDES AND CARBONATES OF METALS USED AS CERAMIC PIGMENTS

Unfired Colour	Chemical Symbol	Oxide Name	Remarks	Normal Fired Colour
Black	Co_2O_3	Cobalt oxide	Coarse particles	Strong Blue
Light Purple	$CoCO_3$	Cobalt carbonate	Fine particles	Strong Blue
Black	CuO	Copper oxide	Coarse particles	Strong Apple Green
Red	Cu_2O	Copper oxide	Medium coarse particles	Strong Apple Green
Pale Blue–Green	$CuCO_3$	Copper carbonate	Fine particles	Strong Apple Green

Red copper oxide seems to have disappeared from the catalogues recently

Yellow	Fe_2O_3	Iron oxide	Fine particles	Brown–Yellow
Red	Fe_2O_3	Iron oxide	Fine particles	Red–Brown
Brown	Fe_2O_3	Crocus Martis	Fine particles	Dark Brown

Iron oxide has several other forms

Black	MnO_2	Manganese dioxide	Coarse (30 mesh) Finer (120 mesh)	Purple–Brown
Light Brown	$MnCO_3$	Manganese carbonate	Fine particles	Purple–Brown
Dull Yellow–Green	Cr_2O_3	Chrome oxide	Fine particles	Dull Yellow–Green

However, as you will have understood by now, the colour given by the fired oxides depends on (a) the composition of the clay or glaze; (b) the temperature to which it is fired; and (c) whether the atmosphere in the kiln is oxidising, neutral or reducing. There are two other factors. The first is that oxides vary in intensity, cobalt being especially strong and yellow iron oxide weak, so that they are difficult to use as paint unless you are experienced. The second factor is that they vary in stability—copper, for instance, runs at the edges, and produces black spots where it is applied in thick blobs (as does cobalt), whereas chrome gives a very stable but peculiarly unlovely green which is difficult to apply as a successful tint. Many enthusiastic potters, however, use nothing else but raw oxides and carbonates because of the accidental qualities which can be exploited for their own particular beauty. There is, though, a great difference between such deliberate exploitation and suffering disappointment because an oxide has been used inexpertly! A wide range of colours has been developed by the ceramic chemist mainly for use in industry, which are predictable for use with many glazes, at temperatures from 900°C–1200°C (approximately).

The colours obtainable from the oxides alone may seem very limited but they can be modified by inter-mixture and very much extended when combined with other (non-colouring) oxides and ceramic materials. This is done by **calcination**—the materials are mixed together and heated in a crucible until the chemical water and carbon dioxide have been driven off. Sometimes they melt together, in which case they are released into cold water and are fragmented by the shock. The fragments are ground to powder and make a coloured stain. A simple example is the chromium pink stain, which is well known to potters, as it is a straightforward calcination of chromium oxide and tin oxide. In recent years the chemistry of ceramics has advanced considerably and the range of stains has been extended and improved by the development of tough and stable colour crystals. Some firms offer a range of 'universal' colours suitable for use as body or glaze stains or as under- or on-glaze paints. Their application is therefore as broad as that of the oxides, but their colour is predictable, and usually the unfired colour is very similar to the fired colour.

Decoration

Before going into the methods of decoration in detail, some of the terms used need further clarification.

Under the Glaze

This is the most hard-wearing form of decoration because it is completely protected by a film of glaze, which is usually transparent, but in some cases can be semi-transparent. All the forms of decoration by modelling and texturing, or by coloured slip on the raw clay, described in the opening chapters, are obvious examples.

Painted decoration under the glaze using oxides or prepared colours is applied to either (a) the raw pottery, damp or dry, or to (b) the biscuit pottery.

On the Raw Glaze

Oxides or colours can be applied to the unfired glaze while it is damp or when it is dry. The glaze can be transparent, semi-transparent or (more usually) opaque. This method used to be known as **on-glaze,** but the practice in the catalogues at present is to use the term **Majolica** painting. Majolica, Faience and Delft are names derived from Majorca (Spain), Faienza (Italy) and Delft (Holland) which were historic centres for the production of painted, opaque, glazed ware. It is also called **in-glaze.**

On the Fired Glaze

This is done using oxides, or universal colours, mixed with a small amount of clear glaze, or more often using prepared colours mixed with a flux which melts at a considerably lower temperature than the glaze on the pot (about 800°C).

The latter are named variously as enamel colours, on-glaze enamels, china paints, or china painting colours. Of course, a further firing is necessary. Decoration on the fired glaze used to be called **over-glaze painting** (it still is by the Americans), but is termed on-glaze in contemporary English books and catalogues. Unless you are quite clear about the stages in the life of the pot at which the decoration is applied, and about the relationship between glaze and decoration, this mixed use of terms is confusing.

To recapitulate in the simplest possible way, colour can be applied:

(a) On the unfired or biscuited pot before the glaze is applied.
(b) On the unfired glaze (as applied to the unfired or biscuited pot).
(c) On the fired glaze (on the fired pot).

In (a) the decoration is protected by the glaze, in (b) the decoration fuses into the glaze but is subject to some wear by abrasion, and in (c) the softer enamel colours stand on the hard glaze surface and are therefore subject to abrasion.

Preparation of the Materials

We must now consider the many ways of using oxides and colours and the tools and preparation required for decorating pottery at the three stages.

In general, then, the sources of ceramic colouring are oxides, carbonates, or prepared stains and paints. The tints produced in the finished articles are dependent upon chemical action and reaction. Only under well-defined conditions can an exact shade be relied upon.

Intermixing is possible but it must not be assumed that the resulting secondary and tertiary colours will be the equivalent of those produced when mixing similar colours in ordinary (non-ceramic) paints. Colours with similar names from different suppliers are unlikely to match. Oxides and colours from the same manufacturers purchased at different times can vary because of variations in raw materials. Prepared colours may be for universal use or specifically as body/slip/glaze stains, or as paints. The uniformity of the colour in a clay or glaze or the smoothness of the paint depends on the size and distribution of the grains of colour.

Oxides tend to be coarse; carbonates and stains are finer; and under-glaze and on-glaze paints are very fine and contain additives to make them suitable for their special role. Grinding in water with a pestle and mortar (a hard porcellanous, stoneware bowl and a stick, like a truncheon, of the same material) is used for larger amounts; or with a palette knife and glazed tile for smaller quantities. This will make any powder, oxides particularly, much smoother. Of course this treatment is not fully effective with very hard granules as in black cobalt and black copper oxides. Some people advise mixing an oxide with boiling water and leaving it to soak, then grinding it and sieving it through something like a 120 mesh (120 holes to the square inch) sieve. Grinding and sieving ensure that there will be no 'specks' due to wild grains in the colour: the finer the sieve the finer the colour. Neither process is necessary for prepared under- and on-glaze colours, which are quite fine.

Oxides or prepared body/slip stains can be wedged into plastic clay to colour it. It used to be possible to buy prepared coloured clays but they do not appear in the catalogues nowadays, possibly because there is little demand. The oxides or stains are mixed with dry, pulverised clay before adding water, to make a coloured slip. If a part-icularly smooth colour is desirable grind the stain first and sieve the slip, drying it out to become plastic if coloured clay is required. On the other hand, coarse oxides mixed directly into the clay by kneading and wedging will give specks and streaks which will affect the glaze when it is fired. A good example is the use of 'Black Spangles' (ferroso-ferric oxide—black oxide of iron deriving from a rock called magnetite!) which give a sparkling texture to clay.

Stains which only partially mix produce an 'agate' appearance in the biscuit clay. The use of coloured slips and clays has been intro-duced in earlier chapters, and will be amplified later when new forms of decoration have been explained.

Nevertheless there are advantages in painting with oxides or pre-pared colours on the raw clay. The colour integrates with the raw clay as it is applied and is baked in during the biscuit firing. As a result it can be handled and glazed without disturbing the painting and the colours are not subject to smudging or running (unless the process is completed in one-firing, in which case the pot must be handled with caution throughout).

Preparation as Pigment

Oxides, underglaze colours or universal colours are all suitable for painting on raw clay. If you are stuck for a colour and all you have is a body/glaze stain this could be used if treated as an oxide, i.e. a coarse-grained colour. The oxides need grinding or else the colour will be very spotty. Do this with a small pestle and mortar, or with a muller on a glass slab. Some potters prepare oxides in fairly large quantities and keep them in small glass jars: they are then ready for a variety of uses and there is no waste. The oxides vary in price, a common oxide like iron being cheapest.

Prepared colours are expensive so use only a salt-spoon at a time—excess colour will only be washed down the sink, whereas more colour can be prepared easily if you run out. With underglaze and universal colours for general use, it is sufficient to grind them lightly when preparing them with a palette knife on a glass slab or on a glazed tile. All colours which need preparation for use as paints should be mixed with: (a) a little transparent glaze or fritt to improve their quality as paint by making them slightly liquid during the first firing, and (b) with a sticky medium such as gum arabic or tragacanth, or with glycerine, to bind the colour; make it adhere; and improve its flow from the brush. Do not overdo the gum: too much gum will dry up, harden, shrink and peel off, taking the colour with it.

Gum is prepared by mixing the water with the granular gum in easy stages and leaving it to steep for a day (if you are in a hurry, use hot water). Gum is cheaper to use than the prepared media which all manufacturers supply to go with their colours. Of course, certain underglaze and universal colours can be obtained ready for use in glass jars.

Methods of Applying Colour Before Glazing

Painting on Raw Clay

As a general practice this method is not used in schools and institutes because of the danger of breakage where communal work takes place. Normally the painting is done with a brush on damp clay which should be no more than leather-hard. Painting on dry clay is possible but not advisable: the porous surface absorbs liquid too quickly so that the colour clots. If the paint is watered down to counteract this tendency it is sucked into the clay and looks thin and weak. A pot which has dried inadvertently should be: (a) biscuit fired before being painted; (b) given a thin coat of gum to seal the pores; or (c) the surface should be moistened by a careful sponging or spraying with water.

The design can be sketched on the pot in pencil or using a thin wash of water-colour or indian ink which will burn away when the pot is fired. The colour of your clay will affect the colours painted on it. It is liable to break into or through them, an effect which is increased at higher temperatures. Some colours, especially reds, change or disappear at high temperatures (data concerning the temperatures which colours will withstand are to be found in the appropriate catalogues). Therefore, it follows that underglaze colours for stoneware are limited, whereas a wide range of bright colours is available in the low-firing on-glaze enamels. To obtain the fullest possible brilliance from underglaze colours they must be painted onto a white body or a white slip.

Any type of colour used for underglaze painting can be made lighter by thinning with water, by adding tin oxide (an insoluble white powder), or by adding a prepared underglaze or universal white. The last two will give a milky or opaque rather than a transparent tint, depending on the proportion of white added. Thin transparent tints are less likely to be effective on a coloured body than opaque tints. On 'red' clay (which fires reddish-brown) colours are rarely effective because of the dark tone—the two extremes, black and white, show up and it is worth experimenting with opaque tints containing a high proportion of white.

It is difficult to advise what sort of brush to use. The pottery catalogues offer a large and varied selection, as do artists' suppliers such as Reeves. The brush should be capable of holding a good supply of paint because it is essential to work freely and quickly in order to avoid patchy colour and should also be firm and springy and draw out to a good point. A sable brush in sizes 6, 8 or 10 is particularly good (and expensive) and there are a number of Japanese and Chinese brushes, at a reasonable price, which are suitable. Broad, flat brushes, of ox hair and/or hog hair, are useful too. A good-quality 1 in (2·5 cm) house-painting brush is also invaluable for all sorts of uses.

Mistakes in painting can be wiped off with a moist sponge, but because the surface of the clay is softened the colour tends to mix into it: it is difficult to remove entirely and to avoid disturbing other parts of the pattern. A more satisfactory solution is to scrape away the colour and a little of the surface using a craft knife.

Underglaze painting on once-fired raw clay is best glazed by spray to avoid disturbing the colour and weakening the clay wall. Another solution is to 'fix' the painting on the surface by firing the pot to 800°C (in other words abandon the once-fired idea, and give it a soft biscuit firing), when it can be dipped in glaze without harm. Applying brush-painted patterns is the first way of decorating that springs to the average person's mind, but it is not the only way of using oxides, etc., under the glaze. As other methods are applicable to painting on biscuit as well as raw clay, they can be explained in both contexts as following the technique of painting on biscuit clay.

Painting on Biscuit Clay

The preparation of the oxides or colours is exactly the same, except that other mediums can be used. Generally speaking because the clay has been hardened the colour will not integrate with it physically or chemically. The clay is more or less porous depending on the temperature of the biscuit firing, therefore it absorbs liquid plus a little of the colour, though most of the colour remains on the surface. Using colour and water alone, the colour would be loose and easily brushed off the surface or it would be washed away when the glaze is applied, especially if the pot is dipped. This is an unfortunate mistake which many beginners make, and there is no remedy because, although the surface colour can be washed or brushed off, the stain in the pores is ineradicable and leaves a 'ghost' pattern on the pot. It is quite satisfactory to mix a little gum with the colour as before to bind it and stick it to the surface. Remember to avoid using too much gum, as this can lift off when the wet glaze is applied, or it may cause the glaze to 'crawl' away. If this persists in happening the answer is to fire the painted ware to 650°C. This is known as **hardening-on**, and it is absolutely necessary when the colours are mixed with an oily rather than a watery medium, in order to burn away all carbonaceous matter and to get rid of the oily surface which would prevent the glaze taking. The oils used are pine oil or turpentine with fat oil; or proprietary oil mediums from the usual suppliers of ceramic colours, who also supply a water-based medium for their underglaze colours (see Plates 13 and 16).

Patterns can be painted on biscuit with coloured glazes, so that the pot is covered with shapes which may either melt into each other or remain distinct, depending on the firing temperature.

Other Methods for Raw and Biscuit Clay

Banding. Even bands of colour can be painted on a pot by holding a well-loaded brush to it as it spins round on a 'lining' wheel or throwing wheel, etc. The width of the band depends on the thickness of the brush and the angle at which it is held. A spiral band is possible, but difficult, because the brush will not hold sufficient colour.

Underglaze Crayons. A solid form of colour which can be used for banding or for drawing patterns; the quality and texture of the colour are affected by the surface of the pot. The colours obtainable are limited, but anyone who is interested could make their own crayons in the same way that coloured candles are made: the paraffin wax medium would have to be burnt off before applying glaze. On raw clay the pot would have to be quite dry in this instance.

Stencils. They can be cut from tissue or toilet paper and made to adhere to a damp, raw pot by finger pressure. Biscuit pots need a thin coat of gum to make the stencil stick. Natural templates such as leaves can be used. It may be possible to peel away the stencil when it is dry otherwise it should be burnt off and the colour hardened on by firing to 650°C, before glazing. The colour can be pounced on with a stencil brush, applied in sweeping strokes with a broad brush, sponged on, or splattered on by drawing a finger along a well-loaded toothbrush, or sprayed on. In each case a different quality of colour is obtained. Be careful not to pull off the stencil if brushing.

Printing. Fine plastic sponge cut to well-defined shapes can be used to print patterns all over the pot or in panels or bands. A whole sponge can also be used to mottle the complete surface of a pot with single or blended colours. Mottling, printing and stencilling can be combined on one pot.

Sgraffito. Scratching through the colours is an effective way of drawing fine lines on a coloured surface. It can be combined with brushwork, stencilling or sponging. On the raw pot any suitable tool can be used as suggested for scratching through slip (see page 56); but sgraffito is effective only on lightly-fired biscuit where the clay is still sufficiently soft to be scratched. A broad pattern painted or stencilled in black underglaze with fine white lines cut through gives an effect similar to wood cutting or engraving. Use the point of a Swann-Morton craft tool or a stencil knife to give a really precise line.

Shading Colours. This can be done with a fine sponge but is particularly effective when an electric spray is used. A suggestion of line and shape can be produced if a card or metal template is held between the spray and the pot: the nearer the pot it is the harder the outline will be. Colours for spraying must be ground and sieved.

Resist. The use of melted wax or prepared emulsions has been described already as a method of slip decoration (see page 72). It can be used equally well on raw or biscuit clay with underglaze colours or oxides. You will remember that the melted wax is thinned with a little paraffin and applied quickly using a brush reserved for the purpose. The pattern is painted on with the wax and the colour is then sprayed, stippled, sponged, splattered or brushed over it. The wax resists the wet paint. When it is burnt away in the kiln, the brush strokes register as an unpainted clay surface, because the wax acted as a guard or template: the pattern therefore has a negative quality, the brush strokes being light and the background dark and coloured. The prepared wax emulsion is easier to use but gives a slightly different effect.

Transfers. Not usually used by amateurs, transferred patterns printed from engraved metal plates (using a ceramic printing ink compounded from oxides, etc.) were once the most popular form of decoration used by the pottery industry. Perhaps the most famous of the earlier designs printed on pottery, utilising the powerful blue produced from cobalt oxide, is the popular Willow Pattern Plate— the picture was adapted from Chinese brush-painted ware. It is possible to make one's own transfers from engraved plates, but patient research and experiment are necessary.

Prepared Underglaze Colours

Underglaze colours range from dull reds through yellows, greens, blue-greens, blues, and purples, to brown, black and white. There is a selection of about thirty colours altogether, none of them particularly subtle. However, they can be intermixed, and it is worth buying a careful selection of primary colours, plus brown, black and white, and exploiting them fully by exhaustive intermixtures painted on clay 'samplers', one set of which should be glazed and fired to the maximum temperature recommended for the colours (usually 1100°C) and another set fired to the minimum temperature suggested for the clear glaze. A low-solubility clear glaze should be used as this gives the fullest effect to the colour and its firing range will be around 1000°C to 1100°C. If you are sufficiently keen you could do the same thing for the colouring oxides. In applying oxides one has to be careful not to get the paint too thick or the oxide will saturate the glaze and register as a black metallic spot, not as colour.

Decoration on the Raw Glaze

Now we come to the practice of applying colour by painting and other methods to the unfired coat of glaze. This has an absorbent quality like blotting-paper. The colour is absorbed immediately to a degree, and during firing melts into the surface of the glaze. It is referred to usually as *Majolica* decoration, as has been explained on page 179.

Majolica Painting

Preparation. There are no specially prepared colours for painting on unfired glaze. Oxides, 'universal' (or general) colours, body or slip stains, glaze stains and underglaze colours, can all be used. Grinding is necessary if you want smooth colour from the oxides (and carbonates) or the body and glaze stains. Stable clear glazes and matt or shiny opaque glazes, white, cream or tinted, are all suitable for painting on. A dark glaze, or a clear glaze over a dark body, is rarely suitable as the colours are unlikely to be effective. A medium is hardly necessary, but it improves the colour to add a little clear glaze or flux so that it is not too dry or harsh when fired; otherwise water is all that is required. If there is too great a proportion of oxide or colour it will not integrate completely and again the effect will be unpleasant. If you purchase prepared colours or stains follow the manufacturer's advice, some manufacturers recommend using a little of their own medium. It is unwise to use gum because this tends to curl as it dries on the powdery surface of the glaze then it lifts off taking the colour with it.

Pots for Majolica painting are glazed by dipping, pouring, or spraying. The glaze should contain a binder to ensure cohesion and a firm surface. As spray falls on the pot in tiny drops, some gum must be included because the surface is granular and without a binder would easily brush off. By using the thickest glaze mix which will pass through the nozzle, or by using a coarser nozzle, a very rough granular surface can be built up, giving texture to the painting.

Painting. It is not possible to sketch the pattern on the glaze with a pencil although a light water-colour wash can be used on a dipped glaze if you are very careful, but it would not be advisable on a sprayed pot. Commercial potteries sometimes use a 'pricked' stencil through which powdered charcoal is dusted to give a dotted line as a guide to the painters. It is best to paint while the glaze is still moist.

Painting technique with the normal pointed water-colour brush, or Chinese brush, should be positive and unhesitating because even a well-loaded brush runs dry very quickly due to the 'blotting-paper' surface. Using the brush in a niggling manner, or attempting to over-paint can disturb the surface of the glaze, mixing the colour into it, so that it becomes messy and patchy and a second coat may result in the brush pulling off the glaze. It is useless to use the normal technique when a granular surface has been produced by spraying because the colour spreads. However, a 'dry-brush' technique with a hog-or ox-hair flat brush and a minimum of paint (squeeze the surplus paint from the brush) is better. The brush is stroked lightly across the surface of the glaze to give a 'broken' quality to the colour.

Banding can be done but is difficult. The addition of a little glaze, as suggested, gives a slight gloss to the brushwork, which some potters enhance by a very thin spray of clear glaze over the painting. Careful experiment on a matt glaze can give soft, non-shiny tones. With experience quite detailed work can be achieved, but because of the directness of the brush-work the repertoire is best expanded by using different sizes of brush. Paler tints can be obtained by watering down the colour or adding some form of white—on an opaque white or cream glaze using only a little of the same glaze will do to lighten the colour. Obviously the technique requires confidence which can come only from experience, so once again it is a good idea to make samplers or practise on discarded pots, etc. Majolica painting has a special quality which is unique to ceramics. The directness of the brushwork in the hands of a sensitive painter gives the patterns a dynamic and lively quality (see Plates 23, 26 and 29).

Other Methods of Decoration

Spraying (as for underglaze or slip). **Do not add gum** to the colour which should be more liquid than for painting. To obtain a softer effect add a small proportion of the clear glaze or opaque glaze which covers the pot. Blend colours into each other or use templates as for underglaze. Spraying is also very effective in applying a number of glazes to a pot, one on top of the other, so that they merge into each other and break through each other. For instance, a clear glaze, heavily but unevenly coloured with copper oxide, could be applied by dipping and then oversprayed wholly or partly with an opaque white glaze: the copper would break through more in some places than in others. Be careful not to let the first glaze become too dry before spraying the second glaze. Glazes and colours can be alternated to produce textures and gradations of colour which cannot be obtained in any other way.

Sgraffito. Light on dark, or dark on light glazes applied by spraying are suitable for scratched patterns. The glazes should be dry, and a needle point or a scraper-board tool used to cut through the top coat of colour or glaze (whichever has been used). It is also possible to scratch right through a glaze to the biscuit. A slightly ragged line may be the result, but this will improve as it softens in the glaze firing. With a very thin top glaze, a dry, flat, hog-hair brush can be used to form a pattern of softly-defined strokes. Fine lines scratched through broad brush strokes look effective.

Resist Painting. This can be done with melted wax or prepared emulsion, but a swift and sure touch is necessary and it is not successful on a granular surface. A resist pattern in wax on a white opaque or clear glaze should be sprayed or splattered with a dark glaze or colour or *vice versa*. Painting over a wax resist is possible but needs thought.

Stencils. In the form of tissue paper templates, stencils gently stuck on the glaze can be used to mask out areas and the colour is sprayed or splattered on. A circle or rectangle, folded twice and cut into a symmetrical pattern, can be used for flat shapes, plates or dishes. Hold the spray as far away as possible, because the force of air tends to dislodge the tissue paper template—it may be necessary to hold it down with blobs of clay. The spraying must be done a little at a time, with intervals for drying, or the colour builds up and runs under the edges of the template. A spray-stencilled pattern can be combined with brush strokes, sgraffito, or both.

Printing. Printing with shapes cut from very fine plastic sponge is possible. Do it with a light touch to avoid pulling away the glaze.

Trailing. It is possible to make a creamy mixture of glaze with a binder in it and use this in a slip trailer, to form patterns—lines of glaze around a raw glazed pot (using a wheel), vertical lines, or circles and other simple shapes. On a flat dish or plate more complicated drawing is possible. The trailed glaze will flatten and sink as it softens into the background glaze during firing. Marbled effects can be produced in dishes by trailing lines of glaze in amongst each other and firing to a high enough temperature to melt the glazes so that they mingle. A tangle of coloured lines on a coat of opaque glaze, in the style of the American Tachist painter Pollock, is effective if not fired too high so that a fair degree of definition is retained. A sort of cloisonné effect can be achieved by outlining shapes with a trailer (similar to the leading in a stained glass window) and filling in with different coloured glazes.

Painting on Fired Glaze

On-glaze Painting

Painting on the already fired glaze with prepared on-glaze colours needs an extra firing, to a temperature ranging between 750°C and 850°C, sufficient to melt the flux into the glaze and seal the colour. A soak at the peak temperature improves the final appearance of the colours, which are brighter generally than underglaze colours, especially in the red range. They are highly synthetic and artificial colours suitable for porcelain and earthenware of a sophisticated type and, of course, for stoneware too. Most of the colours can be mixed together to increase the range. Liquid metals and lustres can be used on fired glaze only, so they are often combined with on-glaze ('china') paints to add to the sophistication of the patterns. These lustres, etc., fire between 700°C and 750°C (see Plates 23 and 26). However, it is not advisable to fire enamels and lustres together because the fumes released from the lustres could spoil the enamel colours. Lustres used alone, especially to cover the whole surface of a pot, look ostentatious in a way which is unsuitable for pottery.

Another method of on-glaze painting is similar to Majolica, except that although the same colours and media can be used, they are painted on the fired glaze and heated to a temperature below that of the original glaze firing (but within their own temperature range as stable colours) somewhere between 900°C and 1200°C. This is really Majolica painting without the hazards, but it increases the expense because of the extra firing and detracts from the special quality associated with directly-painted Majolica.

Preparation. In the case of some prepared on-glaze enamels the colours are mixed with 'fat oil' to a paste and thinned with turpentine, using a palette knife and tile; or a muller and glass slab; or with a liquid medium or water, as recommended by the particular manufacturer. The fat oil is to give a thicker consistency to the colour and make it easier to handle and, although a water base is less trouble, the colour dries quicker and is not so workable.

Painting. This is done in the normal way with a selection of pointed brushes. The paint should not be thin. Lustres—which look brown because of the resin vehicle—do not need to be painted on thickly, and take care to ensure that they do not run. Mistakes are easily corrected on the hard, non-absorbent surface of a fired glaze, the colour is wiped off and you start again! Of course this applies whether you are using on-glaze enamels or painting in the indirect Majolica style.

Other Methods of Decoration

Obviously the methods suggested for direct Majolica apply to both indirect Majolica (on the fired glaze that is) and to on-glaze enamels: namely, spray, splatter, resist, stencil, sponging and printing and sgraffito.

Transfers. This is a commercial method of decorating pottery. Transfers from engravings have been referred to already (see page 185) and modern transfers are printed by lithography and screen printing. Ready-made transfers can be purchased with stock designs or made to order, so that a school, for instance, can decorate hand-made pottery with its own crest. On the other hand, one can purchase or make a screen and print original designs. It is not the province of this book to describe screen printing (information is easy to obtain from Reeves and other firms—see the Harrison Meyer catalogue). The on-glaze colours are mixed thoroughly with silk-screening medium and either printed direct on the ware, or printed on thermoflat paper and given a colloidon film coating. In water the paper comes off and the pattern is left on the covering film, which can be pressed gently on the ware. The pattern is then fired on.

Recapitulation: List of Decorating Techniques

There follows a brief recapitulation of all decorating techniques which have been discussed in this chapter, and earlier in the book, in relation to the exercises in techniques of making pottery.

Clay Decoration
>   (1) Construction patterns (e.g. coils)
>   (2) Integral or applied tool marks and textures
>   (3) Carving
>   (4) Impressing
>   (5) Incising
>   (6) Hand-formed applied shapes and relief modelling
>   (7) Mould-formed applied shapes (**sprigs**)

Slip Decoration
>   (1) Marbling
>   (2) Combing
>   (3) Feathering
>   (4) Slip tracing
>   (5) Dipping
>   (6) Pouring
>   (7) Spraying or splattering
>   (8) Sgraffito
>   (9) Brush painting (banding)
>   (10) Resist
>   (11) Stencils

Colour Decoration
>   (1) Painting (banding)
>   (2) Crayons
>   (3) Stencils
>   (4) Printing
>   (5) Printed transfers
>   (6) Spraying and splattering
>   (7) Resist
>   (8) Trailing

Most of these can be applied as underglaze, Majolica and on-glaze decoration. There are many variations within these broadly-stated methods. It would not be exaggerating to say that there are fifty different ways of decorating a pot. The only way to understand this is to look at pots in museums and shops and analyse their decoration and by doing so, you will increase your range and form personal taste.

CHAPTER TWELVE

POTTERY WITH THE WHEEL

Throwing

Throwing, or spinning, as it is called sometimes, is the technique in which a revolving wheel head assists the potter to open up his ball of clay and form walls more quickly than by hand. It is an acceleration of the 'thumb-pot' process where one hand supported and rotated the clay thus shaping its exterior contour, while the thumb of the other hand pressed into the ball and hollowed it, forming the inside contour of a simple pot. In throwing, as in thumbing, the problem is to achieve height, to produce sufficiently thin, even walls, and to keep outward expansion under strict control.

In throwing, both hands are free to shape the clay wall at any point, as they are not needed to support or rotate the clay. The wheel is operated independently by foot, or electrically, and the faster it goes round the more the shaping process can be accelerated. However, the speed of throwing is also related to the confidence and skill of the potter! The potter's thumb forms a hole in a ball of clay revolving absolutely centrally, then moves away from the centre enlarging the cavity. The clay above is squeezed from the outside with carefully-controlled pressure of the fingers and centrifugal motion assists it to rise into a cylindrical form which is the basis of most thrown shapes (low bowls are an obvious exception). Convex and concave contours in the walls are produced by pressures from the two hands working in unison.

Mankind had been building pots by hand for thousands of years before evolving the wheel to speed up the local supply of domestic ware and to make its distribution to other areas a possibility. Whereas the earlier ware had a sculptural quality, the dynamic nature of throwing and its spontaneity provided a new artistic direction as well as commercial advantages. With mastery of the newly-evolved technique came differences and subtleties of form so that at times and in places beautiful pots were produced for their decorative rather than utilitarian value. In our own times there are many who believe that throwing is the kingpin of the ceramic arts.

The partly-mechanised nature of throwing allows the artist/craftsman to achieve an economic rate of production while preserving his individuality, so that he survives much more successfully in the affluent society than he did at the onset of the Industrial Revolution with its development of ultimate mass-production techniques in pottery.

The fluid, rhythmic manner in which a pot grows on the wheel, like the speeded-up growth of a flower on film, makes throwing fascinating to watch—as if it were a sort of magic. On the other hand the fumbling attempts of complete novices, as exploited in certain television programmes, are quite hilarious. The danger is that anyone who has seen such a programme may get the impression that throwing is too difficult for ordinary mortals. Let us be quite clear that this is not so. Having read how to do it and understood in advance the principles involved, you will be in a better position than those hapless individuals whose innocence (ceramically speaking) is exploited by professional entertainers. Of course in order to throw well personal tuition is necessary for encouragement and advice; but having worked with clay and begun to understand clay is a great help in this, the final technique. Each technique requires suitable clays and throwing is not the exception but, using a good throwing clay, properly and thoroughly prepared, anybody can attain proficiency provided they persevere. Though really good throwing may require a natural talent, competence is a matter of preparation and practice. It is essential not to become neurotic about a few preliminary failures.

Making pottery with the wheel includes turning of course. One aspect of this technique was introduced on page 88, to show how to form certain types of solid models for moulding. Here turning follows throwing as the finishing process by which surplus clay is removed in the leather-hard state, generally underneath and around the base of a pot, although it can be used also to modify and decorate the main shape.

Primitive and Traditional Wheels

Pots have been in great demand as containers and could have been as popular with the ancients as plastic bags are with us. Therefore, necessity being the mother of invention, the potter's wheel, probably the earliest 'industrial' machine, arrived along with the wheeled vehicle in Mesopotamia about 4000 B.C. In Egypt it appeared rather later and it is to be seen in paintings belonging to the Third Dynasty, about 2000 B.C. The primitive wheel was a large wooden stone, or baked clay disc, mounted on a fulcrum and rotated by the potter's free hand or his bare feet, unless he had an assistant. The revolutions were maintained by the momentum of the wheel, but this **slow wheel** was rather ponderous and cannot have been very exciting to throw on.

A step in the direction of greater control was the evolution of the

fast wheel—the kick wheel. This had a longer spindle, attached at the top to the wheel head on which the pots were formed by the potter in a convenient sitting position, and attached below to a heavier flywheel, which powered the throwing wheel and was itself rotated by foot. The speed could not be varied once the throwing had begun.

The logical development was to invent a means of varying the speed of the wheel without losing power. This was a cranked shaft which converted the reciprocal action of a foot-operated treadle into rotary movement. The heavy flywheel attached below the crank gave the necessary momentum and the potter was able to vary the speed

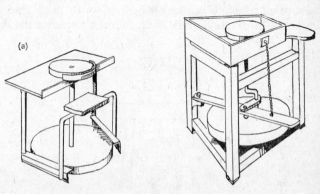

Fig. 159. (a) Direct kick wheel; (b) treadle kick wheel.

with his foot. The entire mechanism was housed in a wooden frame with a seat and so the potter could work quickly and accurately.

A later development was a device where an assistant turned a large auxiliary wheel mounted vertically, with a belt drive to the pivot. Years ago at my art school there was a wheel of this genre: as an assistant was not provided a fellow student had to be cajoled into being the power unit, and variations of speed were by polite request! Learning to throw was therefore a test of control in more ways than one. It is doubtful if this type of wheel has survived in the age of full employment and payment for everything.

In spite of these advances the simpler types of wheel continue to survive. In his well-known *A Potter's Book*, Bernard Leach records that the hand wheel is still used in China and Japan. The wheel has a hollow shaft attached to it underneath which rests on a spindle, and it is twirled round expertly by the potter, who uses a short stick which thrusts into one of a number of notches near the circumference. In parts of the world, wheels are set at an angle facing the thrower.

Contemporary Wheels

Kick Wheels

These provide direct control of the clay and of the speed of the wheel. They are the cheapest form of wheel as their mechanism is simple. They are easy to make and can be tailored to individual requirements. However, to obtain the necessary rigidity in the framework it is best to use welded metal construction, which is generally a professional job as it requires specialised equipment. It is possible to make a rigid frame in wood, of course, but the constant kicking action inevitably loosens the joints. There are a number of kick wheels on the market with different mechanisms:

(a) **The front treadle kick wheel** is built of sturdy angle iron with welded joints, or of tubular mild steel. In order to reduce the shock

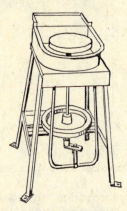

Fig. 160. Front treadle kick wheel.

of the kicking movement to a minimum it should be fixed to the floor. Some wheels have feet to the frame, with holes bored for floor fixing, which makes them more adequate for throwing larger pots. Even then it is difficult to achieve the necessary speed and pressure if the weight of the flywheel is insufficient. Front treadle wheels with light flywheels are frequently found in schools and art schools, presumably because it was thought that a wheel for use by young people should necessarily be light and easy to turn and the consequence is that pupils and students were provided with the means of 'playing at pottery only'. In many art schools these wheels have been relegated to being used solely for turning small pots, for which they are quite adequate.

In the catalogues now there are various front treadle wheels with heavy flywheels, some of which can be fixed to the floor. Another improvement is a ball-bearing crank which gives a smoother action than the old type which is jerky at slow speeds when throwing. It is hardly practicable to provide a seat for a front treadle wheel, but standing on one foot and kicking a treadle back and forth with the other foot affects the balance of the body and forces the arms to rest heavily on the work tray, which detracts from the potter's freedom in throwing.

(b) The **side treadle wheel** has the advantage that the potter can sit at his work. The seat should be close to the wheel head and on a level with it so that the potter can be as near as possible to the clay he is throwing and most wheels on the market have adjustable seats. The size and weight of the flywheel are important, as are the proportions of the crank and **kick-bar** (treadle). These should be related to produce a long kick without a jerk, the ideal in throwing being absolute harmony of foot, hand and eye combined with physical comfort. Unless a wheel is custom built it should be capable of adjustment to the physical idiosyncrasies of the user. Treadle wheels are operated by either foot and on some models the kick-bar is transferable.

The speed and power ratio of wheels vary. There is a wheel based on the traditional timber-framed machine which incorporates an especially heavy flywheel and a one-to-one ratio between the movement of the kick-bar and the rotation of the wheel head, designed to work at a maximum of 120 r.p.m. and to achieve a steady rhythm in throwing. On the other hand there are a number of metal-framed machines (some of them completely enclosed below for safety) which are geared to produce $2\frac{1}{2}$ revolutions of the wheel to one kick of the bar, with a maximum speed of 300 r.p.m.

If ever you are thinking of making your own wheel or having one made locally by anyone who is not a specialist, it is best to consult someone with experience to enable you to prepare or obtain plans. A wheel which is very popular among teachers and craftsmen in England is the St. Ives kick wheel, plans and specifications can be obtained from the Leach Pottery at St. Ives.

(c) A **direct kick wheel** is not cheap. It has a metal frame and cast aluminium flywheel. The address of the suppliers is in the back of this book, on page 286.

Electric Wheels

Geared kick wheels and electrically-powered wheels give comparable results until it comes to using 10 lb (4·5 kg) of clay, when the potter needs the assistance of a motor. The auxiliary wheel device mentioned on page 193 was good in this respect as it allowed an assistant to use all his strength without rocking the boat or getting in the way, as he tends to do on a kick wheel. The weight of clay a wheel can cope with efficiently is stated in the specification. If the wheel does not maintain its speed unaltered, while this weight of clay is centred on it and varying pressures are applied, then it is not worth paying the extra money for it however attractive it looks. Transmission systems vary and on them and the power of the motor the performance of the machine depends. A good range and control of speeds is important too and here again there are differences in design.

(a) **Portable electric wheels** being lighter are less expensive and will not handle more than 6 lb (2·7 kg) of clay. There are bench models and models (not necessarily heavier) with a frame on which the potter can sit. Weights vary, but bench models are not always lighter! A bench wheel with a rather neat fibre-glass chassis and tray combined weighs 110 lb (50 kg) (portable?); one with a frame to sit astride weighs only 70 lb (30 kg). Most wheels have a manual control which can be pre-set at any speed in the range, but some seated wheels can be controlled by foot pedal or by hand lever. In some cases the lever can be removed, if desired, and often the wheel can be set to revolve at a particular speed. Speed ranges vary, covering between 200 and 300 revolutions, with the lowest speed at 35 and the highest at 340 r.p.m. Work trays are plastic. Prices are approximately between £70 and £100.

(b) **Static electric wheels,** originally designed for industrial use, were heavy and ran at the rather high speeds which suited the limited work they were required to do. With the increasing importance of pottery as a craft in schools and colleges, electric wheels appeared some years ago made specifically for the student-potter market, but they were under-powered and had crude control systems—in fact they were little more than toy wheels. But the popularity of the craft increased rapidly and the demand for wheels led to competition, design gradually improved and while some very good machines are made to suit the specific needs of students and individual potters, old-established ceramic machinery manufacturers are offering machines to educational establishments which are suitable also for industry. However, there is still a gap, because such efficient and very heavy machines are two or three times as costly as the lighter school machines. The latter are heavy enough to stand without fixing, but can be moved easily enough by two people and, at a pinch, by one person.

Static wheels do not cost much more than portable models, but they are heavier and handle larger quantities of clay: the greater the load they are designed to take the more they cost, naturally. They need to be flexible in their ability to satisfy the demands of children, students, teachers and individual craftsmen. Therefore an adequate range of speeds is an essential, as is constant speed under any pressure and a method of control which makes changes in speed as effortless as possible—this latter is very important for the learner and for the experimenting craftsman.

Nowadays it is the fashion to fully enclose the works by covering the framework with metal or plywood sheeting, though moulded cases in fibre-glass have appeared and doubtless will grow in popularity as they are simple in shape, have no hard edges and are easy to clean. Adjustable seats are becoming standard equipment also, some are upholstered—could this be feminine influence now that there are so many women potters?

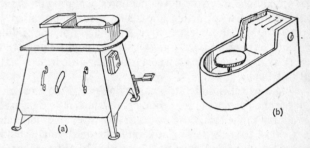

Fig. 161. (a) Static electric wheel; (b) portable electric wheel.

There are a number of systems employed in the various makes of wheel to control the speed of the wheel in relation to the speed of the motor: mechanical transmission by single cones or double cones, by variable pulleys, or by a friction wheel moving across the flywheel and by other similar devices. More recently, electrical control has been introduced by incorporating a variable transformer, and one wheel which has been well tested, decelerates to less than 10 r.p.m. However when the transformer breaks down, which it can do without warning, there is likely to be considerable delay while it is sent away to be repaired; whereas mechanical controls are adjustable for wear and are easily repaired and, if they are inspected regularly, any wear in the parts can be detected and breakdown avoided.

All static machines have a foot pedal or lever to control the speed of the wheel, which is counterbalanced for fine response. On some the lever can be slipped by foot into any one of several positions on a ratchet, when the wheel will revolve at a set speed. The more sophisticated machines, in which the speed is controlled by a variable transformer, have a pedal control which is as light and responsive as the accelerator on a car and a locking device for holding the wheel at any speed. There is an auxiliary hand-lever control (which is removable) for use when the potter is standing and on one type of wheel the foot lever can be converted rapidly to a hand lever. The advertised range of speeds is from 10 r.p.m.–350 r.p.m. for the lighter studio machines—the heaviest industrial-type wheel for use in education, etc., has a top speed of 500 r.p.m. with a minimum speed of 50 r.p.m.

In fact, the studio machine mentioned before does not only decelerate to less than 10 r.p.m. (as advertised), but will creep round in ultra-slow motion. Its top speed is 300 r.p.m. and 50 lb (23 kg) of clay can be centred and thrown on it efficiently. With packing and carriage this wheel costs about £150 and other makes of wheel with a comparative performance are about the same price.

What are known as 'heavy-duty' machines operating on the single- or double-cone-drive principle and using a more powerful $\frac{1}{2}$ h.p. motor are slightly more expensive. They are not so brilliant in performance but are tougher and will stand rough treatment and, if as a teacher you are selecting a wheel for general use in school, this is a point to be considered.

Choosing a wheel is difficult, because one wants the most efficient machine for the particular circumstances in which it is to be used and there is a large range to choose from. In any case it would be unwise to buy a wheel for yourself or anybody else until you have had experience of throwing and have used a number of different machines, unless you seek advice. You will also have to consider whether a particular wheel can be installed in the proposed site, especially if it is upstairs. There are also other factors such as storage of clay, adequate lighting, drainage and electricity supply (electric wheels use less than 13 amps).

Do-it-yourself Electric Wheels

The June 1973 issue of *Practical Householder* has a very clear plan and instructions for making your own wheel at an estimated cost of £45. (This is not so much less than buying one of the portable wheels offered by such firms as Wengers and Podmore's.)

You need to test a wheel before buying it, but this is a feasible proposition—at least it should be easy to find out from the manufacturers where one is in action in your locality and ask to go and see it. One should be wary of buying second-hand machines especially if they are home-made. They should be examined for wear in the working parts and if there is and the parts are not easily replaceable, you could have a large white elephant on your hands.

The Work Tray

Finally a word about the tray, which is usually rigid plastic or zinc lined. The wheel-shaft bearing is fixed in the base of the work tray and the tapered shaft protrudes through it (Fig. 162). Some shafts

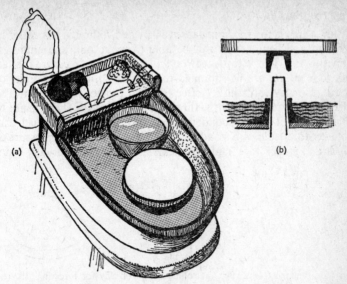

Fig. 162. (a) The work tray; (b) the level of water which should not be exceeded in the work tray, in order to avoid water penetrating between the shaft and the bearing.

have a thread on them, so the wheel head can screw on and off. Otherwise it lifts off, but only if it is not allowed to rust on. In other words it should be removed when throwing is finished or eventually it will cease to be removable! The tray is provided as a receptacle for water and slurry during throwing, but it is also a sink as it has an outlet from which the waste liquid can be piped away into a bucket. The water, etc., should never be allowed to rise above the top of the bearing. A wooden shelf rests across the front of the tray, which should occasionally be treated with linseed or teak oil to preserve it. This is provided as a rest for tools and sponges, etc. Normally one starts throwing on a 10 in (2·5 dm) wheel head and there should be plenty of room between this and the walls of the work tray to hold the tile which takes the pot as it is slid off the wheel: 8 in and 12 in (2 dm and 3 dm) wheel heads are also obtainable and are useful for throwing and turning wider shapes.

Tools and Equipment

A plastic apron or nylon house-coat as throwing can be messy! A water bowl. A fine sponge. Two clay cutters: a thick one for cutting and wedging the clay and a thin wire or twisted nylon for removing pots from the wheel. A flat-edged modelling tool. A sponge on a stick for removing water from pots with narrow necks. A potter's needle.

Preparing the Clay

Clay which is too moist collapses easily and, although it is easier to work up and centre, you will be able to make only the clumsiest shapes with it. If it is too hard you will not be able to centre it at all and your efforts are foredoomed to failure. Within these limits of course, the clay can still be softer (but not too soft) or harder. The softer it is the more direct the throwing must be if the shape is not to collapse and it will respond more readily to pressure. Hard clay is slower to handle, will stand more working, needs more pressure to thin it and is therefore liable to buckle. Naturally, if your clay is not

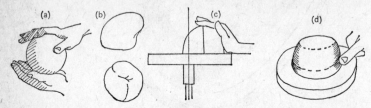

Fig. 163. Preparing to throw: (a) rolling a ball of clay for throwing; (b) bad shapes; (c) pushing the clay on centre; (d) sealing the ball to the wheel using thumb pressure.

homogeneous but contains variations in density it will respond unevenly to the pressure of your fingers and this will throw your work off-centre—eccentric pots are what cause all the laughter on the TV programmes. If you really want to throw well you must make the conditions as favourable as possible and condition number one is to use properly kneaded and wedged clay—no soft streaks, no hard patches, no air-bubbles. (Turn back to Chapter One, pages 6 and 7, and read again about kneading and wedging.)

Preparing to Throw

The two skills in which you must achieve a mechanical perfection before you can throw creatively, are centring and throwing a cylinder. Throwing when demonstrated by a craftsman looks deceptively easy. Like other skills it comes more easily to some people than to others, but with practice you or anybody else can learn to throw. The importance of assiduous practice cannot be over-emphasised, it is as important to the potter as scales are to the pianist.

It is important, too, not to be discouraged by early failure and it is possible, but unlikely, that your first attempts will be successful. The significance of the cylinder is that it is the basic shape from which most (but not all) upright thrown forms are developed. Therefore it is essential to be able to throw any size or proportion of cylinder to order and to be able to judge the quantity of clay required.

In most countries potters throw with the wheel revolving anti-clockwise. There seems to be no particular reason why this should be so and you can use the wheel clockwise if you want to, except that electric wheels rotate anti-clockwise as they are supplied and you would need the services of an electrical engineer to reverse the direction. However, a preliminary twist with the hand will set a kick wheel spinning either way. In Japan the wheel turns clockwise because the thrower needs his strong right arm to keep the wheel spinning (you will remember he inserts a stick in a notch in order to rotate it). Dry the wheel head (the clay slips on a really wet wheel), but leave it damp in the centre so that when you place the clay on it, it will stick. Take one to two pounds of clay and make a ball without creases or wrinkles. Do this carefully because it makes the centring easier. Slap the clay onto the middle of the wheel, spin the wheel slowly and push the clay until it is as central as possible. Wet the clay and your hands and keep them wet throughout the throwing. Spin the wheel quite fast and seal the clay down with your thumbs where it meets the wheel.

Centring Clay

Before you start work on the wheel, position yourself in a comfortable working stance, body well up against the work tray. The potter loves his clay: in throwing, your relationship is an intimate one. Remember this in the way you use your hands—so many beginners stroke the clay gingerly as if they were half afraid of it. Your arms, too, must be firm and steady, so rest them on the work tray and brace

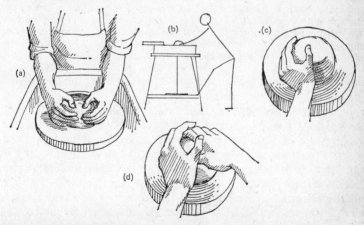

Fig. 164. (a) Standing up to the wheel; (b) the wrong posture; (c) position of the left hand in centring; (d) both hands used for centring.

your left arm against your hip. Now set the wheel spinning rapidly and press the heel of left hand against the rotating ball, the plastic clay must give way before its unwavering resistance. Your right hand, opposite the left, in a two o'clock position, at first assists by pulling the clay into the centre and then, as the clay begins to rise, gently moves over the top to exert a downward force. The two hands should work together wherever possible, steadying each other.

An alternative is to push against opposite sides of the clay with both hands, exerting the downward pressure which controls the top

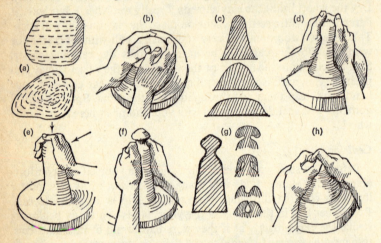

Fig. 165. (a) The diagram suggests molecule patterns in the clay; (b) initial position of hands in raising the clay; (c) sections showing stages in raising the clay; (d) position of hands when clay is raised; (e) beginning to take the clay down (left hand removed for clarity); (f) the result of too much pressure at the top; (g) the sections illustrate various faults to avoid; (h) hands in position when the clay has been taken down.

surface by means of the thumbs and especially using the balls of the thumbs (Fig. 164, page 201).

If your hands are wobbling then the clay is still winning; when they are steady you will know and feel that the clay is centred. Release the pressure of your hands gradually as sudden release causes a reaction from the clay which unsteadies it. Look at the clay now, it appears to be standing still. At this stage most potters like to give themselves and the clay a limbering up exercise. You will recall the spiral twist given to the clay when kneading it, which begins to re-arrange the molecules in a circular pattern after the horizontal wedging. By working the clay up and down on the wheel this process is completed and the clay is then in good form for throwing. Keep the wheel turning rapidly and grasp the clay once more in both hands with the thumbs resting lightly, not pressing, on the clay. Now apply even pressure with both palms and allow them to rise with the clay, forming it into a taller, thinner cone.

Uneven pressure and sudden movement up the clay will cause a break and the top of the clay will come away in your hands. Start again with a fresh ball of clay if this happens! Maintain the pressure of the left hand, while sliding the right hand steadily up and over the clay to rest on the left hand. The pressure exerted by each hand and the angles at which they work must be balanced so that the clay does not mushroom (to understand this fully you can remove your left hand altogether and see what happens!). See Fig. 165 opposite.

Continue taking the clay down in an increasingly broader conical shape until it is a compact shape, low and slightly domed. Be careful not to form a hollow in the top which fills with air and slip, or to spread the clay out on the way down, so that it folds over on itself and traps air and slip in that way. Working the clay up and down improves the throwing texture of the clay but if it is overdone it will become too soft and wet.

Forming the Opening

There are several ways of forming a preliminary hole in the centre of the clay, but only one basic point of difference:

(a) In one method the thumb presses straight down in the centre of the clay to within $\frac{1}{2}$ in (13 mm) of the wheel head. It then moves steadily outwards parallel to the wheel (i.e. horizontally, away from the body) to form a flat base and open out a hole in the clay which is wider at the bottom. The fingers of the right hand clasp the outside of the clay and are supported by the left hand.

(b) In the other methods, both thumbs press down and then away from the body to form a cylindrical hole; or the fingers of the right hand are pressed in and down and then move in the direction of the body and left hand to form a wider opening which is roughly cylindrical. In each case there is a greater thickness of clay below than above.

In any case, there should be $\frac{1}{2}$ in (13 mm) thickness of clay at the base. This can be checked with a $\frac{1}{2}$ in (13 mm) potter's needle (if the wooden handle goes into the clay it is too thick), or the simple device illustrated in Fig. 166.

Thinning

For this you will need to slow the wheel down until you have had considerable experience. In this first complete movement, the object is to use both hands to thin the clay wall and draw it up to produce a

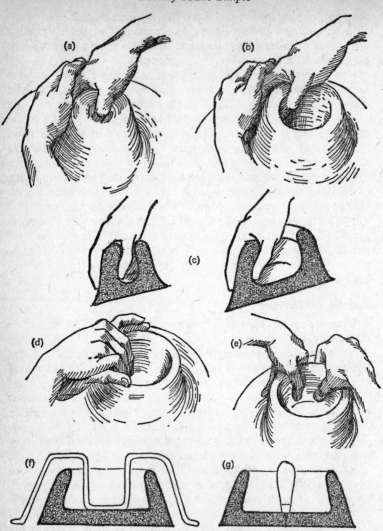

Fig. 166. (a) and (b) The first stages in opening the clay; (c) these stages in section; (d) first alternative method of opening; (e) second alternative method; (f) an improvised wire gauge for measuring the thickness of the base; (g) a short potter's needle for the same purpose.

short cylinder with thick walls, thicker at the bottom and thinner at the top.

The left hand works on the inside and the right hand outside. There is no hard and fast rule, for the index finger or more than one finger can be used in both cases. In fact, most people use the flat surface of the fully bent index finger on the outside as if several fingers are used ridges are usually formed. In this first stage the left thumb, braced on the right wrist, gives extra steadiness.

Having decided on the position of your hands and fingers you start from the bottom and work to the top without hesitation.

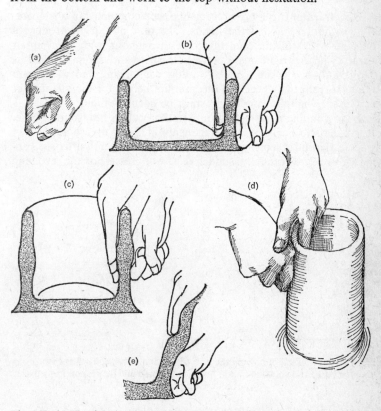

Fig. 167. (a) The right hand as used for knuckling; (b) sectional view of the clay wall with the hands in position, commencing to thin; (c) moving the clay up; (d) spectator's view of the hands at the top; (e) the effect of wrong positioning of the hands.

The pressures on the clay must be equal and opposite and, therefore, allowance has to be made for the thickness of the base. The left hand starts from the wheel head, and the right hand must wait until the left hand is truly opposite it before beginning to rise and exert pressure. This bit of tricky synchronisation is very important; if you get it wrong the left hand will be exerting pressure above the right hand and forcing the wall outwards. Concentrate on a steady rising action of both hands opposite each other. Practise and practise this first thinning action until you have gained confidence before attempting anything further.

Throwing Cylinders

Now attempt two more movements, each completed in one operation without removing the hands. The task now is to produce a cylinder with walls of even thickness throughout, with an even flat base (as near a right angle between the base and the inside wall as possible) ½ in (13 mm) thick to allow for turning and wastage in removal from the wheel and of optimum height for the quantity of clay used. The following points must be borne in mind:

1. No thinning movement should start anywhere but from the base. It is useless to break off and start again half way up a pot.

2. At the end of a movement remove the hands gently after slackening the pressure gradually: sudden release of pressure on the revolving

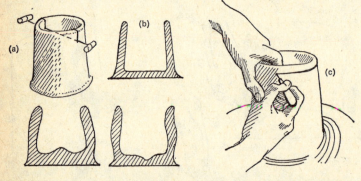

Fig. 168. (a) Method of halving the pot; (b) section of correctly-thrown cylinder with *flat* base: also showing faults: hump in the base and depression in the base; (c) trimming an uneven top.

clay at any time will cause a reaction in the clay wall which will then go off-centre. The wobble is impossible to remove.

3. Greater pressure is necessary where the clay is thicker. Dry hands or dry clay, or too much pressure at the top of the cylinder, can act like a brake and cause the clay to drag in the hands, which distorts the clay wall.

4. Do not thin the top of the wall too soon. The thinning should be done progressively throughout.

5. Keeping the hand and arm steady is of prime importance. The body should be relaxed and comfortable, and so should the mind;

do not get tense but remember that this is only practice. Many beginners are so anxious to make a pot that they will accept the most indifferent results as pottery. All your initial throwing is practice to acquire a skill (like a person practising scales to become proficient as a pianist who takes tape recordings to study his mistakes, not to preserve as music for posterity). You can learn much about your progress by cutting your cylinders in half vertically using a thin wire and studying the cut section (Fig. 168).

Further points for consideration:

1. The cylinder cannot be a completely symmetrical shape because the hands move up the cylinder without stopping as they form and

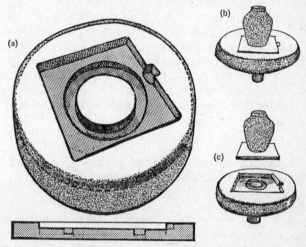

Fig. 169. Rubber tile batt: (a) perspective and sectional views; (b) pot in position after throwing; (c) pot on tile removed from batt.

thin it; the finger marks are not a series of separate rings but they spiral from the base to the top.

If the top of the cylinder is not true it can be trimmed whilst revolving using a potter's needle, or by a quick cut with the twisted nylon wire or brass wire; this needs practice. Support the clay on the inside with a finger when cutting with the needle.

2. There is a relationship between the amount of clay on the wheel and the size of the cylinder. The width of the original clay mound is closely related to the width of the cylinder.

3. What proportion are the cylinders you tend to throw? What is the maximum height? Have you reached 6 in (1·5 dm) yet?

Remove cylinders and standing forms from the wheel by flooding the wheel with water, then take a twisted nylon cutter or brass wire and with both hands hold it very flat on the wheel head and pass it under the pot. The pot can then be slid to the edge of the wheel and onto a wet tile or board and set on one side to dry. Alternatively, if it is a strong pot, clasp it gently and firmly between the hands and lift it onto a board or shelf. A recent device on the market is a 'rubber tile batt' which fits snugly over a 10 in (2·5 dm) wheel head. An unglazed tile fits into it and after the pot has been thrown, the potter's finger is inserted in a small gap to lift out the tile with the pot on it. Throwing proceeds with a fresh tile (Fig. 169).

Task One. Throw a series of cylinders of different heights and widths but equal thickness. Set these on one side to dry for turning practice. Place them upside down for even drying.

Task Two. Continue to throw cylinders until you can achieve a height of 8 in (2 dm). Then do it a second time. Do not throw it at your spouse if he or she is not impressed. The basic cylinder can be developed upwards, outwards and inwards. There is also a question of throwing bowls and flat shapes. Before these developments can be exploited, the student potter must practise shaping movements— but first, as the task one cylinders are probably leather-hard by now, a few words about turning.

Turning

Turning is not as fascinating to watch as throwing. It is a great deal easier to understand but, nevertheless it needs practice.

Tools for Turning

The tools, quite simply, are of three sorts: made from strip steel or aluminium bent to a right angle, and shaped into a variety of straight and curved cutting edges; or they are small-shaped metal blades welded to metal rods set in wooden handles (rather like a paint-shave); or they are narrow metal strip formed into a ring and set into a wooden handle. In all three cases the cutting edge has to be sharpened at an angle, like a chisel.

Turning tools of all types are available from the usual suppliers. Wire modelling tools are also useful. In industry pots are turned on a lathe, but studio potters usually reverse the pot on the wheel when it is leather-hard and centre it by the rings engraved on the wheel. Slow rotation and a tap here and there is used to correct any eccentricity. Some pots need special chucks to hold them in place, but if you are turning cylinders, four blobs of plastic clay pressed firmly against the reversed cylinder and secured to the wheel head by thumb pressure will suffice. The wheel should rotate quite fast for turning. Test the base of the pot for centrality by using the potter's needle to mark a circle as it revolves. Compare this ring with the perimeter of the base and move the pot if it is not truly centred. Make sure the cylinder is held firm to the wheel head as if it moves during turning it is difficult to re-centre.

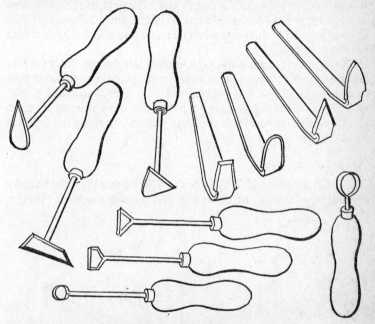

Fig. 170. Various tools available for turning.

Turning Pots

The pot should be leather-hard for turning and if it is of the right consistency the clay will pare off in long shavings as in planing wood. If the cylinder was dried upside down it should have dried evenly. There is less clay in the top of the cylinder so there is a natural tendency for it to dry more quickly than the thick base. As you are not going to re-shape the top by turning it does not matter if it is a little drier, but if it is too dry there will be difficulty in securing the supporting clay lumps, and there is a danger of cracking the walls if the clay is pressed too hard against them. This does not matter on the cylinders which are for practice only, but it will be important later when finishing off pots which are to be fired.

It is fatal to allow a pot to dry more on one side than the other, the difference in response to the turning tool makes turning ineffective. It is unsatisfactory to try to turn pots which are too damp or too dry. The tool churns up damp clay which sticks to the pot and gets in the way and in fact, will not cut clean. Dry clay pares away in powder,

H

and flakes or sometimes chips, the tool judders and produces vertical ridges. Damping down a too-dry pot is not really viable either, since it weakens the texture of most clay and is time wasted. It takes no more time in the end to scrap dry pots and throw a fresh lot. These are hard lessons which all potters have to learn and they are best learned at this stage when there are pots which do not matter on which to practise.

The objects of turning are: (a) to remove surplus clay from the foot and true the base; (b) to do any further shaping the potter may consider necessary. The first process will be sufficient to make a start on turning. Assuming you have a number of tools you can try them all out on the cylinders you make, in this way learning the different ways they cut.

Turning the Foot-ring

1. Level the base with a V-shaped tool. Try using the point to make a spiral ring, starting at the centre and moving outwards; using a

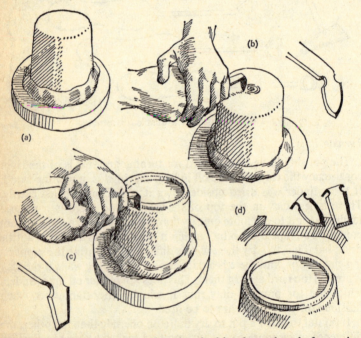

Fig. 171. (a) Inverted pot secured to the wheel by clay and ready for turning; (b) the position of the hands, when turning grooves in the base with a suitable tool; (c) the outside of the foot-ring being formed with a suitable tool; (d) a section of the foot to illustrate the way the tools are used.

fast wheel with steady pressure. Then level the tops of the rings using the edge of the tool sideways and gradually remove the clay until the furrows disappear.

2. Using the point of the tool, mark a ring on the wall just below the base of the upside-down pot. Then use the flat edge vertically to trim the clay above the ring.

3. Finally form the foot-ring. Except for $\frac{3}{8}$ in (10 mm) at the perimeter, the base clay is removed, (about $\frac{1}{4}$ in (6·5 mm) of it) so that the walls of the pot and the base are the same thickness. The base inside the ring may be smoothed or left with the rings which are the mark of the turning tool. As a pot stands on its foot-ring, the base does not damage the furniture.

These are the necessary steps in turning a foot-ring: the main purpose is to remove the extra thickness of clay to ensure even shrinkage in drying and firing. While you have your practice cylinders on the wheel try using all the other turning tools, and even some modelling tools and pieces of saw blade, to learn what can be done with them.

CHAPTER THIRTEEN

POTTERY WITH THE WHEEL: THROWING SHAPES

Throwing a shape is the third stage in throwing. After acquiring skill in centring and in forming true cylinders, shapes can be developed initially from cylinders and, when this third skill has been acquired, they can be blended into one continuous operation. One of the main difficulties in learning to throw is that the hands and the clay must be kept wet. Therefore, the longer the throwing continues the wetter and softer the clay becomes, especially the lower clay, which then fails to support the weight of the clay above and the wall persistently sinks. The more it is drawn up by the despairing potter, the more the water penetrates the clay with consequent accelerated sinking, until the clay wall splits from fatigue and finally collapses (followed by the potter!).

This is why it is essential to practise each stage in turn to perfection, so that it can be completed quickly and satisfyingly. Some potters believe that it helps to re-use the throwing water constantly because it becomes colloidal, which reduces the wetting effect. In America potters have been experimenting with substitutes for water which will lubricate efficiently but not weaken the clay. Another interesting American experiment is a special reversing wheel for extra-tall shapes: a thick basic cylinder is opened up and then the wheel is raised and turned over mechanically. Gravity then assists the potter to extend the walls of the cylinder in a downward direction and there is no question of the pot **sitting** or **squatting** as it is called.

Shapes Developed from the Cylinder

It is best to attempt only subtle changes in the shape of a cylinder because undue distortion after thinning is completed leads to weakness in the walls. For instance, developing a pronounced convex curve developed directly from a straight-walled cylinder thins the walls dangerously at the maximum diameter, and brings down the height. If such a pot survived the throwing process it would probably come to grief in the subsequent drying or firing. Likewise if a cylinder is compressed to form a really concave wall, at its narrowest width the clay will thicken considerably, and the height will increase a little. Therefore, shapes which depart greatly from straight sides are better thrown from the beginning as undeveloped versions of themselves—buds from which the full flowers grow.

212

Practical Work Tasks

Task One: (a) Forming a Neck

Form a cylindrical neck and a slightly wider convex base. As before, bring a cylinder up to its maximum height in three actions. Slow down the wheel and make sure your throwing position is going to be comfortable and relaxed; one arm or the other should be steadied against your body all the time. Only the tips of the fingers need be used as very little pressure is required in shaping. Place the left hand inside the pot at the base and press gently away from the centre to shape the wall in an outward curve: the right hand must be opposite the left hand to support the wall but *not* to squeeze it. Draw the hands up the cylinder as in thinning, and ease off the pressure below half-way; above half-way the hands return carefully to a vertical position. Having reached the top, level it off by supporting the outside of the neck with the palm of the left hand, placing the crook of the right thumb and index finger over the clay. Lubricate with water if there is any tendency to drag, round and thicken the rim with a little pressure.

(b) Collaring

Throw this shape again and place both hands around the neck above the bulge, fingers in front, thumbs behind (throttling position), squeeze firmly but gently. Either the diameter of the neck will be reduced and the clay wall thickened, or the clay will have folded because it was too soft, too dry, or your squeezing was over-enthusiastic.

Task Two: Modified Cylinder I

Throw a third cylinder and shape it similarly to the first, but in one or two complete movements without collaring. Do this by varying the pressure from the inside to the outside, transferring the shaping role carefully from the left hand to the right to produce a continuous convex–concave outline. Finish off the rim (Fig. 172, page 214).

It cannot be over-emphasised that the change in outline is made commencing from the base of the pot. At the start, where the wall meets the base inside there should be as distinct a change as possible from the horizontal to the vertical—an inside curve at this point means extra thickness in the wall which cannot be removed later. The inevitable extra thickness on the outside can be trimmed, during throwing, by a flat-bladed, **wooden** tool (a metal tool roughens the surface of the wheel).

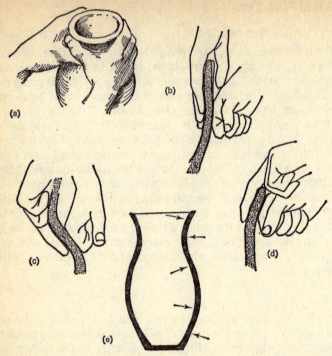

Fig. 172. (a) The hands collaring; (b), (c) and (d) sectional views of the potter's own hands forming the curves of the pot; (e) section of the pot.

Task Three: *Modified Cylinder II*

Throw a tall, thin cylinder into which your right hand will still fit. Working from the bottom flare the wall out a little. Before half-way up begin to come in, finally flaring out to a somewhat wider opening at the top. The outline should be undulating but not too pronounced. The neck may have to be collared in the final shaping if it is too narrow to insert a hand. Form a ridge near the lip by pressing the right-thumb nail into the clay, just below the edge, which is supported between the left hand thumb and forefinger. Above the ridge a rim will have formed which can be wiped clean and firm with a sponge or chamois leather. Alternatively a round-end modelling tool can be used for the ridge, or the lip can be turned over using finger and thumb. There are numerous subtle variations but the main object is to thicken the rim somewhat to strengthen it against distortion in drying and firing. A rim usually improves the look of the pot and gives a better grip for lifting.

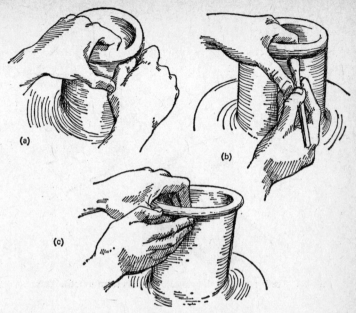

Fig. 173. Forming a ridge below the lip with: (a) the thumb; (b) a wooden
tool; (c) the hands turning the lip over.

Task Four: A Bottle Shape

This is difficult but fascinating to attempt. Throw a tall cylinder
and shape the bottom third into a slight swelling. Bring in the wall
above by collaring, forming a preliminary neck and then thin the
clay wall, again drawing the clay up (you will find that collaring has
thickened the clay wall). Further collaring will reduce the diameter of
the neck to the point where only two fingers, and finally one, can be
inserted. This difficult exercise gives an opportunity to experiment in
the use of the wooden profile—this looks like half a wooden spoon
but is entirely flat. It is inserted inside the pot so that the curve of
the half-spoon shape gently bears against the revolving clay wall to
shape it. The outside surface can be cleared of slip and smoothed by
using rubber or metal kidneys, metal scrapers, or boxwood ribs
which can be obtained from some of the usual suppliers, but are
easily fashioned from hardwood or softwood (the latter wears quickly).
Ribs are a modification of the kidney shape with generally less
pronounced curves. They can be used to thin cylindrical forms (a
slightly convex curve on the rib is best) and to give truly flat vertical
walls. On convex forms, a rib with a slightly concave curve works best.

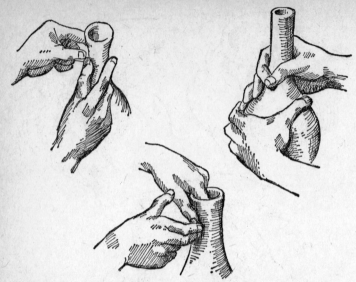

Fig. 174. Three positions showing how hands form a bottle neck.

Task Five: Beaker and Flower-pot Shapes

The simplest form which is not developed from a cylinder is a truncated cone: a cone with its top cut off, reversed, so that the base is the narrowest part. The clay is opened up in the usual way but the walls are immediately thinned and drawn upwards and outwards from the base. If the pressure is not skilfully regulated the sides will be either convex or concave. This is not an easy exercise. As an admission of failure you can try using a wooden ruler or lath to straighten up the sides. It is interesting then to slice the pot in half vertically and study the section.

Throwing Bowls

The clay is centred and opened as usual. Before starting to throw, the support and subsequent removal of open, wide shapes must be considered. The base of a bowl or dish of any size occupies a relatively large area of the wheel and the mouth may be as wide as the wheel, which poses difficulties when it has to be removed. The base tends to cling to the wheel, and the sides are too soft to be handled without distorting the wide mouth. So, either the bowl must remain on the wheel until it has become leather-hard, or else it must be thrown on a support which can be removed with the bowl on it and set aside to dry.

As most potters are not prepared to put their wheel out of action for so long, the popular solution is to throw on a batt. Batts are made of various materials: plaster, biscuit clay, asbestos and wood. They are the same size as the wheel or bigger and, for special uses, as big as will fit inside the work tray. They are fixed to the wheel with soft clay, or else two metal studs are fitted into the wheel so that batts with corresponding holes can be pegged in position. To secure a batt with soft clay, centre and spread all over the wheel and make deep grooves with the fingers. Wet the clay and the batt before sticking down by manual pressure: if the clay is not wet the batt will not adhere and if the plaster or biscuit batts are too dry or too wet they will not take either. The wider batts are essential for throwing plates and they are easily prised off. Absorbent batts accelerate the drying of the bases of pots so that they are ready for turning sooner.

Task Six: Throwing a Small Bowl

(a) Centre and make a depression in a ball of clay. Instead of forming a flat base use the fingers to open up an inverted cone shape. Leave the usual thickness in the centre and very thick walls at the base.

(b) The second action is to open the clay to a broad U-shape, at the same time reducing the thickness, especially around the base.

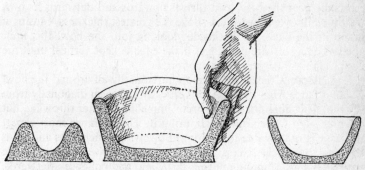

Fig. 175. Three sectional drawings showing stages in shaping a simple bowl.

(c) Commencing from the centre of the base on the inside, and then from the wheel head on the outside, thin the wall and draw it outwards and upwards in a continuous curve, the gain in width exceeding the gain in height.

(d) In the third thinning, the shape is extended once more to its final width and height. The aim of this first exercise is to throw a bowl of medium height and medium width, with a curve inside. If at stage (c) the shape is tall, it will have to be left at that, because the extra pressure needed to force it outwards will thin the top of the wall so much that it will collapse. On the other hand, thick walls widened out too far at stage (b) or (c) will collapse by their own weight and the force of centrifugal motion.

(e) Final shaping, including the modification of the somewhat vertical edge, should be done with very sensitive pressure of the finger-tips. Like all the other movements it commences from the centre. Be very careful not to jerk your hand away from the edge at the end of the thinning. Use a throwing rib to finish off the inside.

Points to Note

1. In stages (a) and (b) where most pressure is applied for thinning, the knuckle of the right-hand index finger can be used.

2. All other thinning and shaping can be done with the finger-tips. Link the two hands for extra support wherever possible.

3. There will always be an excess of clay between the outside of the wall where it meets the wheel and the inside curve where it commences to rise away from the base. On the outside the fingers cannot gain access without disturbing the inside curve, so the final shaping is done by turning, at the same time that the foot-ring is formed.

4. Unless the outside of the wall is well supported during throwing, especially near the base, as it thrusts upwards and outwards its own weight will make it bend just above the greatest thickness, causing a hump in the curve of the inside: looking into the bowl this fault appears as a soft circular ridge. If the edge is kept vertical until the final shaping this gives extra support.

5. Collapse. Cracks can develop horizontally all around the bowl where it flares from the base, or vertically and even diagonally from the rim. This does not always occur immediately after throwing, but often enough while you are admiring it. The beginner must expect this as it is usually due to prolonged throwing which wets and thins the clay too much. Excess water is easy to remove from the inside with a sponge. Slumping during throwing, and collapse afterwards, may also be the result of using **tired clay**: clay which has been reconstituted and used too soon, or without adequate kneading and wedging, is a chief offender. You will remember that in the early exercises in making thumb pots, compression produced by the thumbs pushing into the clay resulted in corresponding tension on the outside of the clay which sometimes caused cracks. Similarly in thinning, if the pressure exerted from the inside of the form is greater than that on the outside, tension is set up which can cause cracking.

Throwing Flat Bowls and Dishes

Use a relatively slow wheel when throwing.

Task Seven: Flat Bowl I

Secure a batt to the wheel and use a ball of well-prepared clay. Open it up as usual and then continue opening it by pulling towards you with the ends of the fingers of the right hand, thus spreading the area of the base and firmly moving the rest of the clay towards the outside where the side of the bowl is to be formed. Repeat this, always working from the centre until the base is as wide as necessary. In doing so be especially careful not to create a series of overlapping folds at the perimeter, which trap air and slip inside each other.

Thin and shape the wall as usual, making it straight and inclining slightly outwards. Finish the inside surface with a sponge and a throwing rib or a kidney, to remove the slip and smooth the surface. Remove the flat bowl on the batt.

Task Eight: Flat Bowl II

Use a fresh batt and a larger ball of clay, as big as you think you can handle, to repeat the opening process. With the larger quantity of clay it may be an advantage to use the fingers of both hands to thin and shape the base, or you can try using the outer edge of the right hand, beneath the palm, to press downwards and outwards simultaneously. When the base has been formed, throw a straight wall, then shape it to a convex curve.

Much practice is necessary, and it can include varying the proportion and size of bowls and dishes. Finishing off should include suitable treatment of the edge: a slight lip, or thickening, strengthens the perimeter of open forms.

Task Nine: A Plate

If you like throwing bowls you will want to attempt a plate form—not the domestic-type plate but a low bowl with a broad, flat edge. Try it first on a small scale until you have some confidence. The problem is to throw a straight-sided bowl and having thinned the wall, to bend most of it over until it is almost horizontal. This is done by supporting the wall with the fingers of the right hand. The left thumb and fingers take hold of it and bend most of it over at an angle, so that a broad, slightly concave edge is formed: concave, of course, to give it strength and prevent it collapsing. (This is done on a slowly-revolving wheel.) One or two more shaping actions bring the edge nearer to the horizontal, depending on the strength of the clay and the skill of the potter. The plate, on its batt, is removed from the wheel. Its shape can be modified a little by careful manipulation and, as the clay grows stiffer, the outside and the base are turned to shape.

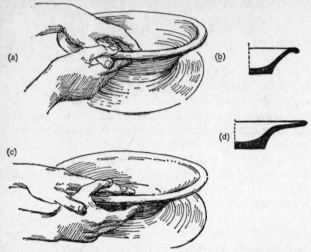

Fig. 176. (a) Hands turning over the lip of a wide bowl; (b) the section of the bowl; (c) throwing a plate with a wide rim; (d) section of the plate.

Altered Bowls. The shape of thrown bowls is sometimes altered by manipulating the walls when the clay is still pliable but not so wet that it marks easily. A wavy edge can be formed by prodding and pushing with the fingers. The rim can be squared, formed into an oval, pulled together to meet in the centre, etc. The base can be made oval while soft by cutting a flame-shaped incision in the centre and squeezing gently until the opening closes. The join can be wiped over or darned if necessary.

Throwing Large Shapes

It is best not to attempt this until you are a proficient thrower. Naturally you need the physique also: it takes strength as well as skill to handle clay in tens of pounds. The heel of the right hand is used to enlarge the opening in the clay after centring, while the left hand supports the wall on the outside. Both hands raise the clay using full pressure. Bowls and large cylinders are possible using this technique (Fig. 177).

Throwing Small Shapes

A procedure known as 'throwing off the Hump' is suitable for small forms which are too fiddly to throw directly on the wheel. As much as 50 lb of clay is centred at one time (this, too, calls for a special technique). Objects such as domed lids, small bowls, egg-cups and spouts can be shaped from the top and removed while spinning

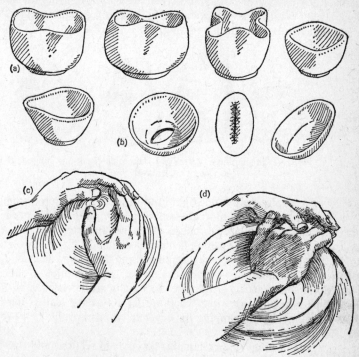

Fig. 177. (a) Five alternative bowl shapes; (b) the conversion of a thrown bowl to an oval shape; throwing large shapes: (c) centring; (d) opening.

slowly with the aid of a bamboo 'spear', and a twisted thread, which is wound into a groove formed in the base and pulled when it overlaps. This releases the pot and leaves a 'shell' pattern on the base.

Enclosed Shapes

Pots with round bellies and narrow necks are difficult to throw in one piece. This type of pot most certainly cannot be developed from a cylinder. After opening the clay the wall is raised in a convex curve, as clearly related to the eventual shape as an uninflated balloon is to one filled with air. The second and third thinning and shaping actions progressively increase the width and height. Subsequent shaping action increases the width and reduces the height. The diameter of the neck remains fairly constant, always allowing access for the left hand. In shaping convex curves the position of the fingers is at right angles to a tangent to the curve at any point. Logically, then, the fingers are equal and opposite at half-way, after which they change their relative positions and roles. At the bottom the outside finger (right hand) does the supporting, in the top half the inside finger (left hand) does the supporting.

Fig. 178. Five stages in shaping a convex pot. The thick black line suggests the section at each stage.

Closing a wholly convex pot right in to form an opening too small for a man's hand, is even more difficult. The clay on the curve of the shoulder tends to collapse because of its unsupported weight. A hollow ball with a small opening is more easily made, especially on a large scale, by throwing two bowls and turning them to as near semi-spherical as possible, so that one has a foot, and the other a neck. Their diameters must be exactly equal, which can be checked with the callipers during throwing. They are joined at the leather-hard stage after scoring and slipping the edges: a wooden profile helps to seal the join on the inside.

Large pots of other shapes can also be made in sections and there are various ways of putting this into practice. For instance, the lower half can be thrown and stored carefully on a batt, while the upper half is thrown separately, also on a batt. When they are firm enough the lower section is replaced on the wheel and re-centred. The upper half is joined to it by scoring and slip, and rapidly centred before it fully adheres. The whole is then revolved on the wheel as one pot making good the join by throwing. This is well-established pottery practice: the end justifies the means. In pottery, as in other arts, technique is not an end in itself.

A further device for forming pots which are too large to make in one throwing process, is to throw the bottom section, ensure that it dries very evenly and, when it is leather-hard, to weld on a thick coil or coils. The fresh clay is sponged and carefully centred and once it runs true it is thinned and shaped to form the next section of the pot. This process is repeated until the pot is complete. Stems are difficult to throw, so they are often 'thrown on' to leather-hard bowl forms. Necks can be added to ovoid forms in this way.

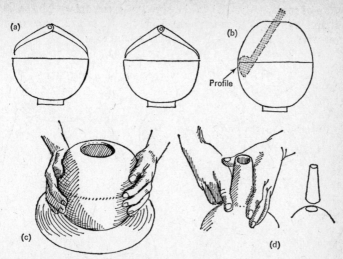

Fig. 179. (a) Two thrown bowls of equal diameter at the mouth (check with callipers); (b) the two pots assembled mouth to mouth with the base of the top one removed and the inside join being welded with a wooden profile; (c) re-throwing the assembled pots on the wheel; (d) adding a neck by re-throwing.

Throwing Jugs (Spouts and Handles)

To be classed as a jug, a pot must be furnished with a spout and a handle. Therefore, the first exercise will be to form a spout on a simple cylindrical form and to make and attach a handle. But as a preliminary and to get your hand and eye in you may like to throw some small cylinders, which can be adapted as drinking mugs.

Task Ten: A Cylindrical Jug

Having thrown a medium-tall cylinder place the middle finger and thumb of the left hand against the rim and use the middle or index finger of the right hand to shape the clay between them, pulling the clay out carefully with a stroking action. Bend the lip of the spout over to form a good pouring shape. Take care not to be too abrupt or the clay will split open and extra clay will have to be grafted in when it is firm enough. The best shape for a spout varies somewhat with the shape of the jug, as this determines the way the liquid flows, and also on the method by which it is formed. There are two further ways to make a spout.

Prepare a spout from the same clay immediately the cylinder has been thrown. Cut a parabolic or triangular-shaped section from sheet clay, fold it into a spout and let it harden with the thrown cylinder. When both are leather-hard cut a V-shaped section from the top of the cylinder and fix the spout over the opening by scoring and slipping. Wipe over the joins with the thumb to integrate the spout with the body of the jug. Apply a handle.

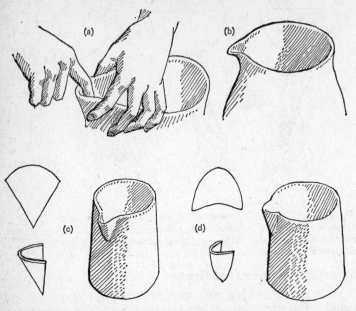

Fig. 180. (a) Forming a lip between the fingers; (b) the lip completed; (c) and (d) sections for forming and adding spouts.

Now throw a modified cylinder. As the clay is drawn up in a thinning action exert a slight pull inwards to make the cylinder grow slightly narrower. When it is leather-hard cut back four-fifths of the top edge of the cylinder. It is rather like cutting a quill to make a pen. Add a handle. It will look like a coal scuttle!

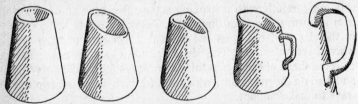

Fig. 181. Truncated cones cut in various ways to make jugs.

Some individual experimenting is necessary to determine what an efficient and good-looking spout looks like.

Handles are formed at the same time as the jugs and dry with them until they are firm enough to retain their shape. For these first exercises use handles formed from flattened clay ropes or with strips cut from thick clay sheet, like those you used for hand-built jugs (see page 49).

Task Eleven: A Rounded Jug

Make a somewhat different type of jug which has a rounded body and a narrow neck, designed to hold more liquid without spilling. It is necessary, therefore, to practise making pots with full, ovoid bodies surmounted by straight or trumpet-shaped necks. As explained already, a slightly ovoid shape can be developed from a cylinder with a gently undulating outline. Mediaeval English potters often used one of these shapes as the basis of a jug. But it holds no more liquid than the cylindrical jug, has rather a narrow base and is less stable. Begin throwing, developing the required shape straightaway, as you thin and draw up the clay. When you have finished thinning develop the full shape from the embryo, and avoid further thickening or thinning action if possible. The position of the hands in relation to each other will change with changes in the form (as described in throwing closed forms on page 221). Potters' methods vary and they use their hands differently, but there are certain logical principles deriving from the nature and behaviour of clay, which again varies as there are clays with different properties, from very 'fat' to very 'lean'. Throwing porcelain involves more limitation than throwing earthenware for instance. Practise making shapes for jugs, some with straight necks, and others which turn out at the top. The latter shape is suitable for the formation of a generous spout with a slight downward curve which prevents dribbles.

The most suitable style of handle for these jugs is formed by the traditional technique of 'pulling'. Immediately after throwing take about 2 lb (0·9 kg) of clay and form a pear shape: the smaller end is moistened and, held in the left hand, is pulled out gradually in a series of stroking actions—rather like milking a cow—until it is the right shape and thickness. Handles which are too round in section are not comfortable to hold and are rarely satisfying to the eye. Decide which is to be the upper area of attachment for the handle and prepare this by scoring. Then support it from inside with the fingers of the left hand, while the thick end of the handle (where it has been severed from the original lump) is pressed home hard. The pot should not be wet, but as soft as practicable to assure reasonably equal shrinkage of the handle and the pot. If the handle should shrink more than the pot it will either crack or break away. Some potters (if their clay is sufficiently plastic) attach a lump of clay to the pot and form a handle by pulling directly from the pot, so that it appears to grow out of the pot as naturally as a willow tree from a river bank.

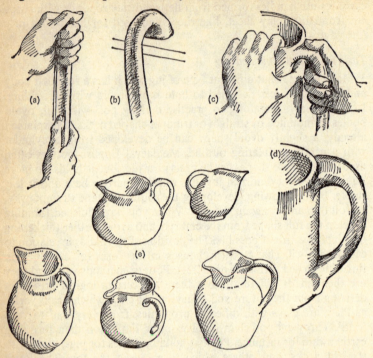

Fig. 182. (a) Pulling a clay handle; (b) the pulled clay left to form a natural curve; (c) attaching the handle by thumb pressure; (d) the handle attached at the top and bottom; (e) selection of five jug shapes.

The potter's thumb is drawn along the upper surface, making a groove in the handle, which improves the grip and the look. If the pulled clay is cut off and attached while still soft, it will bend naturally and form its own curve; or it can be left on the shelf to bend in this natural way and be attached when firm. The lower end is wiped onto the pot if sufficiently soft, or attached by scoring and slip if harder. Elaborately-grooved handles are often formed from clay which has been placed in a wad box and forced through a shaped template. A similar effect was produced more simply in country potteries by drawing a piece of shaped, twisted wire through soft clay.

When making round-bellied pots it is a good idea to make a series of ridges in the neck of one. A ridged lip has been recommended before for strength and, although a series of ridges has no real func-

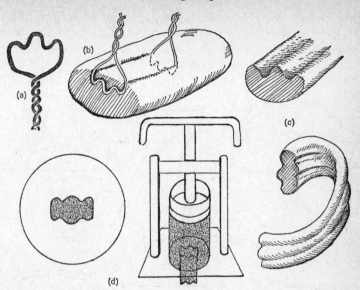

Fig. 183. (a) Wire loop for cutting a moulding for a handle; (b) the loop in position for cutting the clay; (c) the cut section; (d) wad box and die used similarly to (a).

tion, it looks good and gives the neck added strength. The ridges can be produced by using a wooden tool, a hardboard template with semi-circular notches, or just with the fingers. This also could look effective on a jug.

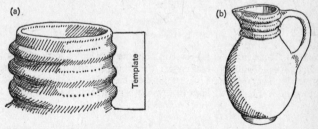

Fig. 184. (a) Wood or hardboard template used to produce ridges on a thrown pot; (b) jug with ridged neck.

Making Lids and Seatings

There is a great variety of lids and Fig. 185 illustrates their intricacies. The lids, which are hollow, are really small bowls and have to be thrown upside down on the wheel. It is easiest to throw them from a clay lump (especially if the knob is integral) and finish them off by

turning since, unless you have small hands, throwing lids directly on
the wheel is difficult. Flat lids with raised edges are small plate
shapes. Lids which are covers are relatively easy to make as they are
flat bowl shapes with no complications, which fit straight over pots
and jars.

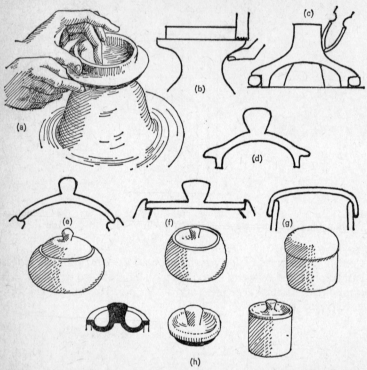

Fig. 185. (a) Throwing a lid (in reverse) from the clay lump. Sectional drawings:
(b) shaping the lid with tool and finger; (c) shaping the top of the lid by turning
(note the clay supports) and (d) the finished lid. Sectional drawings and lids:
(e) domed inset lid; (f) flat inset lid; (g) cover; (h) sunken lid on its own and
in situ.

Task Twelve: A Lid

Your next exercise will be to throw lids until you feel satisfied that
you understand them. Then throw cylinders with seatings to match
one or more of the lids—this, too, is a skill to be practised. Outside
and inside callipers are necessary to match the dimensions of lids
and seatings as the clay will be too wet to try them for fit. Minor
adjustments are possible when the clay is leather-hard, at which
juncture the lids can be tried for fit.

Task Thirteen: A Seating

Throw a fairly wide and short cylinder, leaving extra thickness at the top to provide for a seating which will be situated just below and inside the rim. This is done in the first thinning in the form of a thick, flat edge. Next it is supported underneath by the fingers of the

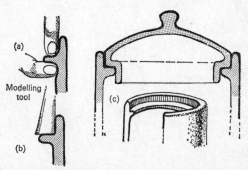

Fig. 186. Sectional drawings showing: (a) the index fingers of both hands forming a seating; (b) trimming up with a wooden tool; (c) the lid in its seating.

left hand and a depression is produced by pressing the edge down to below the rim, using the index finger of the right hand. During the final shaping action this ledge is trimmed to make it flatter, with the aid of a flat modelling tool which removes the slip and imparts definition.

Task Fourteen: A Covered Cylinder

Develop a container with flat sides from a thrown cylinder and fit it with a lid in the form of a simple thrown cover.

(a) Throw another low, wide cylinder and leave an unusually large surplus of clay at the base for subsequent turning. During the first thinning begin to turn the clay in with the object of making a shoulder and a neck.

(b) If it is too difficult to bring the shoulder in and form a neck, leave it and throw a small cylinder separately after removing the pot from the wheel. Also throw the cover and check the size with the callipers.

(c) When the cylinder is sufficiently dry to handle use a paddle to beat four flattish sides on the cylinder, or you can take the pot in your hands and tap it on the bench.

(d) When leather-hard reverse the pot on the wheel and secure it, then turn away as much clay as possible, forming as it were a shoulder underneath the pot and a suitable foot. Add the neck if necessary, and make any adjustments to the cover.

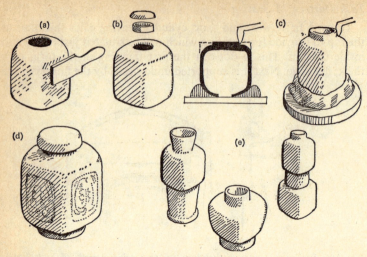

Fig. 187. (a) Beating flat sides on the cylinder; (b) separate neck and cover with the flattened pot; (c) turning a deep foot; (d) the completed pot; (e) variations on this method of construction.

Task Fifteen: Making a Teapot

Make a thrown teapot. The parts required, and the method of assembly, are the same as for a slab-built teapot, described on page 73. This is a test of accumulated skill and knowledge at any stage and for young students, who have not learnt to throw, building a teapot by coiling methods is a challenge in technique and design. However, before a teapot can be visualised and made by throwing alone, the technique for making spouts must be explained. Remember particularly that the rate of drying of all the parts—body, spout, handle and lid—must be controlled carefully or there will be shrinkage problems, which are all very difficult to put right: the spout can drop off, the handle crack and the lid prove too loose. Never leave a drying teapot around—somebody will come along and try to pick it up by the handle!

Throwing a spout from the hump or directly on the wheel is basically the same exercise as that in Task Ten (a gradually-narrowing cylindrical form) only on a smaller scale and the task is to throw a long, thin cone shape. On the outside the left-hand fingers exert pressure slightly above the right-hand fingers inside, pulling the clay wall inwards and narrowing it. Because a very narrow cone is necessary, collaring will have to be used to bring the clay in sufficiently and a straight edge or ruler can be used to help. Beginners often fail

to make the cone tall enough—as the base is later chamfered in order
to fit the spout to the pot at an angle, plenty of spare is necessary.

The exact angle has to be found by trial and error, depending on
the shape and size of the pot. It is a good idea to throw two spouts
in case you make a hash of the first one! Fortunately clay is plastic
and adjustments can be made to the spout after it has been attached
(by scoring and slip). The area where the spout is to be attached must

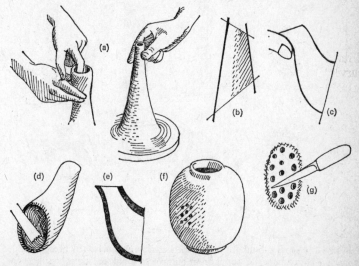

Fig. 188. (a) Throwing the spout; (b) the angles at which the thrown spout is
cut; (c) modelling the spout into the required shape; (d) reaming out the inside
of the spout; (e) sectional drawing of the spout; (f) position for the spout;
(g) shaving the area of attachment to reduce the depth of the holes.

be prepared carefully. At the leather-hard stage it is pierced with
holes which permit the free flow of tea. It is carefully shaved so that
the holes will be large and shallow enough to prevent clogging.

If the spout is placed high on the pot it has to be tipped further to
empty and the lid needs a firm seat. If it is placed lower down this is
not so essential but because the spout must more than reach the level
of the tea in the pot it will be long and consequently easily broken.
Metal teapots, especially those which are more uncompromising in
design, are more efficient pourers than earthenware or porcelain pots.
Of course, a sharp edge to a pottery spout chips easily and looks
unsuitable.

There is a bewildering assortment of shapes and positions for
spouts, because permutations of a number of factors are involved in
their design. These are the force with which the tea issues, the

manner in which it flows, and what happens when pouring ceases which are all affected by the curve of the spout (if any), its position and the angle at which it is set to the body, the relationship between the width of the openings at the top and bottom of the spout and the shape and angle of the lip. For instance, if the opening at the top of the spout is relatively large, the tea crawls out of the pot and

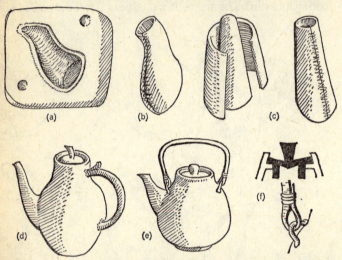

Fig. 189. (a) Press mould for spout with escape channels; (b) press moulded spout; (c) basic shape for spout from clay sheet moulded round a solid cone; (d) tall teapot; (e) teapot with bamboo handle; (f) section of deep sunk lid and clay lug for the handle of the teapot in (e).

dribbles down the spout (which often has a convenient downward curve to help it). A generous opening in the base and a relatively narrow exit from the spout logically eject the tea more forcibly and produce a steady stream. This principle should be used with discretion if the tea is to go into the cup! A slight downward slope to the lip assists pouring, but too much results in dribbling, and so on. It is difficult to pontificate because appearance is a controlling factor also and the spout should harmonise with the general appearance of the pot.

Basic spouts for thrown teapots can be formed in ways other than by throwing, such as by a small two-piece mould for use with pressed-in clay, or by wrapping sheet clay around a plaster or biscuit cone which shapes the inside. As to the shape of the body of the pot, any shape which holds a good quantity of liquid is viable, as long as it can be related sensibly to a spout and handle as, for example, an ovoid form with a pronounced neck providing a good position for a pulled handle. An ovoid teapot can be provided with small clay lugs on the shoulders to which a bamboo handle is attached horizontally, which is heat-proof and gives the same control as a kettle handle. Bamboo handles can be made easily or purchased ready made from the Fulham pottery. A spur of clay can be luted onto a

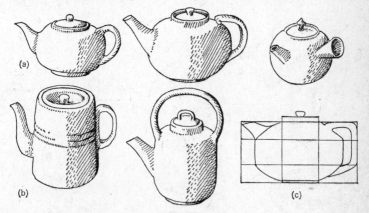

Fig. 190. (a) Three traditional teapots; (b) two contemporary teapots; (c) teapot design based on a rectangular grid.

pulled handle and shaped with the thumb to provide a grip for the thumb when pouring.

A neck with a seating is necessary and can be thrown separately. It also needs a well-fitting lid, with a good deep flange, so that it does not move when the pot is tipped. The final detail is the foot which is turned as soon as the body of the pot is dry enough. The shape of the foot is arbitrary and is more important aesthetically than functionally: its shape can make all the difference to the look of a pot.

Task Sixteen: A Posy Ring

A ceramic gimmick, 'the posy ring', is featured in flower arrangement and is easy to throw, but the technique differs slightly from anything described so far.

Centre the clay on a batt and open it up as usual, then insert the fingers of the right hand and pull the clay towards you, supporting, it outside with the left hand, rather as in throwing a flat dish. Do not leave any clay in the centre as you are forming a ring, but pull it out until it is a thick wall. By inserting the right thumb into the ring, still steadying it with the left hand, form a depression, and then use the hands to thin and shape the wall on either side until the clay is U-shaped in section. Finish off with a throwing rib and chamois leather.

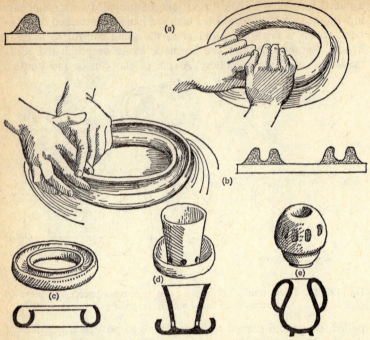

Fig. 191. (a) Shows the hands forming the ring of clay which has no base, as seen in the sectional diagram; (b) forming a central depression in the solid ring and section; (c) an impression of a finished posy-ring with section underneath; (d) one-piece thrown flower-pot and saucer with drain holes (section below); (e) thrown pot with double wall and section.

Repetition Throwing

An affluent society and the mass production of cheap plastic objects have combined to create a demand for craftsman-made objects. Numbers of potters find they can live by satisfying the growing cultural hunger, as a result well-conceived and executed pottery is available in places all over England, much of it being useful as well as beautiful. However, even in an affluent age prices need to be competitive if hand-made ware is to sell in sufficient quantities for economic survival. This means that the individual potter must be able to repeat a limited range of shapes quickly and efficiently, so that he can eat and have some time and money to experiment. An important part of contemporary training therefore is strictly-disciplined repetition throwing. As the result of demand and economic climate, basically the potter is back where he was at the beginning of the Industrial Revolution, and he is not so far removed from the early potters who introduced industrial methods when they invented the potter's wheel in Mesopotamia 6,000 years ago. For the amateur potter there is no such discipline, except perhaps the discipline of enthusiasm. Repetition throwing as a self-imposed discipline should be practised to gain confidence and really accurate control. On the other hand, repetition to the point of boredom is destructive.

A further aspect of repetition throwing is the use of throwing and turning inseparably combined as one technique, established in England since the beginning of industrialisation and never entirely superseded by moulding and casting. Shapes are thrown thicker than they are designed to be and are thinned and finely shaped by another craftsman using a lathe. Non-plastic porcelain bodies are more easily shaped this way, as they need to be especially thin and smooth. Individual craftsmen are also using a similar technique to maintain individuality and yet make the production of personal ware possible on a large enough scale.

More About Turning

Ways of using turning tools have been described previously but only in relation to cylinders. However, the different types of thrown shapes which have been described in this chapter require different types of support. These are now described in detail with some recapitulation of important features of turning technique and practice.

Industrial turning is done on a lathe, but individual potters generally use the wheel. Whether the turning tool is applied to the clay horizontally or vertically the removal of clay is equally effective. It is often necessary to remove excess clay from pots because of the inevitable ratio between the diameter of the base and the maximum diameter of the pot. Only on a very small pot will your fingers manage to throw a small base. Therefore, to form the narrowest practicable foot on a wide pot and shape the bottom, it must be reversed and turned.

At the same time the thickness of the clay in the base and lower part of the pot can be adjusted. Removing clay from the walls or base, gauge the correct thickness by cutting a piece of matchstick to its measure and press it right into the clay. When it appears on the outside during turning you will have removed sufficient. Turning is done on a fast wheel and if the clay is right it will peel off in long, clean shavings. Pots for turning must be dried slowly and evenly, away from artificial heat or draughts. Because the base is thicker than the walls it retains more moisture, so dry the pots upside down.

Before the base of a pot is turned it must be centred accurately, or the tools will cut deeper on one side than the other and eventually penetrate the wall.

Centring

Some machined wheel heads have lightly engraved rings which can be used as a guide in placing the pot—otherwise rotate the wheel and draw a series of concentric circles in pencil. Reverse the pot and fix it temporarily with small blobs of clay then while the wheel spins, assess the accuracy of the centring by eye. If there is any doubt use the potter's needle to score a faint circle as near the perimeter as possible. If the pot is off-centre this circle will be nearer the perimeter on one side, so the pot will have to be moved away from the centre on that side. Centrality can also be checked by eye. Hold the needle steady, very near the perimeter but outside it. Eccentricity may be due to bad throwing, possibly in the upper half of the pot only and in this case the pot would have to be supported off the wheel by a chuck. In this context a **chuck** is any device which secures the pot while it is turned. The chuck is standard equipment on a lathe, but chucks for the wheel are improvised.

Methods of Support

1. Some pots are turned before they are cut off the wheel and set aside for drying. Such pots have flat bases and where a twisted wire has been used there will be a pattern of curved radial lines.

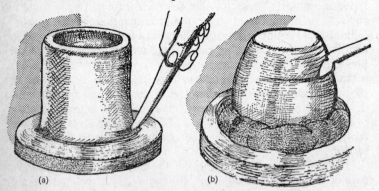

(a)   (b)

Fig. 192. Turning: (a) pot for turning, secured to moist wheel head by pressure from a wooden tool applied to the perimeter of base; (b) reversed pot secured for turning by a ring of soft clay.

2. If the pot has been thrown on a batt, the batt can be replaced when the pot is hard enough to turn.

3. The base of simple form like a cylinder can be secured to the wheel by damping the wheel head, centring the pot and then sealing the bottom edge to the wheel by firm pressure with a modelling tool. When reversed, the rim itself if moistened will stick to a damp wheel

(this can cause minor deterioration of the rim, requiring attention afterwards with a sponge or chamois leather). If there is room between the pot and the wheel, it can be secured with a thick rope of soft clay pressed against the base and stuck to the wheel.

4. Open forms such as bowls are, when reversed, often too wide to be supported on the wheel head. It is possible, though probably risky, to place a bowl so that it fits over the wheel head. In this case, before centring, it must be tested to make sure it is horizontal—that the base is parallel to the wheel head. Make sure the bowl grips the wheel head and support it with the left hand in case it rises, while

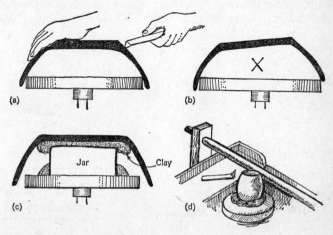

Fig. 193. (a) Turning a bowl larger than the wheel head without securing it; (b) incorrect, the base of the bowl is not parallel to the surface of the wheel; (c) wide bowl supported by a chuck improvised from a tin or jar; (d) broomhandle support for the turner's arm.

doing the turning with the right hand. This method will work provided the wall of the bowl is reasonably thick and damp enough to grip the edge of the wheel.

If it is difficult to turn the bowl with the right hand unsupported, fit a broomstick along the side of the wheel and use it much as a signwriter uses his mahlstick. Otherwise a chuck is necessary. The chuck can be a glass jar, or pot, about the same width as the internal base diameter of the bowl. It is fixed to the wheel by a rope of clay and centred, and a ball of clay is also centred and flattened on top of it as a soft support for the bowl, which is then reversed, placed on it and centred. Alternatively a hump of clay is centred on the wheel and used to support the reversed bowl.

Do not forget that when supporting the bowl in this way that it must be checked to ensure that it is horizontal. If there is any cant the base cannot be centred.

Clay Chucks. The use of a special clay chuck has already been introduced on page 208. A solid clay chuck used to support a large pot can later be reduced in size by turning, to support smaller pots. Chucks should be a little softer than the pots to be turned, but not too soft or they will stick inseparably. A hard chuck may mark the pot. Chucks can be stored in polythene for re-use. Chucks must be accurately centred, of course.

1. If a bowl just fits onto the wheel head or largest available batt, leaving no room to secure it on the outside, stick a thick rope of clay around the wheel's perimeter, centre it and shape it, using callipers

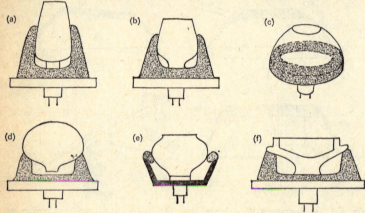

Fig. 194. (a) Tall pot supported in clay chuck; (b) chuck reduced in size to take a smaller pot; (c) thrown clay ring as a support for a wide bowl; (d) clay chuck for an ovoid pot; (e) pot for turning supported in a cup head; (f) clay chuck for turning a deep lid.

to check the diameter and ensure that the reversed bowl will fit exactly over it. (If you have no callipers a pair of compasses or dividers can be used.)

2. An ovoid or spherical form requires a low, thick cylinder as a chuck. The edge of the cylinder is chamfered to match the curve of the pot which is held in position by friction alone.

3. Tall forms need taller cylindrical chucks, almost half their own height.

4. Lids which require turning need special chucks to fit.

Cups heads are obtainable, designed for use with plaster moulds for mass production. These can be used to accommodate pots for turning, though a clay cushion may have to be provided around the edge.

Turned Surfaces

Paring away the surface reveals the texture of the clay. When grogged clay is turned particles of grog catch against the tool and drag along the surface making horizontal scratches. To compress the surface of a turned pot and make it especially smooth, press on it while it is spinning with a broad wooden modelling tool. When there is grog present it will be forced below the surface and there will be no scratches.

Jigger and Jolley

The jigger and jolley are used to form cups, bowls, plates and saucers. The processes involved are a combination of mould making,

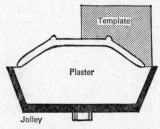

Fig. 195. Jigger and jolley: the sectional drawing shows the hump mould and template used to form the top and underneath surface of a plate.

throwing and turning. The difficulties involved in throwing a plate or saucer on the wheel must be obvious. These difficulties are overcome by making a hump mould for the upper profile of the plate or

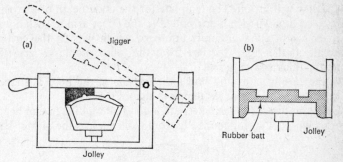

Fig. 196. (a) An improvised jigger arm; (b) rubber batt used to form the hump mould.

saucer, and using a metal template cut to the exact profile to shape the under-surface of the plate.

Factory equipment for jiggering is necessarily heavy and expensive,

but if you are keen to make tea-sets or coffee-sets it is worth improvising the equipment. Fig. 196 illustrates the principle. As you can
see a cup head (which can be purchased) is necessary, although even
here with a little ingenuity a substitute could be devised. Podmore's,
for instance, supply an ingenious rubber tile batt which fits over the
wheel head, on which a cylindrical plaster base could be cast in a
cottle.

Metal templates are necessary for both profiles and zinc or
aluminium will do unless you are going into production in a big

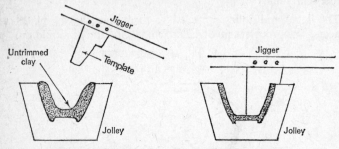

Fig. 197. Mould and template used to form a cup.

way. Having made the plaster block to go on the wheel head, remove
the card or lino cottle wall. Turn the block to shape with the inside
profile, bringing the jigger arm down steadily while the wheel rotates
fairly fast. This forms the hump mould for the top surface of the plate.
The plastic clay is spread out on the rotating mould by throwing
(if you have difficulty use sheet clay). Do not use the hump too dry
or the clay will lift off. The template for the underneath of the plate
is screwed to a wooden block bolted to the jigger arm in such a way
that its height can be simply adjusted, which will fix the cutting
template at the right distance from the jolley mould to give the
plate the thickness required.

In the case of cups and bowls the outside of the bowl is shaped
in the mould and the jigger template shapes the inside.

Extractor heads for the wheel are a good alternative to cup heads
for this work. A spring-loaded bottom plate enables the plaster batt

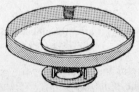

Fig. 198. An extractor head which will eject the thrown pot on the batt.

to be ejected easily. (Cup heads and attachments can be seen at and purchased from the Fulham Pottery (London) to fit on one of the wheels it supplies.)

Recapitulatory Notes on Chapters 12 and 13

Points to remember on throwing and turning.

Throwing

1. Thinning the clay and simultaneously raising a wall are effected by two equal and opposite squeezing pressures with the hands. Pressure is greatest where the clay is thickest.

2. After opening the ball raise the thick clay from the base at the start. Later on it will not work.

3. Shaping is the result of directional pressure unaccompanied by positive squeezing. The position of the hands (fingers, thumb, bent index finger, etc.) is related to the shape being formed.

4. Shaping actions should be rhythmic and continuous (but do not stroke the clay!). The pot grows from the wheel in a series of complete movements.

5. Using too much water rots the clay and causes it to slump. How much is too much water, depends on the nature of the clay.

6. Using too little water causes friction, which can induce eccentricity, rippling and folding. Too much pressure near the top of the pot can have a similar effect.

7. The speed of the wheel is an individual matter. Generally speaking start fast and finish slow.

8. Keep the top of the pot level and slightly thicken the rim for strength.

9. The longer you take to throw a pot the more the clay (and you) will suffer from fatigue; but probably the pot will slump first.

10. Keep hands, arms and body steady. Relax. Do not hold your breath!

Turning

1. Cut the pot from the wheel using:

(a) Steel wire, plain or twisted
(b) Brass wire
(c) Nylon thread, plain or twisted
(d) A steel spatula
(e) A spear.

Pots on batts should be cut before drying. The base shrinks and can crack if it continues to adhere to the batt.

2. Pots for turning should dry slowly and evenly.

I

3. Where a base is horizontally uneven scrape it flat before turn-ing, or use a sharp-pointed turning tool to cut a series of ridges breaking up the uneven surface. After ploughing the surface in this way, flatten the ridges with a broad-edged tool. Repeat the process until the base is flat and level.

4. Give careful thought to the best method of securing the pot for turning. Make sure it is secure.

5. Do not attempt to turn an eccentric pot.

6. Do not attempt to turn a pot unless it is centred.

7. If the base is ragged at the perimeter trim it as accurately as possible by hand. Centre it and cut downwards with a pointed tool to trim any remaining unevenness.

8. Cut a light circular groove, adjacent to the perimeter. Use it as a guide for re-centring if the pot shifts.

9. Do not hold the turning tool parallel to the pot but at a slight angle, or you may cause chattering and juddering. The surface of your pot will look like the shore when the tide is out—interesting but uneven.

Other causes: (a) Blunt tools
              (b) Dry clay
              (c) Eccentricity.

Possible cures, one at a time or altogether:

              (a) Fine grooving before resuming turning
              (b) Damping the clay
              (c) Using a sharper tool
              (d) Reversing the direction of the wheel.

CHAPTER FOURTEEN

POTTERY OF THE PAST

Introduction

The origins of pottery are associated with an early period in the life of man when agriculture was developed as a means of existence, and consequently there was a need for sturdy containers in which to store grain. From coiled baskets to coiled pots was probably a natural development, once it was realised that clay became hard and immutable from prolonged contact with fire; or it may have been due to the chance burning of baskets, sealed with clay to caulk the gaps, whilst the women were cooking food. All early pottery was baked in a fire and blackened on the outside. Fragmented remains have been found buried with the dead, and these are the sole record of various ancient civilisations.

Pot-making was an essential part of domestic life, and thus women were the potters in early times, as they still are in some native tribes. But as men established a settled society and marketing began, so the smith and the potter arrived, and male craftsmanship, once established, became a tradition handed from father to son.

The Middle East and Egypt

The Middle East countries developed pottery making about 5000 B.C. From the primitive, fire-blackened pottery a more cultured ware developed, decorated freely with coloured slips and fired in a kiln. In Mesopotamia the wheel seems to have been used a thousand years later, though it did not reach the great centre of civilisation, Egypt, for yet another thousand years or more. However, the Egyptians had discovered glass, probably through the chance fusion of suitable materials which existed together naturally in the Middle East area—sand and soda, but the use of a glassy coating to make clay water-proof did not occur to them for some time and meanwhile the only improvement in this direction was to burnish the clay with a hard implement in an attempt to seal the pores. Figurines and jewellery from this period can be seen in the museums, made of the so-called Egyptian **faience.** This was a paste concocted from a mixture of silica (obtained by pulverising quartz) with organic material to give plasticity, and soda to make a degree of fusion possible. Bright colours were obtained, especially from copper which gave a lovely turquoise

243

blue. Eventually this led to the development of an alkaline glaze which, fired at a comparatively low temperature, produced bright colours, but did not adhere particularly successfully. Pottery had little more than domestic status in a civilisation where the rich ate off plates of gold.

Crete: the Minoans

The story moves north-east to the island of Crete, occupied by the Minoans, who established a particularly lively civilisation. Their painting and pottery reflected their vigour. The customary **black ware** quickly developed into a variety of vessels of heavy but vital form, decorated with bands of freely-painted geometric motifs in white and black. Learning the use of the wheel, the Minoans developed subtler forms, which they covered with marine and floral patterns. About 1500 B.C., in the final period of this civilisation, the pots were full and rounded or oval. The painted decorations seem imbued with life, especially where they used their very favourite motif, that strange marine animal, the octopus. Painted in dark, flowing brush strokes, it appeared to embrace the pot it decorated with its tentacles. They also modelled charming figurines of Cretan women with bell-shaped skirts and topless bodices.

Mycenaean Pottery

At this time southern Greece was overrun by the Mycenaeans from the north. These people quickly learnt about pottery making from Cretan potters who migrated to the mainland. They developed their own characteristic style. The new shapes they evolved were more refined than the Minoan, for they were to be the genesis of the classic Greek style, with its concept of elegance.

Before the Golden Age began the Mycenaeans were subjugated by the Dorians, a crude people lacking culture. After three hundred years during which only peasant pottery was produced, a creative spirit began to appear again. The Mycenaean shapes of the past were reintroduced and, as the potters developed new skills, they achieved greater refinements of form.

Greek Pottery

Protogeometric and Geometric

The earliest Greek painting on vases is almost Neolithic in character. The **Protogeometric** style consisted of encircling bands filled in with concentric circles painted in a dark slip on natural red clay. The **Geometric** style retained the formal bands but was more complex; it was still severely abstract but more detailed, with triangles, chevrons and swastikas. Soon geometric stylisations of human and animal figures in formal panels were introduced, and a tendency towards naturalism became established.

The next phase showed the influence of trade with Asia Minor. Oriental motifs based on mythology were borrowed and much pottery was decorated with fantastic, highly stylised animal forms. This rather florid pottery was decorative and amusing. Athens became very much the centre of creativity and it was there that the next phase began.

The Black Figure Style

The **Black Figure** style shows a further move towards naturalism. Human figures are silhouetted in black on a red background and the outlines and detail incised in a clear and sensitive line. Homeric themes were illustrated, so the painting becomes pictorial, narrative and dramatic. At the same time the forms of the pots became more elaborate. The shapes were confined to a fixed order of vases, pitchers, jars, bottles and cups. The outline was precise, as if the potter had turned the thrown pot until it corresponded to a prepared pattern. The clay walls were thin and finely finished (see Plate 6).

The Red Figure Style

In the **Red Figure** style the technique became reversed (in the sixth and fifth centuries B.C.) so that the figures appeared in the red of the clay body against a black ground. Detail was painted in black outline using the brush, with highlights in white slip. The slips were highly refined by decanting and thus became virtual glazes. However, glaze as such was not applied to the pot generally as it might have ruined the carefully executed painting. The draughtsmanship was sensitive and beautiful (see Plate 4).

The White Ground Style

In the **White Ground** style the entire surface of tall, thin bottles called *Lekythoi*, and the inside of cups, was covered with white as a ground for black, and sometimes polychrome, painting; unfortunately the white slip used was inclined to flake. The drawing was very delicate and refined, and showed an awareness of foreshortening and perspective. Pots were signed both by the potter and the artist, but this was not a very successful partnership because the artists became too preoccupied with clever drawing and polychrome painting. Decorative harmony was lost, and the art of the potter declined.

Etruscan Pottery

The pottery of Etruria (Italy before the Roman Empire) in the eighth century B.C. was black, not blackened by smoke but fired in a reducing kiln; it is known as 'Bucchero'. The Etruscans were probably the first to use an engraved wheel to roll borders on soft clay. They combined these borders with lively stylised animal forms, engraved or modelled on their pottery. Their latest work included notable life-sized figures and busts in terra-cotta.

Roman (Arretine) Ware

The Romans established potteries wherever they conquered, but the original type-ware was made at Arretium, nowadays called Arezzo. It is therefore known as **Arretine Ware**, and sometimes, but mistakenly, as **Samian** from a fictitious connection with the island of Samos. This is a red, polished, rather waxy and thinly fabricated ware normally formed in a mould and turned on the inside. The designs, which are in medium-high relief, are in reverse in the actual mould. Several seals (stamps) were often used, arranged as a repeating pattern—hence the name *terra sigillata* (sealed clay). There are many good examples, unearthed at Verulamium, in the museum at St. Albans.

Chinese Pottery

Introduction

As in other lands where ceramics were part of a prehistoric culture, Chinese Neolithic pottery was formed from red clay, burnished and decorated with geometric motifs. The first historic Chinese pottery of which we have evidence, dated about 1400 B.C., is a fine white stoneware. The use of high temperatures by the Chinese, so much earlier than by the rest of the world, may have been the result of working closely with metal-workers. Many of the shapes also show metal-work influence.

In the third century B.C. a deliberate use of glaze appeared. Probably this stemmed from the accidental deposits of glaze on pot shoulders and kiln walls, where floating wood ash from the kiln fire had settled, providing potash as a flux to silica in the clay, much as volatilised salt does in salt-glazing. The beauty and variety of pottery made in China over the past three thousand years is due to the unceasing devotion of man with a mystical attitude to the craft, and to the opportune presence of choice ceramic materials such as kaolin and petuntse (China clay and China stone). Continuous pottery making over a long period was bound to build up a great store of knowledge gained by experience and by happy chance. To the Chinese, accidental effects are regarded as a revelation rather than as defects. For this reason a blemish on a pot is prized for its unique qualities. It is difficult for Europeans to understand this, given, as we are, to seeing mud when we look from out our prison bars.

The achievement of Chinese potters is so comprehensive that there are few aspects of form, glaze or decoration which they have not explored. A visit to the ceramic galleries of the Victoria and Albert Museum will convince you of this; the collection of Chinese pottery is amply representative of the various periods and styles.

It is fairly easy to identify the Chinese characteristics of a pot, especially if it is decorated. However, most pots have a local and contemporary, as well as a national, style. It is much more difficult to pinpoint where and when a pot was made. Identifications of Chinese pottery are made by reigning dynasties (lasting one hundred to three hundred years approximately) and more precisely by reigning emperors (rather like our own Georgian, Victorian, etc.), as well as by names of individual potteries, official titles, European nicknames, etc. Chinese words and names mean little to most of us, and so as far as possible only those will be used which are fairly commonly encountered in general reading.

200 B.C. to A.D. 200

In China, as in many ancient civilisations, pottery was buried with the dead. During the period between 200 B.C. and A.D. 200 this included red clay models of everyday creatures and objects, such as servants, domestic animals and buildings. The glaze is shinier than that on earlier pottery. This was due to the use of lead as a flux, a process which may have been learnt from Western Asia or which may have been adopted from glass-making, which the Chinese already understood. **Celadon** is a French term for pottery covered with a very subtly coloured and textured glaze derived from iron oxide fired in a smoky atmosphere. It resembles green jade which the Chinese prized particularly for its delicate beauty. The olive and brownish-green glazes on stoneware of this period were the fore-runners of celadon. The glaze is used most often over delicate carved or incised decoration, where it emphasises the depth of the intaglio line. Celadon glazes occur during many periods in China, Korea and Japan and have been copied recently in Europe.

T'ang Dynasty

T'ang is the name of a three-hundred-year dynastic period from about A.D. 600 (see Plates 15 and 17). There is evidence that translucent porcelain was first made in this period. The name T'ang is well known, the commonest pottery being of a highly porous buff body, partly covered with monochrome and dappled coloured glazes, applied with a sponge. As much as two-thirds of the vessel might be left unglazed, emphasising the beauty of the glaze, and the contrast of colour and texture with that of the clay body. Marbling, by mixing coloured slips on the clay, or by mingling different coloured clays with each other, is used at times. Beautiful animal figures, up to three feet high, were made for inclusion in the tombs (see Plate 19).

Sung Dynasty

Sung (A.D. 960–1279) is regarded as the classical period of Chinese pottery. The main characteristic is an emphasis on beauty of form. Sung is stoneware with a brilliant glaze based on feldspar. Decoration (impressed, incised, carved) is not frequent (see Plate 12). However, there are many types of ware belonging to this dynasty (see Plates 11, 13 and 20). The most common is a superb celadon taking its name from Lung Ch'üan, where pottery was first made in the tenth century. This ware was very popular because there was a tradition that a celadon dish would change colour if it contained poisoned food (see Plate 10). A scarce type of Sung is **Kuan** (meaning *official*) which has a 'crackle' with wide divisions, the craze lines being filled with brown oxide to emphasise them.

Chün ware is known for its lavender glaze suffused with crimson purple. This is what is sometimes called a 'transmutation' glaze, but is better known as **Flambé**—the first example of the reduction of copper oxide to the metallic form during the firing of a glaze. **T'zu Chu** ware of the Sung dynasty is especially admired and emulated nowadays. The kilns were working before A.D. 900 and were still working in 1960. In the Sung period the T'zu Chu potteries made wine-jars and pillows from a greyish stoneware with a transparent glaze. For the first time, surprisingly for a people to whom writing with a brush is second nature, painted decoration was introduced. Floral motifs were painted very freely in black or brown; one variety of ware had black painting under a blue glaze in the manner of the Persians. They also employed scratching through the slip (under glaze sgraffito) and scratching through a dark brown glaze (glaze-sgraffito) (see Plate 20). Finally red, green and yellow, rather primitive enamel (on-glaze) colours were introduced.

Tenmoku was the name given by the Japanese to a black-brown glaze breaking to rust over a dark stoneware body, made in the Sung period. It was prized by them and used in the tea ceremony.

In the next hundred years the wholesale manufacture of white porcelain commenced, and the use of painted decoration was developed further. One innovation was a copper-red used under the glaze (see Plate 14).

Ming Dynasty

During the **Ming** Dynasty (1368–1644) pottery making acquired new vigour, becoming exuberant, masculine and more decorative. Polychrome painting on thin fine porcelain became popular, and replaced stoneware. The largest and most popular group of Ming pottery was painted in underglaze blue (see Plate 16). At first, because the native cobalt contained manganese, it was imported from the Middle East. By the end of the sixteenth century the Chinese knew how to refine their own.

Early in the fifteenth century a style of decoration was evolved using flowers, leaves, fish and birds as motifs. With these, there was an extensive use of a conventional border of rocks and stylised waves (which gave rise to the nickname 'Rock-of-Ages') which typified Ming in European eyes. Other wares of note in the Ming period were the **Wan Li** five-colour ware (green, yellow, dark purple, iron red and blue) and the pierced ware called by the Chinese the equivalent of 'Devil's Work', because of the diabolical skill necessary to make it. An innovation was the use of enamel colours directly on the porcelain body.

In the first half of the eighteenth century the vogue for Chinese porcelain increased in Europe and huge quantities were exported from China. This was during the **Ch'ing** (1644–1912) Dynasty, but the European name for blue-painted porcelain was **Nanking Ware.** Underglaze blue was used as a ground colour, applied by blowing through a bamboo tube with a gauze, and known as 'powder blue'. Ginger jars were most popular right into the early twentieth century. They were decorated with plum blossom in white on a divided blue background representing the cracking ice in spring. Copper red was used for monochrome decoration and known as **Sang-de-boeuf** (oxblood). **Peach Bloom** was another European name given to a white porcelain bearing a pink glaze tinged with green, with reddish spots.

The Emperor K'ang-hsi

The Emperor K'ang-hsi was a very special patron of the arts. It was in his reign that the **famille wares** were produced: best known is **famille verte**, a particular development of the Wan-Li five-colour ware (using on-glaze enamels) with a green ground, but there were also **famille noire** (black ground) and **famille jaune** (yellow ground). The extent of the painted decoration was such that the white of the porcelain was completely hidden. Near the end of his reign, the Chinese obtained an opaque rose-coloured enamel from European sources, and **famille rose** was initiated and developed in the next reign. In the nineteenth and twentieth centuries there has been little further development.

Islamic Pottery

In the seventh century A.D. the Arabs, inspired by Mahomet and the Islamic faith, spread from Arabia, conquering the Middle East and spilling into North Africa and Spain. When things had begun to settle down a characteristic Islamic art evolved: bright colours and abstract and floral motifs were used on the traditional arabesques and inscriptions from the Koran, especially on tiles for the mosques. On pottery these were interpreted in flowing, colourful brushwork (see Plates 5 and 8).

The Near-Eastern potter (like the European in later times) suffered the disadvantage of inferior materials. Competition from China gave the native potter little chance of finding wealthy patrons. Naturally the latter preferred fine white porcelain to the rugged work produced from sandy clays lacking plasticity. In an attempt to rival Chinese pottery the Islamic potters revived the tin-lead glaze which had been used by the Persians as far back as 500 B.C. This gave them a white ground on which they were able to paint freely in bright colours. Temperamentally they inclined towards brilliant colour, which was the sole asset which low-fired pottery offered them. A further development in this direction was to adapt the use of lustres to pottery, which had been used on glass already in the eighth century. These were perfected in the twelfth century and they gradually spread to Europe, where factories were established for their manufacture.

Islamic Influence

The Moors in Spain

Meanwhile the Moors from Mauritania had taken over Spain. There, and in Majorca, they produced some very lively and highly-decorated **lustre work**. The richness of effect almost rivalled that of real gold and silver, which were very scarce at this time, and the possession of sets of lustre ware, decorated mainly with the family coat of arms, became a prestige symbol among the great families. (In this context it is probable that early Egyptian pottery never developed greatly, because of the competition from gold, which was so highly esteemed and comparatively plentiful.) Large platters, about 18 in (4·5 dm) in diameter, were typical. The well-known dish in the Victoria and Albert Museum bears the arms of Isabella of Castile and Ferdinand of Sicily (the date of this is probably 1469). Many platters were mad to imitate Renaissance gold and silver plate, ribbing and gadrooning (an inverted fluting) and applied reliefs were used to imitate metal forms. Added to this the surfaces were covered with painted decoration, mainly in lustre, and the total effect can only be described as sumptuous. The plates and other vessels are thick and of a heavy form, bold but lacking refinement (as is all Islamic pottery) doubtless due to the difficulty of throwing with a lean and sandy clay.

After the Turks had obtained power in the Middle East in the sixteenth century, Turkish potters developed a distinctive style based on a conventional treatment of sprays of identifiable flowers, such as the tulip and carnation, neatly painted and disposed over the surface of the pottery. The painting was polychrome but with a leaning towards the traditional blue.

Italian Majolica

The Italians were first introduced to **tin-glazing** through Hispano/ Moresque wares bought in the course of trade with Majorca. The earliest Italian **Maiolica** (as the Italians called it) is mostly painted with manganese purple and copper green or turquoise (see Plate 23). Antimony yellow was added later. The drug-jar is a favourite shape: basically cylindrical, but with slightly concave walls, it is easy to grasp. Central subjects are human portraits, badges of hospitals for which the jars were made, and heraldic motifs. In the fifteenth century an unvarying stylised **oak-leaf pattern** was used to fill the spaces, so the jars are known as **oak-leaf** jars.

Many styles developed in the next three hundred years as pottery making spread throughout Italy, certainly too many to record. Painting became more elaborate, and was influenced by the Renaissance painters. Finally pottery became a vehicle for the display of virtuosity in painting—overcrowded and confused.

The delicately-modelled terra-cotta statuettes, lead-tin glazed and tastefully coloured, made in the fifteenth century by Luca della Robbia, should be mentioned here although they are well known. He specialised in Madonnas, naked cherubs, etc., altar pieces and fonts, and other objects connected with the church. Tin-glazed earthenware had a long run in Italy but finally lost favour in the nineteenth century when cream-coloured earthenware, perfected by Wedgwood, proved more attractive. The main centres for the production of Majolica in Italy were Florence, Faienza (Faience), Urbino, Castel Durante, Pesaro, Diruta, Forli, Caffaggiolo, Gubbio and Siena, all with their own characteristics.

Delft

In Europe, tin-glazed tiles were made in 1500 at Delft in Holland, decorated with scriptural subjects. The painting was in cobalt, using a fully-loaded brush on the raw tin-glaze. It is possible that a clear glaze was applied over the top, in which case the painting may have been fired first, then the clear glaze applied, and fused in a third firing. This would account for the richness and softness of the blues. Dutch potters introduced this craft to England, working at Lambeth in the latter part of the seventeenth century. One of the della Robbia family introduced tin-glazed ware to France in the second half of the sixteenth century. The French ware was painted with blue in-glaze, and further colours were added in the form of on-glaze decoration by enamels.

At about the same time Bernard Palissy spent all his money and burnt most of the furniture in his home in repeated experiments to obtain a tin-glaze. His most typical (and horrible) work is covered with lifelike replicas of reptiles such as lizards and frogs, which look as if they have been cast from moulds made from natural animals.

English 'Delft' Ware

The tin-glaze technique was introduced into England about 1550 by Flemish potters. By 1780 it too was eclipsed by Wedgwood's cream-coloured earthenware. English tin-glazed pottery is usually referred to as English Delft ware. Main centres of production were at Bristol and Lambeth. The ware is painted all over, but rarely overpainted: the treatment is lucid and fresh, and often contains an element of humour. All the usual oxide colours were used and subjects were royal and other portraits, heraldic, biblical, floral, and abstract patterns, mainly imitating Italian and Dutch styles.

English Peasant Pottery

All that remains of English peasant pottery of very early date usually consists of fragments carefully pieced together. What evidence there is shows that a raw lead glaze was used as far back as the ninth century. By the twelfth century glaze was often used, but generally confined to the insides of pots. In the early work the methods of decoration most in favour were incising, impressing and applying stamped clay reliefs; in a few potteries they used bold brushwork in oxide or slip. The native clays were buff, red and dark brown. On later pottery trailed and sgraffito decoration appears, using a white slip under a honey or treacle-coloured glaze, probably made from the red clay, and lead in one form or another. A black glaze, probably containing manganese, was used on the well-known **Cistercian ware,** so called because many fragments have been found on the sites of Cistercian abbeys such as Fonteins. The most popular shape was the 'Tyg'—a two- or three-handled mug designed to be passed easily from hand to hand amongst the monks.

Up to the seventeenth century the potter sold his wares in his own district. They were simple and unaffected, serving many daily domestic uses: bowls, dishes, tygs, jugs, candlesticks and jars (see Plates 27 and 28). Special pieces were made occasionally in honour of a birthday or similar event, and decorated enthusiastically. During the seventeenth century this was altered, as centres for pottery making began to be established. Stoke-on-Trent figured first among these, as it had the natural advantages of good clays, good water, and plenty of coal to supplant wood as fuel, since the latter was no longer plentiful.

The work of Thomas Toft bridges the change. Thomas' platters are well known; their immense size (up to 22 in wide) and bold slip trailed decoration, white on red clay, challenge the eye wherever they are displayed. The subjects, ranging from kings to mermaids, are depicted in a naive style which could only be English. Soon slip decoration was superseded by the use of a raised line produced from an engraved biscuit mould. The decoration was carved or incised on a leather-hard clay hump mould which was baked before it was used for making dishes. The raised lines enclosed areas which were filled with coloured slips.

Peasant pottery was still made in Sussex in the eighteenth century and Brighton Museum has some excellent examples of this local ware. The local clay contained undigested impurities which gave a characteristic speckle to the pottery. The Sussex potters were also fond of marbled, runny and speckled effects. Novelties are an English feature and a special Sussex novelty is the Sussex Drinking Pig. Its body, sat on its haunches, serves as a jug and the head twists off to become a cup.

John Dwight's Stoneware

One of the first developers on the pottery scene was the scholarly John Dwight who founded the Fulham Pottery, still extant. He introduced stoneware to the British market, taking out a patent for its manufacture. A glaze was not essential, as the high-fired vitreous body was waterproof, so he compromised by using the cheap **salt-glaze** technique which did not require a second firing. Fulham produced jars, bottles and mugs for public houses, bearing their own particular device in the form of a raised clay seal applied to the pot surface (see Plates 25 and 30).

Josiah Wedgwood

Others copied Dwight in spite of his patent, and the popularity of stoneware increased until Josiah Wedgwood and his cream-coloured ware caused a slump. Wedgwood started as an apprentice to his brother in 1744 and in twenty years he dominated English pottery. He produced well-made and designed ware at a low price, but later turned to making expensive copies of antique pottery.

European Porcelain

English pottery making became efficient and competitive until the end of the nineteenth century. Continental potteries had been playing the status game in pursuit of an indigenous porcelain, and in 1770 the Germans succeeded in making the hardest porcelain ever, using their own china stone. The French invented an artificial porcelain (soft paste, as it is known) by the mid-eighteenth century, and succeeded in making true porcelain a hundred years later. The English joined in the game rather later with a soft paste of their own, and from then on were involved in turning out expensive ceramic fine art on the one hand, and mass-produced tableware on the other. It was not until the Martin brothers set up their three-man pottery in Southall in 1877 that the contemporary studio potter was born.

POTTERY MACHINERY AND EQUIPMENT

A brief description of some of the machinery designed to lighten the task of preparing materials or to assist in the manufacturing processes follows. Much of this is available to non-industrial pottery establishments and is to be seen in the educational catalogues.

Bench Whirlers, Heavy Bench Whirlers, Decorators' Lining Wheel, Banding Wheel. These have been referred to already on pages 28,

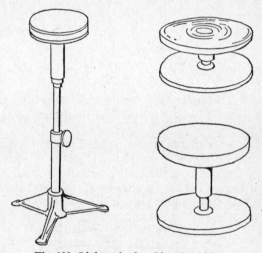

Fig. 199. Lining wheel and bench whirlers.

39 and 183. The heavy bench whirler is cast iron and runs on ball-bearings. The lining wheel is adjustable for height and is also useful as a modelling stand.

Blunger. A heavy machine for mixing clay slip, consisting of a hexagonal vat with a rotating paddle operated from above, which reduces raw lump, powdered or plastic clay to slip. The slip is run off through a tap at the bottom, usually into a sifter. It has a $\frac{1}{2}$ h.p. electric motor (see Fig. 200).

Damp Storage Cabinets. These are made of galvanised sheet metal, with nylon sealing strips behind the hinged doors and are about 4 ft

(12 dm) × 3 ft (9 dm) and 1–2 ft (3–6 dm) deep. They are very useful for keeping work damp. Do not buy the sliding-door type, since clay dust and bits get in the grooves and interfere with the action.

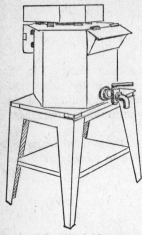

Fig. 200. A blunger.

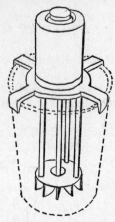

Fig. 201. Electric mixer.

The Electric Grindstone. It is used for grinding stilt marks and glaze drops from the bases of pots and for sharpening potter's knives and turning tools.

Electric Mixer. Similar to an electric paint mixer, it is more sturdy as it is especially designed to mix slips and glazes. It is probably the most helpful item of motorised equipment for a small pottery or school as it can be left to get on with the job and does it more efficiently. Costs about £40 at present.

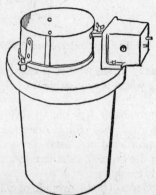

Fig. 202. Electric sifter.

Electric Sifter. Used for sifting wet or dry materials (portable).

Vibratory Screen. Used for sieving quantities of slips and glazes rapidly. Both machines take standard sieves (lawns) and work on the oscillatory principle, working off an ordinary electric light socket or plug if necessary. The screen is static, being fixed on its own 5-gallon tub, but the sifter is portable and is not attached to a container.

Filter Press. A machine in which slip is fed into cloth-lined compartments and the water is pressed out to form moist layers for pugging.

The Gauge Post. An aid for repetition work in throwing: the arms have rubber pointers to indicate the height and width limits when

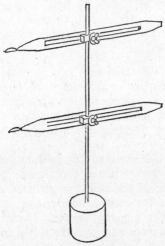

Fig. 203. Gauge post.

throwing. A similar arrangement is easy to devise using wood and wing nuts. Even simpler are two pieces of pointed dowel stuck in clay!

Hand Presses and Power Presses. Industrial tiles are made from powdered clay by machine. The powder is swept into a metal mould, a die comes down on a screw thread, or by power-operated mechanical action, and presses the clay to the predetermined thickness. An ejection device operated from below then lifts the tile out of the mould, it is removed and the process is repeated *ad infinitum*.

Jar Mill. Raw materials, fritts, glazes and colours can be ground in porcelain jars which contain round pebbles or porcelain balls (therefore otherwise known as a **ball mill** which is larger, with a

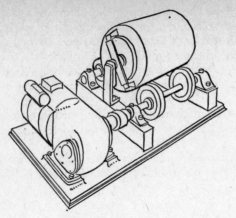

Fig. 204. Jar mill.

lined cylinder, for industrial use) and is suitable for schools or studios. Models are made to accommodate one jar or two jars at a time. The rollers which rotate the jars are adjustable to take more than one size of jar. A vibration mill is a later development which uses an opposed reciprocating action to grind faster than the ball mill.

Pottery Lathes. Made especially for finishing pottery by turning on a chuck. Spindles are provided for turning plaster models for moulding. Moulding as you will have gathered is used extensively, if not exclusively, in the pottery industry.

Pug-mills. Used for 'pugging' the clay. The mill is rather like an oversize mincing machine and gives the clay a rehash. It consists of a metal barrel or cylinder, tapered at one end to a die (a type of metal template) through which the clay is forced by a screw. A pug-mill is very useful for adding extra materials to clay such as sand and grog, as well as reconstituting used clay. Large versions are fitted with a vacuum pump. They are made in two versions, horizontal or vertical. They are not self-feeding so they have to be attended and fed. If clay is allowed to dry in the barrel some mills are very difficult to clean out (check this point if ever you think of buying one).

A more recent version is the Doughmixer–Pug-mill which will also produce plastic clay from powdered materials and water. In the normal pug-mill the clay is fed into a hopper and a pressure plate attached to a lever is used to force in the clay. In the doughmixer the clay is taken from the hopper by rollers so no pressure is necessary.

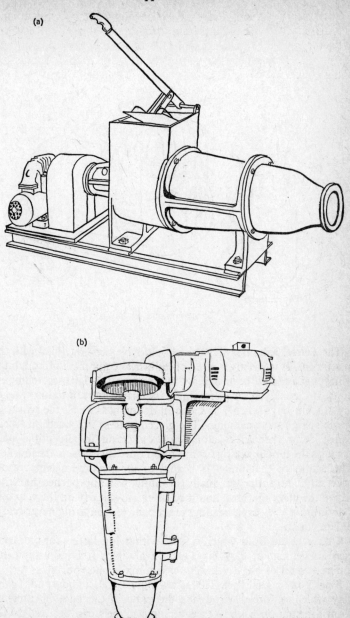

Fig. 205. (a) Horizontal pug-mill; (b) Vertical pug-mill.

Spray Gun and Booth. These have been referred to on pages 55 and 157. Used for slips, glazes and decoration, the booth has an extractor fan, filter, and exhaust tube to connect the apparatus to the outside atmosphere via a window or vent. Mobile booths are obtainable.

Fig. 206. Spray gun and compressor.

The Tunnel Kiln. Possibly this should have been included with the other kilns. It is strictly a piece of industrial equipment although the concept may have been based originally on the Japanese climbing kilns. It has played an increasingly important part in industry since my student days when I saw one in action at Carter's tile works in Poole some forty years ago. The glazed pottery is loaded on trucks which draw themselves along a track at an imperceptible pace through the tunnel, taking twenty-four hours to complete the journey. The centre of the tunnel is heated to the maximum temperature necessary. The pottery gradually gets hotter as it approaches the centre where the glaze matures, and it cools equally slowly on the way out. This ensures very even heating, exact control, and firing never ceases day or night.

Universal Bin Dolly which is fitted with nylon casters for quiet and easy movement of clay bins, etc. Invaluable! It is adjustable for different sizes of bin. (N.B. You could make one yourself.)

Wad Box or Dod Box. This is a simple metal cylinder, filled with clay which is forced through a die plate in the base by pressure from a piston on a screw thread. Some models can be fixed to the edge of a shelf or table, others are fixed over a hole in a bench. Wads —strips of fireclay—were used to seal the lid on saggars (the protective fireclay boxes in which glazed ware was fired). Nowadays the wad box is used to produce coils or strips for handles, etc., the extruded section is shaped by the hole in the die.

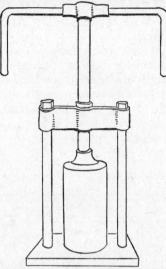

Fig. 207. Wad or dod box.

Wheel and the Jigger and Jolley. These have been mentioned before, on page 239. Heavy industrial-type wheels cost (at present) £300–£400 as against £150 or so for the studio electric wheel. The industrial jigger and jolley is not something you would expect to meet in the local school or even art school, because this also costs about £300.

The Ceramic Workshop

The basic equipment for a classroom or studio pottery should include the following:

Necessary Items

1. Kiln, kiln shelves, interlocking props, stilts, pyrometric cones, placing powder (flint, etc.).
2. Clay bins (3 for each sort of clay) i.e., red clay, grogged clay, white clay, etc.
    (a) Clay fresh from supplier.
    (b) Too-dry-to-use clay.
    (c) Clay in soak for reconstitution.
3. Wedging surface (concrete paving slabs built up on bricks).
4. Benches
    (a) One for Clay Work—slate or hardwood surface.

    (b) One for Glazing—hard or soft plastic cover.

    (c) One for Decorating—(with shelves above for colours and brushes).

5. Cupboards

    (a) Wooden or metal cupboard for glazed pottery awaiting glost firing.

    (b) Cupboard for biscuit pottery (or shelves with clear plastic sheeting hanging in front of them).

    (c) Damp cupboard or cellar (this is the best place to store unfinished work—underground!).

6. Plaster slab for drying clay—this is made from fine white plaster and should be about 3 ft × 4 ft × 4 in (9 dm × 12 dm × 1 dm) thick to dry 1 cwt (50 kg) of clay slop.

7. Bin for plaster.

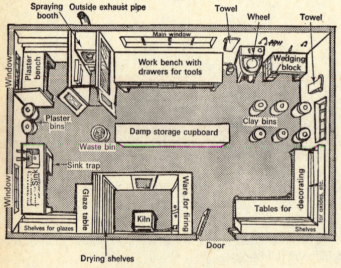

Fig. 208. The ceramic workshop.

Optional Items

These are the machinery and equipment already described. The most useful in a small pottery are:

Throwing wheel, cupboards, extractor heads, plaster batts, jigger and jolley.

Spare set of kiln elements.

Pyrometer. Electric grinding wheel.

Electric mixer. Electric spray and spraying booth.

Bins for sand, grog, powdered fireclay.

Tools not Illustrated

(a) Surform tool (with non-clogging teeth) for planing leather-hard clay.

(b) Carborundum stick for grinding off stilt marks, etc.

(c) Hacksaw blades (old ones will do).

Equipment Illustrated

Plastic Ware

1. Square storage containers for oxides, etc., with recessed lid: easy for stacking.

2. Plastic buckets with recessed snap-on lids with metal carrying handles for storing glaze, clay and slip.

3. General-purpose bowl for mixing plaster, glazing, slip coating etc.

4. Plastic funnels for transferring liquid slips and glazes, and for filling slip trailers, etc.

5. Measuring jugs.

6. Small and large scoops for measuring and weighing materials generally.

7. Small storage bowls with snap-on lids.

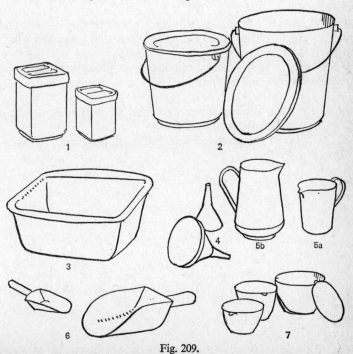

Fig. 209.

Equipment for Preparing Glazes, Slips and Colours

8. Scales.

9. Metric weights.

10. Spring balance.

11. Potter's measure—for measuring the pint weight of a slip or glaze.

12. Glass muller for grinding oxides, colours, and small quantities of glaze etc.

13. Glass slab for use with the muller.

14–15. Pestle and mortar for grinding raw materials and colours by hand.

16–18. Brushes for passing slips and glazes through sieves and lawns. Obtainable from potters' suppliers. No. 19 is a hog hair which can be used for splatter.

20. Domestic (sink) brush, obtainable at your local hardware shop, also very good for passing slips, etc., through lawns and sieves.

21. Sieve with wooden frame and fixed phosphor-bronze mesh (various mesh sizes from 30 to 200).

22. Cup lawns are provided with 100 mesh (for slip).

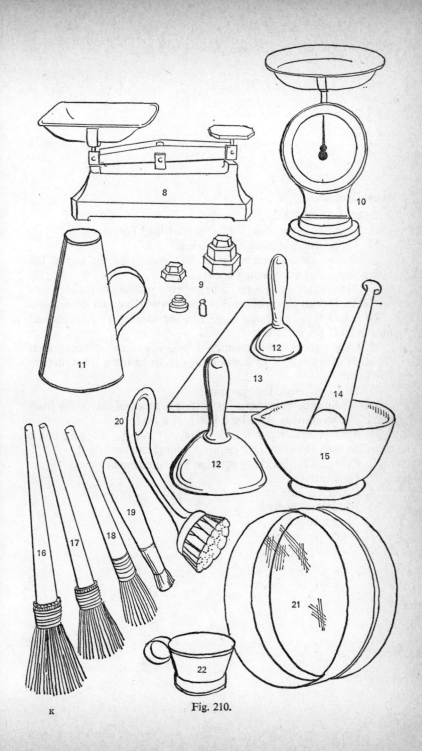

K

Fig. 210.

Tools Illustrated

Bamboo Tools (23 to 27)

23. Comb: for grooving and cross-hatching (darning).

24. Knife: for trimming and scoring.

25. Spear: used to remove pots, lids, etc., from the top of the hump; also used for shaping spouts.

26. Fluters: used like a plane to cut even grooves in the clay surface. The fork at the other end is used for scoring and decoration.

27(a) and (b). Small and large ribs for shaping clay forms and finishing off the surface.

28. Clay cutters (cheese-cutter type), nylon or stainless steel (twisted) wire attached to wooden toggles, or to brass rings (improvised cutter).

29. Small harp used for trimming.

30. Medium or large harp for cutting a series of clay slabs from one block by moving the wire a notch at a time.

31. Spatula or scraper for cleaning clay off the wedging block etc., also used sometimes for removing pots from the wheel.

32. Callipers for checking external measurements.

33. Hole cutter.

34. Potter's needle.

35. Natural sponges.

36. Sponge stick.

37. Synthetic sponges.

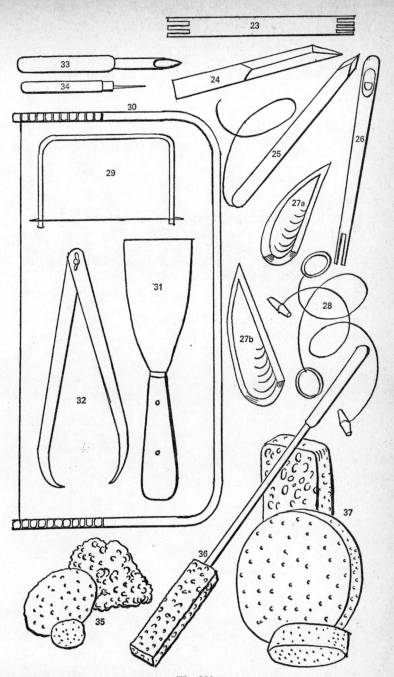

Fig. 211.

Further Tools

38–39. Kidney-shaped and rectangular steel palettes.
40. Kidney-shaped rubber palette.
41. Boxwood modelling tools.
42. Steel modelling tools for leather-hard and dry clay and plaster.
43. Wire modelling tools.
44. Potter's knife.
45. Slip trailers.
46. Scissors for templates and stencils.
47–48. Rolling-pin and rolling guides.

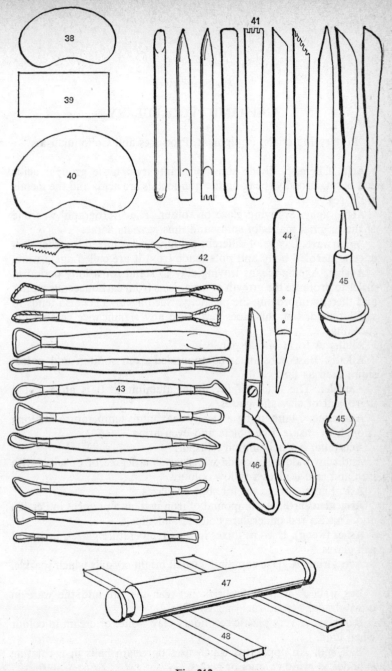

Fig. 212.

A CERAMIC VOCABULARY

Pottery Materials, Equipment, Processes and Colloquialisms

Acid. Chemists divide substances into two basic groups: acids and bases. Broadly speaking the non-metals are acids and the metals are bases.

Aerography. Spraying glaze or colour. The 'Aerograph' was one of the original makes of spray and thus gave its name.

Agate ware. Layers of different-coloured clays mixed together produce a marbled body and pots made from it are called agate ware.

Ageing. Ageing means leaving clay to stand for a long period in order to promote the growth of organisms from carbonaceous matter and thereby improving the plasticity. Such ageing clay also tends to smell putrid, but this does not have any significance ceramically speaking.

Albite. A form of feldspar.

Alkalis. Base substances compounded from sodium and potassium, used as fluxes.

Alumina. The oxide of the metal aluminium. It is an essential ingredient of clay and glazes.

Annealing. Maintaining a steady maximum temperature for long enough to ensure a complete and even firing.

Anorthite. An uncommon feldspar.

Antimony oxide. An oxide which gives a degree of opacity; with iron and lead it gives a yellow colour.

Ark. Large storage vat for slips or glazes.

Armenian earth. A compound of iron used as a pigment in Persian and Turkish red underglaze colours and slips.

Ashes (wood). Used as fluxes in high temperature glazes, i.e. wood ash glazes.

Aventurine. A glaze containing small bright crystals which sparkle.

Bag wall. A wall of firebrick between the fire and the ware in down-draught (solid-fuel or gas) kilns.

Ball clay. A very plastic secondary clay, white or cream in colour when fired.

Ball mill. An apparatus which uses porcelain balls in a rotating cylinder to grind colours or glazes.

Banding. Application of bands of colour by hand or machine.

Bank kiln. A kiln built on a sloping surface, e.g. a natural bank.

Barium (baryta, barytes). A rare metal (its oxide, the common ore).

Barium carbonate. A small addition to a clay body prevents surface scum forming.

Basalt ware. Black vitreous body so named because it resembles the black basalt rocks: first made in 1768 by Wedgwood.

Batts (bats). Refractory shelves used to support pottery during firing; or discs of clay used in jiggering plates and saucers, etc. In industry batts are beaten out on a batting machine.

Batt wash. Infusible water and flint, etc. A mixture used to paint shelves as a guard against ware sticking.

Bauxite. Rare ore containing pure alumina.

Bedding. Supports ware in sand during biscuit firing.

Bentonite. A fine clay resulting from the weathering of volcanic ash. Assists suspension of particles in glaze.

Bichromate of potash. Used to make an orange-red pigment.

Bisque or biscuit. Once-fired pottery (bisque kiln).

Biscuit stopping. Cracks in biscuit ware are filled before glazing. A piece of biscuit (or pitcher) from the same firing is ground to a fine powder and mixed with flux or gum (or both) to make a stopping paste. The pot is dampened and the 'stopping' forced into the crack.

Bismuth oxide. This has a similar action to lead oxide, but greater fusibility.

Black cores. Caused when the outside of the body becomes dense too early, with the result that the carbon is unable to escape and forms a black core.

Blisters. The result of bubbles formed in a body or in a glaze due to the rapid escape of gases.

Bloating. Blistering on a large scale.

Blowing. The bursting of pots due to too rapid heating or air trapped in the body.

Blunger. A hexagonal vat with rotating paddle for mixing slip.

Body. The natural clay of which a pot is formed; materials mixed together for the formation of pottery; or the main part of the pot as distinct from the glaze.

Bond. Glossy materials formed between particles during firing.

Bone china. English soft porcelain blended from calcined ox-bone, china clay and flint.

Bottle-oven. A coal-fired kiln once used extensively. As its name implies, it is shaped like a huge bottle.

Borax. A compound of boric oxide and sodium oxide: a flux.

Boric acid. This acid is used instead of borax where sodium is not required.

Boric oxide. Another important low-temperature flux.

Borocalcite (colemanite). A mineral containing boric oxide: a natural fritt.

Borosilicate. Boric oxide and silica fused together.

Brass wire. Used for cutting clay because it does not corrode.

Bung. A pile of saggars or ware.

Calcareous clays. Lime-bearing clays.

Calcination. The firing of materials before grinding them for use in pottery making, whereby volatile substances are driven off by heating.

Calcite. Another name for calcium carbonate (the material from which whiting is prepared).

Calcium carbonate. Whiting, chalk and limestone, as far as glaze making is concerned.

Calcium oxide. Known familiarly as lime, as it is corrosive it is obtained by using chalk, marble, limestone or whiting.

Callipers. Hinged arms for measuring round openings, covers, etc.

Cane ware. Light buff stoneware used in filters and sanitary ware. Old-fashioned hot-water bottles were made of it.

Carbonates. A fine form of metal used as pottery stains, etc., in preference to coarser oxides.

Carbon dioxide. Freed by the decomposition of carbonates in a glaze when fired.

Case mould. Replicas of the prototype from which production moulds are made.

Casting. Forming hollow shapes in a mould using a liquid. In the case of pottery slip is used (casting slip).

Celadon. Originating in Korea and China, this is a ware covered with a very subtle pale grey-green glaze (obtained from a small amount of iron), fired in a reduction atmosphere.

Cement. Cement is formed from a mixture of calcined lime and clay.

Ceramic (Greek—keramos). A general word for all pottery and pottery processes. Also used today in connection with industries such as glass and cement.

Charging. Packing the kiln.

Chatter. When turning, a blunt or incorrectly held tool may produce ridges which *bang* against the tool.

China. In England this name is in common use to describe English bone china, but the original reference was to Chinese porcelain. It is used colloquially to describe almost any form of pottery, and so it ceases to have any real significance as a specific term.

China clay. Primary clay sometimes called kaolin from the Chinese word for clay. Very large amounts are used in the paper industry.

China stone (Cornish stone). Partly decomposed granite.

Chromium oxide. Used as a glaze stain for green, pink, orange and brown.

Clamming. A mixture of sand and wet clay used to seal the kiln door.

Clay. $Al_2O_3 \cdot 2SiO_2 \cdot 2H_2O$. A stable chemical compound resistant to chemical attack.

Clay press (filter press). A machine which filters and presses out water from clay slip.

Colloidal (Greek—Kolla; glue). Refers to properties of viscosity and plasticity, especially in clays.

Combing. A blunt rubber or wooden comb used to produce patterns in wet, coloured slips, similar to those used in decorative book-papers.

Combined water. Water which, being combined chemically with clay, requires heating to a comparatively high temperature before it is driven off.

Copper oxide (cuprous oxide). An oxide used as a green stain, but it also gives red. Originally mined in Cyprus.

Cottle. A wall of stiff waterproof material used to contain liquid plaster until it hardens.

Crackle (craquele). Crazing used intentionally as a form of decoration and emphasised by rubbing oxides into the cracks (then usually re-fired).

Crank. A form of kiln shelf.

Crawling. Bare patches where the glaze has failed to adhere or has retracted.

Crazing. A mismatch of glaze and body. The glaze has greater contraction and therefore splits, causing fine cracks: these are usually, but not always, distributed fairly evenly.

Cristobalite. Quartz heated to a high temperature: a form of silica.

Crockery. General term for kitchen and table ware.

Crystallisation. Crystals forming in slowly-cooled glazes.

Cullet. Crushed or ground glass. (The French word from which it is derived is *collet*—a little neck.) Actually the little neck is that left on the glass-blowing iron when the blown shape has been removed.

Damper. Shutter used to control draughts in a kiln flue.

Deflocculent. A chemical added to slip to increase fluidity (without adding water).

Delft. Dutch opaque (tin) glazed earthenware imitating painted Chinese porcelain.

Devitrification. Crystallisation in a cooling glaze.

Dishing. Warping of flat ware: the edges rise.

Dolly. A tool for stirring ceramic liquids.

Dolomite. A common rock found in England, containing calcium and magnesium carbonates.

Drawing. Unpacking a kiln.

Dunting. Chipping caused by cold draughts on fired ware or by too rapid cooling.

Earthenware. Non-vitreous opaque pottery, usually white or ivory. It fires between 1050°C and 1180°C.

Efflorescence. A scum on the surface caused by soluble salts in the body.

Embossing. Decorating with small relief decorations called 'sprigs' pressed from moulds and applied to the surface of pots.

Enamel. Coloured soft-firing flux painted or transferred onto the fired glaze, then fired between 700°C and 800°C.

Encaustic decoration. This decoration is an inlay of contrasting coloured clay and it is usually seen in the form of encaustic tiles.

Eutectic. A mixture of two substances which has a lower melting point than either of them: as this is an unpredictable phenomenon it can produce freak results in glazes.

Extrusion. Forcing clay through a die.

Faience. The French name for tin-glazed earthenware originating at Faienza in Italy. The term is sometimes used loosely to describe earthenware in general.

Fat clay. Highly plastic clay.

Fat oil. This comes from evaporated turpentine and is the traditional vehicle for underglaze and on- (over) glaze painting.

Feathering. Dragging the tip of a feather through bands of coloured slip to form a thin line.

Fettling. The removal of the seam from slip cast ware and finishing off the surface of leather-hard pottery.

Filter press. See Clay press.

Fireclays. Found beneath coal seams, they are pure, plastic, and capable of withstanding high temperatures.

Firing. Subjecting pottery to heat in order to develop a vitreous bond.

Flaking. Raw slips and glazes flake off if they contract too much when drying: also dust or grease on the biscuit can cause flaking of the glaze, as can over-firing.

Flambé. Term for Chinese pottery with red and purple glazes.

Flat ware. Potter's term distinguishing dishes, plates, etc., from hollow ware.

Flint. Found in knobbly pebble form in chalk country, it is almost pure silica.

Flocculation. The addition of a suitable electrolyte to aid suspension ('flocking of particles') in a slip or glaze.

Fluorspar or fluorite. A mineral which is more fusible than feldspar as a flux.

Flux. A substance which lowers the melting point of the materials to which it is added.

Fritt (or frit). Ceramic materials heated until they form a glass; they are then cooled and pulverised.

Frizzling. The term used to describe curling and lifting of painted or transferred decoration, because too rapid firing makes the binding medium erupt.

Fusible clays. These clays vitrify and partially collapse at below 1200°C.

Fusion. Any treatment which melts a solid substance.

Galena or lead sulphide. Used in the past as a lead glaze on red clay ware. It is highly poisonous.

Gilding. This is effected by the use of very fine gold dust, or gold compounds, fired on the vitrified glaze at 800°C.

Glaze and glass. These are produced by the fusion of silica.

Glost. An adjectival form of the word 'glaze': thus 'glost kiln', 'glost firing', 'glost ware'.

Green ware. Unfired clay ware.

Grog. Pulverised biscuit (pitchers, shards).

Gypsum. The mineral from which Plaster of Paris is made.

Hard paste. Another name for true porcelain (feldspathic).

Hollow ware. As distinct from flat ware, is the trade name for pots with necks narrower than the widest part of the body.

Hovel. The brick structure enclosing a bottle-necked kiln.

Ilmenite. An oxide of iron and titanium.

Impermeability. The non-porousness of a vitrified glaze or body.

Impressed decoration. This is stamped into the damp clay when it is just hard enough to withstand the pressure.

In-glaze. This term is used to describe the majolica technique: the pigment is applied on the raw glaze and fused into it.

Intaglio. The old term for pottery transfers printed from engraved metal plates.

Intermittent. Where the kiln is filled with ware, fired, then emptied, this is known as an intermittent kiln, as distinct from a continuous kiln.

Iridium oxide. This is used as an underglaze black.

Iron. More than any other metal iron is used as a ceramic pigment and stain. There are a number of forms of iron oxide including black, red and yellow.

Ironstone china. A hard, fine earthenware, it is not china at all: 'ironstone' implies strength.

Jasper ware. A fine stoneware manufactured by Wedgwood from 1774 onwards.

Jigger and jolley. A wheel, or an attachment to the wheel, used to shape flat ware by the use of a template (jigger arm) and a rotating plaster mould on the wheel head (jolley).

Joggle. The 'natch' incorporated in a piece mould to ensure correct alignment of one part with another.

Kaolin. The English version of the Chinese word for clay.

Kidney. As the name suggests, a small tool shaped like a kidney, made in metal for scraping and in rubber for smoothing.

Kiln. A potter's oven for baking ceramic products.

Kiln furniture. All devices such as shelves, props, stilts, etc., used to support pottery in the kiln.

Lawn. Phosphor-bronze gauze used in clay/glaze sieves. Sometimes the complete sieve is referred to as 'a lawn'.

Lead antimoniate. Also called 'Naples Yellow' it is used as a yellow glaze stain. It is highly poisonous.

Lead oxide (PbO). The common name is litharge, a grey-black ore. There are also white lead oxide and red lead oxide, which are chemically slightly different. Once traditional fluxes, their general use in raw form is banned nowadays because of their poisonous nature. Lead fritts are safe to use, lead bisilicate being the most popular.

Lean clay or short clay. This clay lacks plasticity and is the opposite of 'fat' or 'long' clay.

Leather-hard. Rigid clay, still sufficiently damp to receive attachments such as handles and to be cut, scraped or planed.

Lime. See Calcium oxide.

Limestone. See Calcium carbonate.

Lining. Thin banding with colour.

Litharge (PbO). Lead oxide.

Lithium. A rare metal: the oxide is used occasionally as a flux.

Loss on ignition. Commonly called L.O.I., the loss of weight when carbon and hydrogen are driven off by heating.

Low solubility. The catalogue term is 'Low Sol' or 'L.S.' before the name of the glaze. Defined by the Pottery Health Regulations as a glaze which does not release more than 5% of its dry weight of soluble lead.

Lug. An attachment for fixing handles to pottery.

Lump or lumpware. The lowest grade of saleable defective ware; the better grade is known as 'seconds'.

Lustre. An iridescent sheen produced by a very thin coat of metal on the glaze which is achieved by reduction firing.

Luting. Joining leather-hard clay surfaces with slip, e.g. handles to cups.

Magnesia. An alkaline base used as a flux.

Magnesite. Magnesium carbonate.

Magnetic iron or iron spangles (Fe_3O_4). A distinctive form of iron oxide.

Majolica. Opaque tin-glazed ware originating in Majorca. Now it is applied generally to soft-fired decorated earthenware with an opaque glaze.

Marbling. Random effect produced by the mingling of coloured slips while wet.

Marl. A clay containing a high percentage of lime. Loosely used to describe red clay.

Matt glazes. These glazes have a partially crystalline structure which gives a dull surface.

Maturing. This means either glaze 'soak' to produce even development, or clay storage to improve plasticity.

Minerals. Natural substances, mainly of crystalline structure. Rocks are mixtures of minerals, therefore clay should be classed as a rock.

Ming. Seventeenth-century dynasty in China: Chinese porcelain of the era with blue-painted scenes on it is identified as Ming.

Model. A prototype shape modelled in clay or plaster.

Mosaic. Small squares of glazed clay (also, of course, stone and glass) used to decorate flat surfaces such as floors, and walls, with abstract patterns or formal pictorial arrangements.

Mould runner. This used to be the job of a hard-worked lad, who carried the slip-filled moulds to and from the drying rooms.

Muffle. Protective inner chamber of fireclay often used in solid-fuel and gas kilns to shield the ware from flames and gases.

Mullite. A substance formed when clay is heated over 1100°C.

Neutral. This describes a firing in which oxidation and reduction atmospheres alternate: theoretically it is an atmosphere balanced between them.

Nepheline syenite. A feldspar containing a high proportion of potassium and sodium.

Nickel oxide. On its own it tends to give dirty greens, but it is used for modifying the colouring effects of other oxides in glazes.

Nitre. This is potassium nitrate, sometimes called saltpetre.

Once-fired. Where biscuiting is dispensed with and body and glaze mature together in one firing.

On-glaze decoration. This is painted, sprayed or transferred to the surface of a fired glaze and fired again at 700°C to 800°C.

Opacifier. Material added to a glaze to make it opaque. Stannic oxide, usually known as tin oxide, was used traditionally, and where this is so it is called a tin glaze. Antimony, titanium and zircon are used as well, especially the latter.

Open clays. Porous clays.

Open firing. Where the flames pass among the wares.

Opening material. A material added to clay to reduce its density and shrinkage, such as sand or grog.

Organic matter. Generally applied to vegetable substances in clay and raw materials, but it may refer to organic chemicals which are added to them.

Orthoclase. A common feldspar containing a large proportion of potassium.

Oven. Old name for 'bottle' kiln.

Overfiring. Heating ware well in excess of the optimum temperature.

Overglaze painting. Sometimes used instead of on-glaze painting. Generally there is some confusion between the uses of the terms in-glaze, on-glaze and overglaze.

Paste. Obsolete word for European 'porcelain' bodies.

Pate-sur-pate. A method of decoration where a positive relief effect is built up in successive layers of slip applied with a brush (paste-on-paste)

Pearl ash. A name for potassium carbonate, an alkaline glaze flux.

Pebble mill. A ball mill where flint pebbles are used instead of porcelain balls.

Peeling. A glaze fault also known as flaking or shivering.

Pegmatite. A feldspathic rock with large crystals.

Peptizer. Another word for deflocculent.

Petuntse. The Chinese word for China (or Cornish) stone.

Pinholes. The result of gases erupting through the glaze.

Pitchers (shards or sherds). Discarded biscuit, used for making grog.

Placing. Packing the kiln.

Placing sand. Clean white sand used to support pots in the biscuit kiln.

Plucked ware. Faulty, because the glaze has touched the kiln furniture.

Porcelain. A vitreous (glassy) white pottery with a translucent quality due to its glassy nature.

Porosity. This refers to the proportion of pores or air passages between the solid particles making up a body.

Potash. Potassium oxide or carbonate; one of the two bases known as alkalis, sodium being the other.

Pressing. Use of a two-piece mould to press (or squeeze) out small pieces such as handles.

Primary air. The main air supplied to solid-fuel or gas kilns.

Pug-mill. A machine which minces up (pugs) reconditioned clay.

Pyrometer. An instrument for measuring high temperatures which indicates the rate of rise (or fall).

Pyrometric cones and bars. These bend at predetermined temperatures.

Quartz. The common(est) form of silica.

Quenching. Molten fritt is poured into a **bosch** (bath of water) to fragmentate it for subsequent grinding.

Raku. A thick, soft, once-fired ware used in a Japanese tea ceremony. It is made, fired and used to drink from during the ceremony. Therefore it has to be fired, and cooled rapidly by plunging it into water.

Raw glaze. Either a glaze in which none of the materials has been fritted, or a glaze applied to green ware.

Red iron oxide. The most common form of iron oxide, it is used in clays, slips and glazes.

Reduction. This takes place in an atmosphere starved of free oxygen: oxides are reduced to lower forms, giving colour variations.

Refractory materials. These stand up to very high temperatures without fusion.

Resist. Wax (or other materials) can be used as a shield which resists water; thus parts of a body or glaze can be protected from an application of colour or glaze over it.

Rouge flambé. French term for Chinese pottery with particularly richly-coloured red and purple glazes obtained by reduction.

Rutile. Crude ore of titanium oxide with iron present.

Saddle. A bar of refractory clay, triangular in cross section, used to support pottery in the kiln.

Saggar. A fireclay box in which ware is placed to protect it during firing.

Saggar maker's bottom knocker. A man who flattened out wads of fireclay to make the bottoms for saggars.

Salt glaze. Salt is introduced into the kiln at 1200°C, it volatilises and settles on the ware, combining with the silica and alumina in the body to form a glaze.

Sand. Sand is finely-ground quartz and is therefore almost pure silica. It is used for 'opening' clay, for 'placing' biscuit, for making 'clamming', and as a glaze ingredient. It is the principal material used to make glass.

Screens. Similar to sieves, they are used for grading particles by size.

Scum. The result of efflorescence.

Secondary air. This passes over the fuel to complete combustion.

Secondary clay. Any clay which has been moved by nature from the place where it was formed: it is more plastic than primary clay and contains impurities.

Sedimentation. The settling process when particles of clay sink to the bottom of the container and form a 'pan'.

Setting. Another word for 'placing'.

Sgraffito (or sgraffiato). The Italian for 'scratched'. Scratching through a covering of coloured slip to expose the different colour of the clay underneath.

Silica. Basic material for clays, glazes and glasses, cement, and a great part of the earth's crust.

Silicon carbide. Local reduction around the particles gives red speckles in glazes.

Slip. Clay suspended in water.

Slurry. Sloppy clay.

Soak. Maintaining a steady temperature in the kiln for a period.

Soda or sodium oxide. With potassium forms one of the two main alkaline fluxes.

Soft paste. An imitation porcelain firing at 1100°C.

Souring. Ageing of clay.

Spangles. Magnetic iron oxide.

Sprigging. Applied decoration using small moulded relief patterns and motifs.

Spurs (cock-spurs). Triangular supports for plates in the kiln.

Stains. Proprietary colours, other than those usually obtained from oxides, for tinting slips and glazes, e.g., lemon yellow, grass green, maroon, and slate blue.

Stannic oxide. Another term for tin oxide.

Stanniferous. This means 'tin-bearing': so a stanniferous glaze is an opaque tin glaze.

Starved. Describes the appearance of a glaze which has been too thinly applied.

Stoneware. Dense, vitrified, hard body fired to about 1300°C; often looks like stone.

Sucking. Volatile constituents are sucked from the glaze sometimes by porous bodies such as new kiln bricks.

Suspending agents. Materials which support the suspension of glaze or clay particles.

Talc or steatite. Magnesium silicate: used as a flux in bodies and as a secondary flux in glazes.

Tenmoku. An iron glaze which fires black breaking into rust red.

Terra-cotta. Low-fired earthenware, 'cooked earth'.

Terra-sigillata. The finest clay particles are obtained by decanting a number of times, and are used as a glaze on red ware giving it a 'sealing-wax' appearance: a process used by the Romans.

Tesserae. Small cubes of flat glazed clay used for mosaic pavements, etc. ('tessellated' pavements).

Tessha. Lustrous metallic Tenmoku.

Thermal shock. Sudden heating as used in the Raku process.

Tin enamel. Tin glaze. Both terms refer to a glaze containing some 10% of tin oxide as an opacifier (see also Stanniferous).

Titanium oxide. Used as a matt opacifier.

Trailing or tracing. Squeezing a trail of slip from a flexible container to make a ceramic decoration: glaze can be trailed also.

Turning. Shaving surplus clay from a leather-hard pot.

Underglaze. Decoration applied under and seen through a clear glaze.

Uranium oxide. Gives yellow in glazes.

Vanadium oxide. Produces yellow in a glaze containing tin or titanium.

Viscosity. Resistance to flow.

Vitreous. Having a glassy character.

Vitrification. The progressive fusion of ceramic substances as the temperature increases.

Wad. A strip of fireclay for sealing lids on saggars: the wad box was used originally to produce such strips.

Weathering. Exposing clay to all weathers to improve its plasticity.

Water smoking. Steam issuing from the kiln between 100°C and 250°C as previously unevaporated water escapes.

Wedging. Repeated cutting and banging of the clay to expel air and condense the particles.

Whirler. Hand-operated wheel to support pots during coiling and banding, etc.

Zinc oxide. A high-temperature flux, it brightens the colour response of the oxides in a glaze.

Zirconium oxide. An alternative to tin as an opacifier, but needs adding to glaze in a proportion of 15%–20%.

RECOMMENDED READING AND VISUAL AIDS

Recommended Reading

Billington, D. M. *The Technique of Pottery.* Batsford, 1962.
Cardew, M. *Pioneer Pottery.* Longmans, 1969.
Christy, J. and R. *Making Pottery.* Penguin, 1969.
Clark, K. *Pottery Throwing for Beginners.* Studio Vista, 1970.
Clark, K. *Practical Pottery and Ceramics.* Studio Vista, 1964.
Colbeck, J. *Pottery: The Techniques of Throwing.* Batsford, 1969.
Cooper, E. *Taking up Pottery.* Longman, 1972.
Drake, K. *Simple Pottery.* Studio Vista, 1966.
Drawbell, M. *Making Pottery Figures.* Tiranti, 1961.
Fieldhouse, M. *Pottery.* Foyle, 1952.
Green, D. *Experimenting with Pottery.* Faber and Faber, 1971.
Green, D. *Pottery: Materials and Techniques.* Faber and Faber, 1967.
Green, D. *Understanding Pottery Glazes.* Faber and Faber, 1963.
Kenny, J. B. *Ceramic Design.* Pitman, 1964.
Kenny, J. B. *Ceramic Sculpture.* Pitman, 1967.
Kenny, J. B. *The Complete Book of Pottery Making.* Pitman, 1972.
Lauder, I. *The Home Potter.* Barrie and Jenkins, 1970.
Leach, B. *A Potter's Book.* Faber and Faber, 1945.
Nelson, G. C. *Ceramics.* Holt, Rinehart and Winston, 1971.
Powell, H. *The Beginner's Book of Pottery.* Blandford Press, 1963.
Powell, H. *Further Steps in Pottery.* Blandford Press, 1962.
Powell, H. *The Pottery Handbook of Clay, Glaze and Colour.* Blandford Press, 1968.
Riegger, M. *Raku: Art and Technique.* Studio Vista, 1970.
Rhodes, D. *Clay and Glazes for the Potter.* Pitman, 1967.
Rhodes, D. *Kilns, Design, Construction and Operation.* Pitman, 1969.
Rhodes, D. *Stoneware and Porcelain: The Art of High Fired Pottery.* Pitman, 1960.
Rosenthal, E. *Pottery and Ceramics.* Penguin, 1949.
Roscoe, W. A. *Manual for the Potter.* Tiranti, 1948.
Tyler, K. *Pottery Without a Wheel.* Dryad Press, 1966.

Useful books for primary and junior schools are obtainable from Podmore & Sons, Ltd. (see Appendix Five).

Periodicals

Pottery Quarterly from Northfields Studio, Tring, Hertfordshire.

Visual Aids Suppliers

Educational Productions Ltd, 27/28 Maunsel Street, London
    SW1P 2QS.
Craftsmen Potters' Association, William Blake House, Marshall
    Street, London, W1.
Diana Wylie Ltd, 3, Park Road, London NW1.

MUSEUMS WORTH VISITING

Ashmolean Museum, Oxford	Early cultures
Anthropological Museum, Cambridge	Prehistoric
Brighton Museum, Sussex	English slip ware
British Museum, London	All periods
The Craftsmen Potters' Shop, Marshall Street, London W1	Contemporary pottery
Fitzwilliam Museum, Cambridge	Famous collection
Guildhall Museum, London	English mediaeval
Hanley Museum, Stoke-on-Trent, Staffordshire	Many periods
Horniman Museum, London	Native pottery
London Museum, Kensington Gardens	Pottery connected with London's history
Victoria and Albert Museum, London	Comprehensive collection
Wallace Collection, Manchester Square, London	Italian Majolica

Note for the enthusiastic student. A visit to The Craftsmen Potters' Shop, mentioned above, is recommended in order to keep abreast of contemporary trends. Associate Membership of the Craftsmen Potters' Association is open to anybody sufficiently interested to pay an annual subscription of £2 (junior membership, under 21, is 37½p).

POTTERY SUPPLIERS

Acme Marls,   Kiln furniture
   Clough Street, Hanley, Stoke-on-Trent,
   Staffordshire.

Applied Heat Co., Ltd,   Kilns
   Elecfurn Works, Otterspool Way,
   Watford, Hertfordshire.

Blythe Colour Works Ltd,   Materials and
   Cresswell, Stoke-on-Trent, Staffordshire.   colours

W. Boulton and Co,   Wheels
   Burslem, Stoke-on-Trent, Staffordshire.

R. M. Catterson Smith Ltd,   Kilns
   Adams Bridge Works, Exhibition Grounds,
   Wembley, Middlesex.

Cromartie Kilns,   Kilns
   Dividy Rd, Longton, Staffordshire.

Dryad Handicrafts,   Materials and
   Northgates, Leicester, LE1 4QR.   equipment

Ferro (Gt. Britain) Ltd,   Materials and
   Wombourne, Wolverhampton, WV5 8DA.   equipment

Fulham Pottery,   Complete service:
   210, New King's Road, London SW6 4NY.   materials and
               equipment

Harrison Meyer Ltd,   Complete service:
   Meir, Stoke-on-Trent, Staffordshire,   materials and
   ST3 7PX.   equipment

The Leach Pottery,   Plans for the
   St. Ives, Cornwall.   Leach wheel

Mills and Hubball, Ltd,   Materials and
   Victoria Rise, North Side,   equipment
   Clapham Common, London, SW4.

The Oxshott Pottery,   Plans for wheels
   Potter's Croft, Oakshade Road,   and kilns
   Oxshott, Surrey.

Pike Brothers,   Clay
   Wareham, Dorset.

Podmore and Sons Ltd,
  Shelton, Stoke-on-Trent, Staffordshire.

Complete service: materials and equipment

Pot Clays Ltd,
  Brick Kiln Lane, Etruria, Stoke-on-Trent,
  Staffordshire, ST4 7BP.

Clay

Potter's Equipment Co.,
  73–77, Britannia Road, London, SW6.

Wheels

Price Brothers,
  Burslem, Stoke-on-Trent, Staffordshire.

Clay

Reeves & Sons Ltd,
  Enfield, Middlesex.

Materials, brushes

A. Tiranti, Ltd,
  72, Charlotte Street, London, W1.

Vinamold and tools

Technical Art Products,
  202, Turnpike Link, East Croydon, Surrey.

Cold wax resist

Watts, Blake and Bearn Ltd,
  Newton Abbot, Devon.

Clay

Wengers Ltd,
  Etruria, Stoke-on-Trent, Staffordshire,
  ST3 7PX.

Complete service: materials and equipment.

INDEX

The page numbers in **bold type** refer to illustrations and those in *italicised type* to the Ceramic Vocabulary.

Decoration—*cont.*
  trailing, 58–60
  techniques, 190
  under the glaze, 176, 178–9, 181–3
Deflocculent, 100, *273*
della Robbia, 252
Devil's work, 249
Dipping, 54, 155, **158,** 186
  double, 156
Discolouration, 148, 175
Draught kilns, 134, **135,** 141, 142, 149
Drying, cooling, frame, 13, 73
Duckboard, 9
Dunting, 175, *274*
Dwight, John, 253

Earthenware, 3, 4, 145, 146, *274*
Electrolytes, 100
Elements,
  chemical, 170, 172
  electric, 135, 136, 138
Enamel colours, 179, 182, 188, *274*
Encaustic, 70, *274*
Engobe, 51
Epsom-salts, 155
Equipment, 13, 78, 98, 199, 255–69
  drying, **13**
  storage, 8–9, 263
Equivalent weight, 173
Extractor head, 240–1

Famille ware, 249
Feathering, 95–6
Feldspar, 162, 168, 169, 170
Fettling, 60, 86, *274*
Findings, 122, 123
Finishes, surface, 19–20, 38–9, 60
Firing, 145–52, *274*
  biscuit, 145–8
  chamber, 134
  glaze, 148–50
  neutral, 177, *277*
  oxidation, 150
  Raku, 150
  rate, 138, 140, 145, 147, 148, 149, 151
  reduction, 141, 150, 151
  salt glaze, 151
  your work, 13–14
Fish, 127–8
Flange, 103, 121, 233
Flashing, 105
Flint, 149, 168, 173, 174, *275*
Flue, 134, 140, 141

Fluorspar, 168, *275*
Flux, 159, 160, 161, 163, 166, 167, 168, 169, 170, *275*
Foot, 51, 75, 85, 87, 90, 91, 106, 149, 153, 229, **230,** 233
Fuels, 134, 140–2, 152
Fritts, 160–2
Fuse heat, 139
Fusion, 3, *275*

Galena, 155, 161, 168, *275*
Gas kilns, 140–1
Glass, 159, 160, 243, *275*
Glaze, 153–74, *275*
  appearance of, 161–3, 165–6, 168, 169
  binder, 154, 186
  colours from oxides, 163–5
  contraction, 174
  defects, 174–5, 183
  expansion of, 173
  firing, 148–50
  fritts and, 160–2
  opaque, 162–3
  preparation, 154–5
  procedures, 155–60
  recipes, 167, 174
  simple, 162–3
  stacking, 148
  transparent, 162
Glazing, 153
  procedure, 155–60
Green ware, 18, *275*
Grog (grogging), 4, 8, 51, 100, 147, 150, 239, *275*
Gum, 58, 154, 158, 181, 183, 184, 186, 187
Gypsum, 77, *275*

Hacksaw blade, 12, 20, 80
Handles, 49–50, 75, 86, 110, 224–7, 232–3
Hardening-on, 183
Harp, **43,** 44, 266
History, (*see* Pottery)
Hydrogen, 2, 171, 173

Impermeability, 38, 146, 159, *275*
Improvisation, 23, 90
In-glaze, 179, *275*
Iron, 164, 177, *276*

Jelling, 72, 100
Jewellery, ceramic, 121–3

Wedgwood, Josiah, 253–4
Wheel,
  fast, 193
  fly, 193, 194–5
  lining (or banding), 39, 157, 183, 255
  potters, contemporary, 194
    electric, 195–8
    kick, 193, 194
  primitive and traditional, 192
  slow, 192

with or without the (*see* Pottery)
Whiting, 166, 169, 171
Willow pattern, 185
Wiping, 35, 45, 50
Work tray, 198–9

X.P.M., 53

Zinc, 170, *282*
Zircon fritts, 162
Zirconium, 162, *282*